Economies of Scale,
Competitiveness,
and Trade Patterns
within the
European Community

Economies of Scale, Competitiveness, and Trade Patterns within the European Community

NICHOLAS OWEN

CLARENDON PRESS · OXFORD

1983

Oxford University Press, Walton Street, Oxford OX2 6DP

London Glasgow New York Toronto
Delhi Bombay Calcutta Madras Karachi
Kuala Lumpur Singapore Hong Kong Tokyo
Nairobi Dar es Salaam Cape Town
Melbourne Auckland

and associated companies in
Beirut Berlin Ibadan Mexico City Nicosia

Oxford is a trade mark of Oxford University Press

Published in the United States
by Oxford University Press, New York

British Library Cataloguing in Publication Data
Owen, Nicholas
Economies of scale, competitiveness and trade
patterns within the European Community.
1. Competition   2. European Community
countries—Commercial policy
I. Title
338.6'048'094   HD41
ISBN 0-19-828457-8

Library of Congress Cataloging in Publication Data

Owen, Nicholas.
Economies of scale, competitiveness, and trade
patterns within the European Community.
Bibliography: p.
Includes index.
1. European Economic Community.   2. European Economic
Community countries—Commerce.   3. Automobile
industry and trade—European Economic Community
countries.   4. Truck industry—European Economic
Community countries.   5. Electric household appliances
industry—European Economic Community countries.
I. Title.
HC241.2.094 1983   382'.094   83-13399
ISBN 0-19-828457-8

Typeset by Hope Services, Abingdon, Oxfordshire
and printed in Great Britain
at the University Press, Oxford

To
Cecily
and
Charles

PREFACE

This book is based on a doctoral thesis accepted by the University of London in 1982. It reflects on the European Community, twenty-five years after its formation, in order to discover whether the competitive developments within the Community have been important to the industries directly affected, and more generally, to Europeans' standards of living. To do justice to the subject it was felt that the book should try to combine three elements: a theoretical discussion of the economics underlying intra-European trade, an analysis of this trade as a whole, and detailed studies of the structures, technologies, and trade patterns of individual industries on a European scale. The author is grateful to Denys Gribbin for suggesting, prior to Britain's entry, the theme of competition within the Community, and to Basil Yamey for encouraging its pursuit. The author is particularly grateful to Jürgen Müller and John Graham, Stephen Smith, Francine Bougeon-Maasson, Alistair Nicholson, and Brian Hindley for their assistance and advice. He is also most grateful to Vivienne May for her help in preparation. The responsibility for any factual or analytical errors is, of course, entirely the author's.

Thanks are also due to the North-Holland Publishing Company for permission to draw upon the author's article 'Scale Economies in the EEC', published in the *European Economic Review* (1976); to the Controller of Her Majesty's Stationery Office for permission to reproduce Fig. 4.4 from *The Future of the British Car Industry*; and to the Royal College of Defence Studies for permission to draw on material from a study carried out by the author at the College in 1979.

CONTENTS

CHAPTER 1

INTRODUCTION

This study explores the economics of the European Community's[1] internal trade in manufactures. It attempts to identify the economic forces which have shaped the pattern of internal trade, and specifically, the role which economies of scale have played in determining the competitive positions of the four major member countries' industries within the Community markets. The study concludes with an assessment of the scale-related welfare benefits arising from Community trade.

These themes have not been convincingly treated in the literature. Trade patterns within the Community are not easily susceptible to economic analysis within the traditional framework of international trade theory because the majority of Community members are advanced industrial societies, possessing similar factor endowments. For this reason there is little on which international trade theory, which looks primarily for explanations of trade patterns in the differences in countries' factor endowments, can get a grip upon. Casting about for an alternative source of explanations of trade patterns, one looks in vain for the kind of detailed industry-specific study spanning the Community as a whole which would be capable of explaining why particular national industries have succeeded and others failed to cope with European competition. Without either a general explanation of the kind trade theory attempts to provide, or a detailed grasp of the circumstances and performance of individual industries, it is no easier to understand the successes and failures of individual industries in Community markets than it is to understand why individuals or teams from one country win particular athletic events or football tournaments.

The role played in Community trade by economies of scale has not been satisfactorily explained either. The Community's founding fathers regarded economies of scale as being of fundamental importance to the success of the Community. They envisaged that the creation of the Community would secure for its members levels of productivity comparable to American levels through the creation of integrated continental markets comparable in economic terms to that of North America. As Layton[2] put it: 'For roughly a hundred years, or since the end of the American civil war, the long-term trend of growth in the US economy was faster than that of Western Europe as a whole. One major reason was economies of scale. For the first time in history, modern industrialism developed within a continental economy.' But this view has not received sympathy let alone confirmation in the economic literature, where it has been argued that in most industries in the larger member countries, national markets were by themselves sufficiently large to accommodate plants of minimum efficient scale. The authors of what is arguably the major single piece of empirical work on comparative industrial structure[3] expressed disappointment at what they perceived as a lack of any Community stimulus to the construction of larger plants. And to the extent that increases in scale have been observed in the Community, they have not been demonstrated to be conditional upon the removal of national tariff barriers. This contrast between the aspirations of the architects of the Community and the perceived out-turn is puzzling and invites further exploration.

The same gap between aspiration and achievement exists also in respect to the economic benefits of Community membership. Whereas the political impetus of the Community, and the attractions of seeking its membership, derive in part from expectations of higher economic growth within than without the Community, all the estimates of these benefits have been of a derisory order — fractions of a per cent of GDP.[4] There is clearly much to be explained here. Intra-Community trade has grown considerably faster than the Community's GDP, yet its significance and its pattern have not been explained; it has not, it is alleged, promoted economies of scale nor has it enhanced material living standards by more than a fraction of a single year's growth. These judgements are completely at odds with the perceptions of industrialists, politicians, and administrators involved with European integration and of the electorates of Europe which have evidently been prepared to make a number of political sacrifices in the presumed interests of greater economic and social benefits of Community membership. Only two conclusions seem possible: either thousands of informed people have been misleading the millions of less informed about the economic benefits of Community membership; or economic analysis has so far failed to understand, interpret, and quantify the economic forces at work in the Community. This is the starting-point of this study.

SCALE AND INTEGRATION OF MARKETS

The scale factor is the linking thread running through this study. Policy-makers have considered it to be a fundamental economic reason for integrating the markets of the Community. The founding fathers looked across the Atlantic to the USA — the world's largest integrated common market — and judged that the size of American markets had fostered the development of large-scale production technologies which in turn were partly responsible for American productivity levels being the highest in the world. The size of the productivity gap between the USA and Europe is indicated in Table 1.1. In 1960, American productivity levels in manufacturing were three times greater than Britain's and Germany's. By 1975, Germany had narrowed this gap slightly, Britain had not.

Subsequent research provides some support for the industrial logic underlying the instinctive aspiration behind the Community's formation. Cross-sectional studies of international productivity differences at the national level found that market size contributed to explanations of these differences.[5] More recent and detailed studies of American and European industrial structures and levels of performance support this finding, indicating both the scale difference in the Americans' favour and the causal link between scale and productivity. Pratten's[6] study of the operations of multinational companies with comparable manufacturing operations on both sides of the Atlantic suggested that the average length of production runs in the companies' American operations were between two and three times greater than in the European operations. Thus, even when the same manufacturing experience is applied by the same company in the USA and Europe, a substantial scale difference is apparent in its application.

TABLE 1.1. *Comparisons of manufacturing productivity* (USA = 100: comparisons on a purchasing power parity basis)

	1960	1970	1975	1978
USA	100	100	100	100
Germany	36	43	43	44
Britain	35	35	34	33

Source: S. J. Prais, A. Daly, D. T. Jones, and K. Wagner, *Productivity and Industrial Structure* (London, 1981), p. 279.

Significant differences emerge also in the other dimension of scale, the size of the plant employed. The study of plant sizes in twelve industries in six major industrial countries (USA, Canada, Sweden, Germany, France, and Britain), by Scherer and his colleagues,[7] calculated the minimum efficient plant size in each industry (the size of plant which exhausted the known economies of scale in each of the technologies concerned) and then compared the representative plant size in each country with these minimum plant sizes. From this research it is possible to deduce that whereas the average American plant size was 75 per cent of the minimum efficient size in ten industries, the corresponding figures for the three major Community countries were 50 per cent for Germany, 40 per cent for Britain, and 35 per cent for France.[8] This configuration was found to be no coincidence; the study proposed and confirmed a rationale for investment decisions in respect to plant size, according to which the size of a plant depended on the transport costs of the product concerned, the importance of scale economies in its manufacture, and the size of its market. Using this analytical framework Scherer was able to explain three-quarters of all the variations in national plant sizes in the sample; by far the most important explanatory factor was market size.

These scale differences feed through into productivity. Scherer's study found a significant relationship between plant size and productivity; a doubling of plant size was associated with an increase in productivity of nearly 40 per cent. Even if this relationship applied across the whole of manufacturing it would not in itself be sufficient to explain all of the American–European productivity differentials. If, as Scherer suggests, American plants are double the size of their European counterparts, this would explain about one-third of the 100–120 per cent productivity differentials noted in Table 1.1 between the USA and Germany. Part of the unexplained differential can be explained by differences in the other scale dimension, namely, the extent to which managements organize work in particular plants so as to achieve long production runs. American managements have pushed plant specialization much further than their European counterparts. Pratten reported that this factor emerged as the main explanation of Atlantic productivity differentials, mentioning as reasons for this difference the scope for using high-capacity units of plant and machinery with little or no extra labour to operate them, for mechanizing more operations, for reducing set-up times for machinery, and for economies in indirect labour in stores and in production and quality control. As the figures shown in Table 1.2 indicate, the greater the difference in average production run lengths between four major countries covered in Pratten's analysis, the greater the productivity differential.

TABLE 1.2. *An International Comparison of Productivity and Run Length*

	Productivity differential over United Kingdom level (percentage)	Production run length relative to UK level
USA	50	3.4
Germany	35	1.6
France	20	1.3

Source: Pratten, *Productivity Differentials*, pp. 9 and 34.

Nowhere is the scale differential greater or more decisive than in the high technology industries, such as aerospace. Table 1.3 compares the lengths of production run for American and European combat aircraft. The American production run advantage is of the order of five, compared to the twofold or threefold advantage in manufacturing overall. This differential is an exact reflection of the differential in market and company size; whereas eight American companies shared an aircraft market of $18 billion in 1977, with average sales of $2 billion each, nineteen such companies in Europe shared a market of $7 billion, with an average sales of only $0.4 billion.[9] These scale differences translated into substantial productivity differences. A study by the Rand Corporation for the British Government in 1969 on the productivity of the national aircraft effort[10] concluded that: 'it is the scale of production more than any other single factor which accounts for the 3:1 difference between the United States and the United Kingdom in the value added by the aircraft industry for each man it employs.'

Against this background of expectations of scale-related productivity gains being achieved within integrated Community markets the study considers first, in Chapter 2, the economic basis of trade and integration. It then combines two complementary types of empirical analysis. Chapter 3 provides an interpretation of an early 1960s snapshot of the entire trade pattern in manufacturing between the three largest original members of the Community, France, Germany, and Italy, in terms of the structural characteristics of 70 industries. Chapters 4, 5, and 6 each offer industry case studies (cars, trucks, and white goods); their coverage extends to the fourth major Community member, Britain, which acceded in 1973. These two types of analysis have been brought together in this book for reasons which should be appreciated at the outset. The strengths of each type of approach constitute at the same time their respective weaknesses.

TABLE 1.3. *Length of Production Run: Combat Aircraft*

American Aircraft	Run Length	European Aircraft	Run Length
F4	5,000	Mirage III	1,150
A7	1,300	Lightning	300
F5	1,150	Buccaneer	200
F111	500	Harrier	200
F15	750		
F16	1,000		

Source: Roger Facer, 'The Alliance & Europe: Part III: Weapons Procurement in Europe — Capabilities and Choices', *Adelphi Papers*, No. 108, Winter 1974/75, Table 15, p. 19.

The large sample approach allows the researcher to abstract from the detail in order to test, with a degree of statistical rigour, general propositions about industrial behaviour, but the process of abstraction also drains the material of any feel for any particular industry's character and operating characteristics. Conversely, industry studies offer a richer texture of detail but much of it is difficult to interpret without the assistance of a tested general model of behaviour. The insights which case studies can offer tend to be suggestive, rather than scientifically testable, precisely because case studies are essentially narratives, offering little opportunity to bring scientific testing procedures to bear. One might learn from such accounts that particular companies expanded, contracted, were profitable, went bankrupt, but in the absence of a background of tested hypotheses these occurrences cannot be adequately explained.

Until the 1960s, the case study approach was the accepted style of addressing industrial economics. At that time, the advent of econometric techniques and the growing anti-trust market for generalizations about industry structure and behaviour largely displaced the case study in academic writings. The casualty of this development was any real feeling for industrial life because companies and industries were reduced to abstractions — science without understanding. An industrial economist required only a computer and a census of industrial production for his work. One now senses that academic industrial economists have begun to appreciate that the two types of study are complementary; that it is possible to develop rigorous models of behaviour while at the same time reaching down into the industrial detail. The landmark in this context, as in others, is the study of multi-plant economics by Scherer and his team which spanned a dozen industries in six countries. It was informed throughout by an understanding of each industry's technology and history; the mass of detail was made intelligible by tested theory. Although more modest in scope, the present book is written with the same approach in mind, in that the theoretical discussion and the insights derived from the cross-sectional analysis of Community trade patterns in the early part of the book provide a basis for interpreting the case study material in Chapters 4, 5, and 6.

The industry studies reflect the differing nature and availability of data in respect to each industry. They focus initially on trade patterns within the Community and test their conformity with each industry's relative unit cost positions within the Community; they then proceed to explore the extent to which these unit cost positions can be explained by economies of scale and the respective structures of production of each industry. This approach requires detailed consideration of the industries' production technologies and allows the effect of different dimensions of scale — company volume, plant volume, model volume — to be explored. The industry studies span a spectrum of product differentiation from the fairly standardized domestic refrigerator to the highly differentiated heavy truck.

Chapter 7 addresses the question: to what extent has the Community raised the living standard of its members? Drawing on the preceding empirical analysis it concludes that scale-related welfare gains have been very substantially greater than previous estimates. It is important to distinguish at the outset what is claimed from what is not. The book does not claim that, thanks to the Community, economies of scale are now fully or even substantially realized in most industries; there are many areas such as electronics where this is manifestly not the case. Nor does the book claim that, but for the Community, movements towards efficient scale which have occurred in the last twenty years are entirely attributable to the existence of the Community. This would be a naïve claim; internal competition within member countries, fortified by the stimulus of the growth of international trade under the auspices of the GATT, would undoubtedly have pushed European producers towards the full exploitation of scale economies, even without the Community.

The welfare arguments in the book anchor themselves to the wealth of literature testifying to the trade-creating effects of the Community. This literature is in broad agreement about the size of these effects. The book is not concerned to question these estimates; it is concerned with the significance of this increment in intra-Community trade and applies to that increment the lessons to be drawn from the analysis of trade patterns in Chapter 3 and the industry studies in Chapters 4, 5, and 6. The book does not attempt therefore, to demonstrate that the Community has enabled scale economies to be fully realized, or that it can be credited with the totality of such moves in this direction as have occurred over the last twenty years. The book does claim, however, that by providing an impetus to trade, the Community's existence can be credited with important scale-related welfare benefits which appear to be associated with the undisputed trade-creation effects and which are possibly as great as the amount of incremental trade which induces them. The evidence for these scale-related effects is not by any means conclusive since, as was mentioned above, industry studies are essentially narratives which attempt to make sense of a confusion of detail. The estimates are offered in the belief that it is better to be approximately right about the important but less quantifiable aspects of a subject than it is to be precisely correct about minor aspects which do happen to be measurable.

NOTES

1 For ease of reference, the European Community is referred to hereafter simply as 'the Community', West Germany as 'Germany', The United Kingdom as 'Britain'.

2 Christopher Layton, 'The Benefits of Scale for Industry' in *The Economics of Europe*, ed. J. Pinder (London, 1971).

3 F. M. Scherer *et al.*, *The Economics of Multi-plant Operation* (Cambridge, Mass., 1975). 'We had expected these trade-expanding measures [of the Community] to have a major impact on the adaption and survival of sub-minimum optimum scale plants. To some extent our expectations were disappointed. With only a few prominent exceptions, the effect of customs union membership on plant sizes was either so weak or so entangled with other forces that it received little weight as an explanatory variable.' (p. 155).

4 Scitovsky concluded that Western Europe would gain an increase in GDP of 0.05 per cent (T. Scitovsky, *Economic Theory and Western European Integration* (London, 1958)). H. G. Johnson ('The Gains from Freer Trade with Europe: An Estimate', *The Manchester School of Economic and Social Studies*, No. 3, 1958) concluded that the British GDP would benefit by at most 1 per cent. J. Wemelsfelder ('The Short-Term Effect of the Lowering of Import Duties in Germany', *Economic Journal*, Mar. 1960) estimated Germany's gain at 0.05 per cent of GDP. Marcus Miller and John Spencer ('The Static Economic Effect of the UK joining the EEC', *Review of Economic Studies*, Feb. 1977) estimated that, disregarding outward transfers related to the Common Agricultural Policy, Britain gained only one-sixth per cent of GDP as a result of a 50 per cent increase in imports of manufactures from the Community.

5 H. B. Chenery, 'Patterns of Industrial Growth', *American Economic Review*, Sept. 1960, p. 633.

6 C. F. Pratten, *Labour Productivity Differentials Within International Companies* (Cambridge, 1976).

7 Scherer, *Multi-plant Operation*, p. 86, table 3.13. Two industries were excluded from the table in making this comparison — batteries and bearings — due to the presence of extreme observations.

8 The superiority of American plant sizes is understated or concealed altogether in some comparisons. It is a convention of censuses of manufacturing, from which comparisons are often drawn, that plant size is measured in terms of employment, on which basis of course, plants which operate at low levels of labour productivity appear substantially larger than they would in a comparison in terms of achieved or designed *output*. Since average labour productivity in European plants is only 30–40 per cent of American levels, comparisons of plant sizes in terms of employment are highly flattering to European plants, putting them on a par with American plants, despite their inferior outputs.

9 'A European Armaments Policy', *Report to the Assembly of the Western European Union* (Document 786, Oct. 1978).

10 *Productivity of the National Aircraft Effort*, Report of a Committee appointed by the Minister of Technology, Ministry of Technology, HMSO (London, 1969).

CHAPTER 2

COSTS, SCALE, AND TRADE:
SOME THEORETICAL CONSIDERATIONS

International trade theory sees trade as deriving from international differences in unit manufacturing costs. This proposition is central to this study. The objection could be made, of course, that a cost-based approach to intra-Community trade misunderstands the nature of this trade, which is as much if not more to do with non-price factors such as quality and product differentiation and which has grown more strongly along the within-industry route than along the between-industry route, as Europeans swap different brands of clothing and marques of car, rather than cars for clothing. This observation does not imply that unit manufacturing costs are of marginal significance. Quite the contrary, as is recognized in the recent developments in trade theory, which are discussed below, intra-industry trade in differentiated products has its origins in economies of scale and hence in the cost advantages of specialization. Moreover, the important non-price dimensions of competition, which underlie this product differentiation, themselves respond to differences in unit costs. Not only do profit-maximizing producers exploit a reduction in their own unit manufacturing costs by reducing price and increasing sales volume, but, as the mathematics in Appendix 1 demonstrates, they will also increase their expenditures on non-price dimensions of competition such as marketing because the marginal productivity of these expenditures increases as price–cost margins widen. By so doing they reinforce the effect of the cost-induced price changes on sales volume. This suggests that when consideration of the response of marketing and any other non-price expenditures is taken into account, the sensitivity of sales volume to unit cost changes, and of trade to international cost differentials, will invariably be strong, even when non-price aspects of competitiveness are important. These considerations justify the central role accorded to unit costs in this study.

According to international trade theory, international unit cost differences arise from national differences in factor endowments; countries in which one factor of production is relatively abundant are able to produce relatively cheaply those commodities whose manufacture makes intensive use of that abundant factor. Industrial structure and performance have no place in this scheme of things. Industries are assumed to be perfectly competitive and to operate in their entirety in the most efficient possible way. According to this account of international trade, integration yields no benefits from economies of scale whatever; these are assumed to be already achieved within national boundaries.[1]

There are two obvious weaknesses in this approach. In focusing on factor endowments it cannot explain why trade developed so rapidly in the Community, between countries whose factor endowments are so similar. It fails to come to terms with the fact that most industries are known not to be operating in their entirety in the most efficient way, to judge by the existence of substantial sub-optimal capacity and of wide dispersions in productivity levels and in unit costs *within* national industries. It also fails to acknowledge the fact, which is evident from a glance at any trade catalogue, that markets and companies do not operate in terms of the broad categories such as 'steel', 'aircraft', 'electric motors'. Markets are finely segmented and within any segment, the achievement of efficient scale is typically bounded by the market.[2] A high proportion of trade can be characterized as of the intra-industry type (for meaningful definitions of products such as 'family cars of 1000–2000 cc', rather than, say, Volkswagen and Renault). Once it is acknowledged that all product varieties cannot be produced within one country at minimum efficient scales, it is intuitively clear that producers must find compromises between efficiency and the number of varieties they offer. Widening the market by trade allows greater specialization in respect to product varieties.

The reason why traditional trade theory shied away from the manifest existence of economies of scale and their under-exploitation was that once economies of scale are allowed into trade models, the models can generate indeterminate solutions involving complete specialization but without it being theoretically clear which country would specialize in which product. Recent theoretical developments have succeeded in reworking trade theory to include economies of scale. Ethier[3] and Krugman[4] have demonstrated that not only are the familiar trade theorems preserved in the face of economies of scale, but that similarity of factor endowments — a feature of the Community — tends to promote intra-industry trade. They showed, moreover, that this trade derives ultimately from economies of scale.

The world which is described in Krugman's elegant model is in one important sense a comfortable one: each firm produces one, differentiated product. No firm is eliminated by trade, nor even is the volume of production of any firm affected by trade. What appears to happen is this: the variety of products produced in one country is limited by the existence of scale economies in production; and the increase in size of the market through trade makes a greater variety of products available, to everyone's benefit. Trade does not extend economies of scale because each firm's output remains unchanged, but it extends consumer choice.

The element of intra-Community trade which can be characterized in this way could be significant. For reasons which will become clear, it is not as important a source of benefits as other components of trade but its benefits are none the less quantifiable, as the author's own simplified version of this approach illustrates, before an alternative approach is developed. Suppose that a firm has the option of manufacturing two distinct versions of a product (let us call them Y and X), which are assumed for analytical convenience to cost the same to produce at any given volume. The firm could specialize entirely in the production of one or the other variant, or it could produce both, but the existence

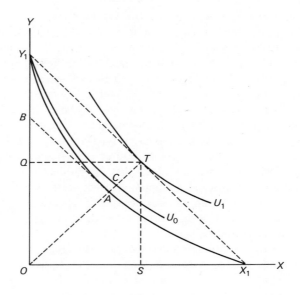

Fig. 2.1. Specialization and economies of scale

of economies of scale determines that, with a given quantity of resources, the firm could produce more units by specializing. The firm's options are represented in Figure 2.1 by the line Y_1AX_1 (in analytical terms its transformation curve is convex to the origin). Consider the case where in the absence of trade the firm chooses to specialize, and produces OY_1 units of Y. Suppose also that in a prospective trading partner, an identical firm, with the same costs, has opted to specialize in the production of the other variant, X, and produces OX_1 units for its domestic market. Trade would enlarge consumer choice because the two variants can be traded on a one-for-one basis, along the line Y_1X_1, making available to the consumers of both countries combinations of the two variants which would not be available so cheaply under autarchy.

To take a symmetrical case, the firm producing variant Y could export half its output Y_1Q in exchange for QT of variant X in order to offer its domestic customers a combination represented by T. How much better off would they be, in respect to their original position, Y_1, as a result? The answer depends on two factors: their preferences as between the two variants, and the importance of economies of scale, reflected in the curvature of Y_1AX_1 (greater the economies of scale, greater the curvature). The upper bound to the answer can be judged by considering the case in which consumers as a group had preferred A to Y_1; in other words, where they had valued the greater variety at A more than the lower prices made possible by manufacturing Y at a higher volume. In this instance, trade would have encouraged specialization and the gains in real income in respect to the original position A would be $AT/OA = BY_1/OB$.

However, in the case we are addressing here, where producers already specialize before trade, as Krugman's analysis assumes, the gains from trade must be less than this. The community indifference curve, U_0, passing through Y_1 is less convex to the origin than Y_1AX_1 and therefore lies above it. The gains from trade would be CT/OC, less than AT/OA. The lower bound would be zero. If the two variants were near-perfect substitutes — trivially differentiated, in respect to colour, for example — the benefits from trade would be negligible. But the fact that we are discussing cases where competing models require different model-specific production facilities argues that the differentiation is substantial. The community indifference curve probably lies closer to Y_1AX_1 than to Y_1X_1, and the gains from trade (CT/OC) are probably of the same order as those associated with the first case. The magnitude of these gains is determined by the economies of scale. Succeeding chapters suggest that unit costs in manufacturing typically fall by 10 per cent with each doubling of volume. Appendix 2 shows that on this assumption the gains from enlarged consumer choice are equivalent to something approaching one-quarter of the value of the imports involved. This is an interesting result, to which the study returns in Chapter 7, because it suggests that, even without shifting resources within countries, intra-industry trade can generate significant welfare gains.

The point of departure for this study is the observation that international trade between similarly endowed countries is much more of a brawl than is allowed in the analysis stylized above and that it does reallocate resources quite significantly. There are winners and losers in this process: some manufacturing units expand and prosper; others are eliminated. This is the aspect of trade which interests businessmen and policy-makers: which firms will be the winners and which the losers, and why? To put the matter in more analytical terms, the new theoretical approach developed by Krugman and others is based upon the theory of monopolistic competition: each producer produces its own unique product. This approach enables the authors to integrate economies of scale into trade theory within an equilibrium analysis in ways which are all full of insights and satisfying, save one: the approach ignores 'industries', those loose collections of firms which produce products which are sufficiently similar for it to be possible for the firms to eliminate each other by direct competition, rather than through the more generalized competition for consumers' purchasing power assumed by monopolistic competition. The everyday experiences of international trade furnishes examples of casualties or near-casualties of this kind of direct competition. Empirical studies of trade therefore have to be carried out on an industry basis. Once this approach is adopted, economies of scale become a critical factor because size differences between competing firms give rise to cost differences both within industries, and between countries. If economies of scale are admitted, as they must be, as an important ingredient in the analysis of trade, it becomes necessary to consider industrial *structures*: why they exist at all; and how they interact with international trade.

The first major industrial study which linked economies of scale with international trade was the Wonnacotts' analysis[5] of the potential economic effects of free trade between the United States and Canada. This was a significant departure from the traditional customs union approach. Customs union analysis assumes away economies of scale; the foreign trading partner is assumed to be capable of supplying unlimited additional imports at constant cost; the domestic industry is assumed to run up against (external) diseconomies of scale. The Wonnacotts, however, predicted that trade would lead to the fuller exploitation of economies of scale[6] and that these gains would account for the major benefits from free trade. They concluded that the gains to Canada could be over 10 per cent of GDP, an estimate which is several times higher than those which emerged from the traditional customs union approach. Their approach was adopted by Williamson[7] in an interesting contribution to the assessment of the benefits of European Community membership in which he also arrived at estimates of benefits which were many times greater than those based on customs union theory, which reckoned that the benefits would only be a small fraction – less than the pre-Community internal tariff – of any induced Community trade.

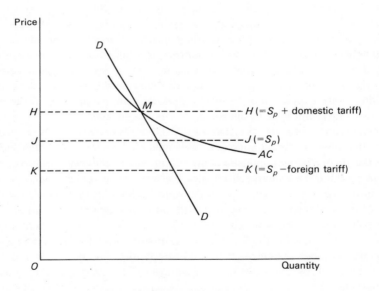

Fig. 2.2. Trade, tariffs, and scale

The Wonnacotts' approach is illustrated in Figure 2.2, adapted from one of theirs by Williamson. It shows a representative industry facing a domestic demand DD and the opportunity to sell abroad at a price OK. Competition in its domestic market from foreign producers is represented by a supply curve JJ, which is modified by a domestic tariff to HH. There is no domestic supply curve as such. The Wonnacotts argue that the most important of the conditions which generate the conventional upward-sloping domestic supply curve — the industry-specific nature of fixed capital and labour skills — will disappear over normal replacement cycles. They argue that many of the industries affected by North American free trade are subject to major economies of scale. Accordingly, the responses of the domestic industry to trade opportunities are determined by the behaviour of its average costs (AC in the diagram). The condition for the existence of the industry is that domestic demand is sufficient, at a price OH, to allow the industry to recover its costs at M. It is assumed that there is no price discrimination between domestic and foreign markets, for anti-dumping reasons. Whether or not the industry exports under conditions of protection depends on whether AC ever falls below KK, the price level realized by exporters to the foreign market. If both tariffs are abolished, all producers can realize the same price in both markets (JJ). The domestic industry's average costs will need to fall to JJ or below if it is to survive. If AC lies below JJ but above KK, the industry would not have found it economic to export previously but does find it so under free trade.

The Wonnacotts' analysis provided for the first time a framework for linking trade and scale in an integral way. The significance of this analysis relates primarily to the calculation of the benefits of free trade of an order of difference higher than those arrived at on other assumptions. The novel consideration in the calculation is that any increase in the industry's output through exporting will reduce the cost of *all* its output for the domestic market, yielding benefits over and above those accruing directly from trade expansion, measured by the familiar customs union welfare triangles. This is a subject to which this study returns in Chapter 7. The analysis does not say very much about the mechanics of the process it predicts, namely, which industries will expand and which will contract under free trade; and how will industry structures be affected. It did not consider cost differentials within the industry, the origins of these differentials, and the way in which these bear on the responses of individual producers to the opportunities offered by free trade. As in the trade literature discussed above, the structural dimension has been assumed away. Only by considering cost differences at the company level can the impacts of industry structure on trade, and of trade on industry structure, be explored. To this subject the analysis now turns.

AN APPROACH TO TRADE AND INDUSTRIAL STRUCTURE

It is helpful to imagine a starting position in which two national industries, each producing a homogeneous product and each paying identical factor prices, confront one another. They employ a common technology which is subject to economies of scale; these economies apply only to fixed factors of production. Short run marginal costs are horizontal up to full capacity, at which level all producers are operating. Fixed equipment is assumed to require replacement for technical reasons after a predetermined period of use (let us say 10 years).

Until its retirement its operating costs remain unchanged except in respect to capacity utilization.[8] Let us introduce industrial structures, that is to say, dispersions in the sizes of the producers within each industry. These size dispersions give rise to unit cost differences and it will be assumed that they are the only reason for unit cost differences. For reasons which will become clear, substantial suboptimal capacity exists in both industries. Assume also that the marginal producers in both countries happen to be of the same size, although the industries' size structures are in other respects different.

Suppose that hitherto, trade had been totally discouraged by prohibitive tariffs, but is now completely open. Prior to trade, the price levels in both countries are the same, because they both accommodate the unit costs of the marginal producers, which are therefore just able to survive. All other producers earn profits in excess of the opportunity cost of capital. Once each industry is allowed unimpeded access to the other's domestic market, it is open to any producer, existing or potential, in either country, to install new capacity in order to compete for market shares in its export market (new capacity will be necessary to achieve this because existing equipment is assumed to be already fully utilized). The incentive to do so is that any producer in either country which installs capacity of a larger scale than that of the marginal producers will achieve unit cost levels below the prevailing price level in the export market, and can therefore undercut and displace marginal foreign producers and still secure a return in excess of the cost of capital. The recognition that industries have size structures which include suboptimal capacity explains a phenomenon which is inexplicable in terms of trade theory, namely, bilateral trade in homogeneous products by industries with a common technology, facing identical factor prices. It is not necessary to introduce product differentiation to explain bilateral trade in this situation, though this factor obviously provides another important explanation. It is sufficient that low-cost producers in both countries have an incentive to displace marginal producers in export markets.

But this explanation for international trade raises in turn a more basic question about competition and the stability of industrial structures, which needs answering if this explanation is to be credible. If it is open to any producer to build new capacity of any size in order to displace the high-cost capacity of others, why would the industrial structures described above have survived *internal* competition? Why would not the displacement process have started at home, eliminating suboptimal capacity, until all producers operate at their respective minimum efficient scales, as is assumed in trade theory? What factors are we looking for which limit the profitability of displacing less efficient competitors and contain this displacement process? Two factors in particular suggest themselves; managerial constraints on company growth, and the expectation of short term losses for the company prepared to take on and drive out competitors.

It is recognized in the literature on the firm that the firm is more than just a collection of productive resources, which can be extended at any required rate in response to new opportunities. There always remains the problem of

co-ordinating them effectively; while the administrative factor is not fixed and
therefore need not lead in the long run to managerial diseconomies of scale, as
Penrose[9] pointed out, its ability to cope with *changes* in volume is limited by
the surplus managerial resources available for managing growth, over and above
those required to cope with existing levels of operations. This surplus is presumably limited by the fact that the expertise required to manage larger scale
operations is not freely available on the market; in large part, it resides in those
already in the firm with experience of operating at a scale close to the new,
higher scale, and who are capable of developing that experience to handle the
next increment in scale. In other words the organic growth of the firm is the
result of on-the-job learning and not the result of a series of capricious hops.
There is therefore a strong expectation that the size ranking within industries
remains fairly stable, particularly in mature industries.[10]

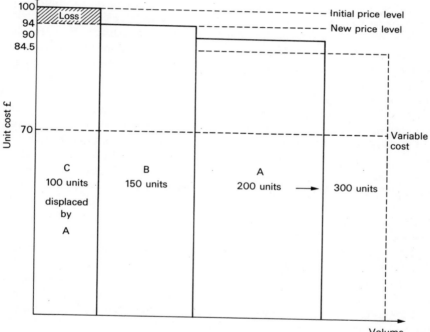

Fig. 2.3. Competition and structural change

The industry in this analysis operates in a closed economy and is composed
of just three producers, A, B, and C, producing respectively 200, 150, and 100
units, whose relative unit costs are determined only by economies of scale and
fall by 10 per cent with each doubling of volume (see Figure 2.3). Suppose
that initially, the price level is just sufficient to maintain the marginal producer,

C, in business. The two larger producers, A and B, earn rates of return above the competitive level by virtue of their cost advantage over C (of 10 per cent and 6 per cent respectively). The economies of scale apply only to the fixed costs; average variable costs are invariant to scale, at £70 per unit. The average fixed costs of the three producers at full capacity operation are respectively £20, £24, and £30.

The question at issue is whether or not this is a stable structure. This largely depends on the competitive strategy most likely to be adopted, within the given technological and cost parameters, by the firm in the most advantageous position to make predatory moves, the lowest-cost producer, A. Views will differ as to the basis for such a strategy. It is assumed here that producer A has a precise view about the likely casualties of aggressive behaviour and of the risks which it incurs by attempting to drive out a competitor. It is assumed to disregard the effect of price reductions in market demand. In focusing on competitors, rather than on the market as a whole, this account is the converse of the Cournot model which has it that the firm anticipates the effects of its price decisions on market demand but totally disregards the likely responses of competitors. Brander[11] has demonstrated that this model can yield determinate solutions to bilateral trade in a homogeneous product. The lack of realism of the Cournot assumptions strains belief. Not only are business-men operating in an oligopoly assumed to start out by disregarding the probable responses of their competitors; they are assumed to fail even to respond to their competitors' actual responses when this assumption proves incorrect. It must be questionable whether businesses which fail to learn from their mistakes are fitted to survive. The analysis offered below makes no claim to the elegance and determinacy offered by Brander's analysis but the reader may agree that it more than compensates for this by its competitive realism; it captures the flavour of business decisions and provides a heuristic way of exploring the relationship between trade and industrial structure.

Predatory moves are more likely to come from A, the lowest-cost producer. Suppose that A's 200-unit plant is due for replacement. A has the options of replacing like with like and retaining its existing market share, or installing a 300-unit plant with a view to increasing market share by driving C out of the industry and at the same time deterring any other producers from entering the industry. A could achieve this by installing the capacity to replace C's sales and lowering its price to around £94 when (or possibly before) C's plant is due for replacement in order to deter C from replacing it. It would of course be possible for A to force C to close down before its plant is technically due for retirement by reducing prices to below £70. This would be a very expensive option for A, since the price reduction might need to be sustained indefinitely. So long as C's plant remains closed down but intact, it is not wearing out and can be switched back into operation if A raises the price again. Moreover, C would know that A would be losing money by adopting this degree of aggression and may decide to hang on in the hope of A raising the price. The new price needs to be somewhere close to £94. A would gain little by lowering the price below £94 since such a price would also deter B, which will become the new marginal producer, from replacing its plant. This would create excess demand (since A would not have planned capacity to cope with B's sales) which would pull the price back up to £94. A price much above £94 increases the likelihood of new entry, because the industry's new marginal producer, B, would be earning more than a competitive rate of return. It is for consideration of course whether C would respond by installing a larger plant capable of covering its full costs. This looks unlikely within this particular structure; even a 150-unit plant would yield no profit with the price at £94 and in any case, C would face the problem of driving out B in order to make room for this capacity.

Producer A has to reckon with the likelihood that C will resist these pressures in so far as C can continue operating its capacity, provided that sales revenues more than cover variable costs. The question for A is whether the additional costs of running a larger plant well below its capacity during the period before C's plant is retired are more than compensated for by additional profits after C retires, taking account of the lower costs of the larger plant and the lower price level (assumed to be £94) which will prevail after C's departure. The answer turns on the life still left in C's plant when A has to replace its own. If A replaced its existing 200-unit plant with another, it could expect to earn profits (referred to from now on in the sense of profits in excess of opportunity costs of capital) of £2,000 a year throughout the plant's life. If A chose instead a 300-unit plant, its unit cost would increase slightly during the period prior to C's withdrawal (£91.75, composed of an average variable cost of £70 and an average fixed cost of £21.75),[12] and its annual profit would be reduced to £1,650 during this period. After C's withdrawal, A's new plant achieves full utilization; its unit cost falls to £84.5 and A's profit margin almost totally recovers, to £9.5 (£94 less £84.5) even though the price has been reduced to discourage C from replacing its capacity. Annual profits increase to £2,850. It turns out that so long as C withdraws within seven years, the (undiscounted) profits over the life of the new plant would be higher than they would have been with a 200-unit plant. In the average case, where C's plant is half way through its 10-year life when A has to renew (or expand) its plant, the undiscounted profits from the 300-unit plant exceed those from the 200-unit plant by £2,500.[13]

To return now to the discussion of international trade, the question was posed earlier: if international trade is to be explained by the displacement of the high-cost producer in one country by the low-cost producer in another, why has this competitive process not already occurred *within* countries? If it has occurred, suboptimal capacity will be the exception rather than the rule, and cannot be used as a general explanation for trade. And if competition has not removed suboptimal capacity at home, why should it do so in the international context? The stylized illustration above underlines a sufficient reason why some suboptimal capacity always survives internal competition. The additional profits which will accrue to the larger, low-cost producer over the life of its plant as a result of driving out the smaller competitor can be outweighed by the short term penalties which arise from the need to operate larger capacity at below full utilization during the period prior to the withdrawal of the high-cost competitor, more especially if the low-cost competitor feels it necessary to reduce prices prior to the retirement of the smaller competitor. Suboptimal capacity is a general phenomenon which can, along with the scale factor, therefore legitimately feature as part of a general explanation for international trade. This conclusion leads on to the next question: why should competition on an international dimension bring about displacement of high-cost by low-cost producers *additional* to that which occurs domestically?

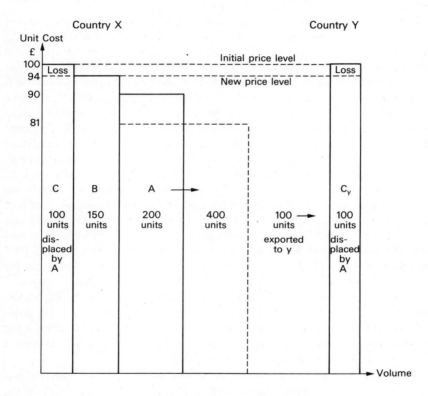

Fig. 2.4. Trade and structural change

An explanation which immediately suggests itself is that predatory adventures abroad are more attractive than those at home because they need not disturb domestic price levels and therefore incur fewer short run penalties in the form of foregone profits. But this explanation is not convincing because it assumes that price discrimination between markets can be maintained more or less indefinitely, which seems very doubtful for commodity product markets if we assume that the removal of trade barriers facilitates parallel trade and is likely to be inhibited for all products by anti-dumping measures. In any case, price discrimination does not solve the difficulty that the larger capacity necessary to serve export markets (we are ignoring marginal export sales which may well be secured by prices less than full costs) will be under-utilized until such time as the foreign high-cost producers withdraw.

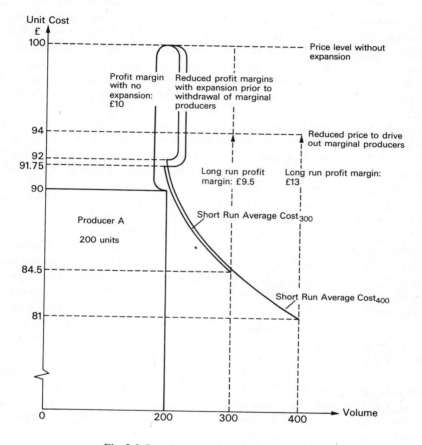

Fig. 2.5. Investment options for producer A

A more satisfactory explanation is that the additional opportunities which the export market opens up for the low-cost producer improve the economics of displacing high-cost producers *both* in the domestic and in export markets (Figure 2.4). Suppose that the marginal producer, C_y, in the trading partner — a 100-unit producer with unit costs of £100 — is due to replace its plant at the same time as C does. A could now double its capacity to 400 units to displace both marginal producers, bringing down its unit cost to £81 at full capacity.[14] At one-half capacity its unit cost is £92 (unit variable cost £70 plus £22 unit fixed cost). Using the same reasoning as before, A's profits will be lower in the period prior to the retirement of the two marginal producers than they would be if A simply replaced its 200-unit capacity because its profit margin will be lower (£8 rather than £10). But once the marginal producers withdraw, A's volume doubles to 400-units and its profit margin will increase to £13 (equal to the new price – £94 – less the full capacity unit cost – £81), as illustrated in Figure 2.5. The profitability of an aggressive policy by A in two markets simultaneously is considerably greater than in one market alone. Whereas in the domestic market alone, aggression would not pay off if the marginal producer survived longer than seven years, in the wider market created by the removal of tariffs, aggression will pay (at zero discount rates) even if the marginal producers survive for nearly nine years, that is, until A's new capacity is almost at the end of its life. In the average case, where the marginal producers' capacity has only a half-life of five years to run, the additional undiscounted profits over the life of A's new plant is £14,000, compared to the corresponding figure of £2,500 for the 300-unit plant built for the domestic market alone.[15] Expressed in terms of discount rates, the latter investment would be deterred by a discount rate of 20 per cent, whereas the former is justified even at a discount rate of 50 per cent.[16]

The inhibiting role tariffs play in this context is worth considering, by asking how great would the tariff have to be to deter A from constructing the 400-unit plant, assuming that A is prepared to accept a 19 per cent rate of return. It turns out that A would find the investment in the 400-unit plant attractive provided that the tariff were no higher than 31 per cent.[17] This would entail A selling free on board (f.o.b.) at £72 a unit in order to get into the export market at £94 a unit. It therefore appears to be worth while exporting at little above marginal cost (£70) in order to reduce unit cost and hence improve margins on the domestic market. Tariffs might therefore not seem to be particularly inhibiting to the exploitation of economies of scale; 31 per cent is, after all, a very high tariff, beyond the range of tariffs now imposed by developed countries on each others' trade. However, this is an attractively profitable project. A more realistic appreciation of the choice as between the domestically-orientated 300-unit plant and the larger, export-orientated plant would attach a risk premium to the larger expansion in plant size, partly for technical reasons, partly in recognition of the unknown difficulties likely to be encountered in the export market. To illustrate; if the management demanded a return of just below 20 per cent on the smaller project and a return of 40 per cent on the larger in recognition of its greater riskiness, a tariff of only 12.5 per cent would be sufficient to chill off the larger project. In the absence of any 'animal spirits' stimulating expansive entrepreneurs, tariffs can be a powerfully inhibiting factor on the exploitation of scale through trade.

CONCLUSIONS

The first and fairly obvious conclusion to draw from this discussion is that international trade extends the opportunities of larger, low-cost producers because it brings a greater number of vulnerable, high-cost producers within their range. The less obvious corollary is that trade accelerates the structural change of the *exporting* industry, as well as that of the industry in the importing country. Marginal producers in the exporting industry become more vulnerable once trade becomes possible, because the economics of jointly displacing marginal producers of equivalent size in both export and the domestic markets are more attractive to the larger producer than displacing marginal producers in the domestic market alone. A powerful piece of evidence which supports this proposition is to be found in the Scherer study. In a regression designed to explain representative plant size (defined as the mean of the smallest number of plants which accounted for 50 per cent of an industry's employment) the elasticity of the dependent variable (mean plant size/minimum efficient scale) with respect to export performance defined as 1 + (exports/production) was nearly four (3.78 in one regression, 3.94 in another) and was in both cases significant at the 0.01 level.[18] To illustrate the significance of this, if an industry which has not previously exported, exports 10 per cent of its production, its representative plant size increases by over 40 per cent. This high figure is difficult to explain on the basis of exports alone. Even if one new plant was built to supply the entire export market, equivalent to 10 per cent of total industry production, it is difficult to envisage, given the typical industrial structure in advanced countries, that it would pull up the average Top-50 plant size by as much as 40 per cent. The strength of this effect can only be due to the displacement of smaller plants in the domestic industry by the newer, larger plants, as predicted in the discussion of the economics of displacement outlined above.

This discussion can be extended to yield predictions about the effects of industry structure on both the *level* of bilateral trade, in relation to the combined output of two trading partners, and the trade *balance* between them. If, as has been suggested, trade originates in part from within-industry unit cost differentials, and these in turn originate from company or plant size differentials within industries, one would expect to find a positive *ex ante* relationship between the dispersion of company sizes within the two competing industries and the amount of bilateral trade between the two trading partners.

A good statistical representation of inequality in company size within an industry is provided by the Herfindahl index of concentration.[19] It correlates closely with the so-called concentration ratio — the share of industry sales or employment accounted for by a small number of the largest firms.[20] This observation opens the way for a straight-forward test of the link between industry structure and the level of bilateral trade. Other things being equal, one would therefore expect to discover a positive relationship between the average of the two competing industries' concentration ratios and the volume of bilateral trade between their two countries in the product concerned, measured in relation to the two industries' combined output. This relationship could of course be dislocated by any recognition of 'spheres of influence' by the two industries which might occur at high levels of concentration, which would inhibit exporters in either industry from making excursions into each other's domestic markets.

The trade balance will reflect the relative strength of the constraints and opportunities facing the two groups of companies. Firstly, the rate of expansion of all producers alike is constrained by managerial factors. For the purposes of this discussion, let us assume that no producer feels capable of more than doubling his capacity at each ten-year replacement. Within this limitation, the initial responses will be conditioned by availability of finance and the profitability of expansion, both of which are dependent on size. In so far as the availability of finance depends on internally generated funds, the larger producers are better able to finance further expansion. Whereas the marginal producer is just able to replace its capital, the 200-unit producers' margin on sales is 10 percentage points in excess of this requirement. The larger producer also finds it more profitable to expand, either by a given absolute amount − for example, by 100 units to displace a marginal producer − or by a given proportion. For example, whereas the 200-unit producer would earn an additional profit of £2,500 over ten years by displacing the marginal 100-unit producer, the 150-unit producer would earn an additional £1,600, on similar assumptions (a price reduction of £6, at the time of the withdrawal of the marginal producer after 5 years). And whereas a doubling of capacity in order to displace 100-unit producers yields additional profits of £14,000 for the 200-unit producer, it only yields an additional £6,000 for the 150-unit producer.[21]

These considerations suggest that the growth rate of companies in response to new exporting opportunities is positively related to their initial size. Marginal producers can probably do no more than replace their existing capacity, whereas larger producers will begin to plan to displace marginal producers at home and abroad. The balance of trade will be determined by the outcome of these plans in aggregate, and will therefore tend to favour the industry whose units of capacity are on average of greater scale. Each industry will lose its tail of marginal plants as the price level is forced down; the industry with more low-cost capacity will tend to occupy the greater share of the spaces left by these departing producers.

This analysis of the economics of trade informs the remainder of this study. In general terms, it underlines the importance of relative costs in determining competitive positions and hence trade balances, even in industries in which non-price dimensions of competitiveness are important. More specifically, it provides three testable propositions about trade and industrial structure in the European Community:

1. Particularly in the early stages of the Community, industries which achieve the greater average scale in their manufacturing operations will tend to secure trade advantages over their counterparts in partner countries. An equilibrium position will eventually be reached in which both trading partners operate on comparable scales; trade will have eliminated suboptimal capacity in both

countries. The trade balance will still favour the country whose industry first achieved superior scale, because more capacity will have been eliminated in the net importing country. *Ex ante*, scale shapes the trade pattern. *Ex post*, there may be no observable relationship between scale and trade advantage.

2. Intra-industry trade is positively associated with industrial concentration. Trade originates in part from unit cost differentials within industries; these derive from company or plant size differentials which characterize concentrated industries.

3. In the process of European integration, industrial structures will tend to change with market leaders expanding at the expense of smaller producers.

Welfare Considerations

The discussion in this chapter began by estimating the benefits of pure exchange between countries, without involving shifts of resources, and proceeded then to consider how trade generates competitive pressures which do shift resources and change the structures of the competing industries. This analysis offers insights into the benefits which arise directly i.e. disregarding any induced efficiency gains by the survivors. If it is assumed that producer A would not have expanded to 300 units in the absence of free trade but that the favourable economics of expanding in the export and domestic markets simultaneously induced its expansion from 200 units to 400 units, the benefits attributable to trade expansion are as follows:

1. cost of producing A's 400 units before trade: £38,000[22]

less:

2. cost of these units after trade: £32,400

Benefit from trade expansion: £5,600
Value of trade: 100 units @ £94 = £9,400
Value of benefit as a proportion of increased trade: 60 per cent.

This order of magnitude is considerably greater than was estimated by Williamson, who estimated the direct scale-related benefits (including the resource implications of price-induced increases in demand for the product concerned) to be 38 per cent of the trade expansion, on the assumption of much greater economies of scale (20 per cent cost reduction per doubling of volume).[23] The benefits which can be derived from trade are even greater than those calculated from the Wonnacott–Williamson approach, when account is taken of the structural implication of trade within, as well as between industries.[24] These benefits are reviewed in Chapter 7, in the light of the empirical analysis which follows.

NOTES

1 See, for example, the discussion by Nils Lundgren, 'Customs Unions and Industrialised West European Countries' in *Economic Integration in Europe*, ed. G. Denton (London, 1969). Arguably the best analysis of the static benefits of Community membership ever carried out, within an equilibrium world trade framework, by Miller and Spencer, *Economic Effects of UK Joining the EEC*, ruled out economies of scale by adopting constrained Cobb-Douglas production functions.

2 This is true in a number of industries, even in terms of the stylized picture of the world composed of 'steel', 'aircraft', and 'electric motors'. A large European country cannot always attain minimum efficient scale (MES), even with trade. A survey of published MES estimates (*A Review of Monopolies and Mergers Policy*, HMSO Cmnd. 7198, May 1978, Annex C) revealed that MES exceeded UK levels of production in electronic calculators, turbo generators, TV tubes, and aircraft, and exceeded 50 per cent of production in industrial diesels, electric motors, and refrigerators.

3 Wilfred J. Ethier, 'National and International Returns to Scale in the Modern Theory of International Trade', *American Economic Review*, 72, No. 3, June 1982.

4 Paul R. Krugman, 'Intraindustry Specialisation and the Gains from Trade', *Journal of Political Economy*, 89, No. 5, 1981.

5 Ronald J. and Paul Wonnacott, *Free Trade between the United States and Canada* (Cambridge, Mass., 1967).

6 'major gains from free trade . . . depend primarily on the exploitation of economies of scale, broadly defined to include not only engineering economies but also managerial and organizational efficiencies associated with specialization and competition in a larger market.' (*Free Trade*, p. 336.)

7 John Williamson, 'Trade and Economic Growth' in *The Economics of Europe: What the Common Market Means for Britain*, ed. J. Pinder (London, 1971).

8 There is an admitted degree of artificiality in this assumption. It would be more realistic to assume that plant is physically durable and is retired only when prices do not cover variable costs. However, to explain the process by which this occurs requires a vintage model incorporating rates of technological change, which would unhelpfully complicate the analysis discussed here.

9 Edith T. Penrose, *The Theory of the Growth of the Firm*, 2nd edn., (Oxford, 1980), p. 201.

10 This assumption comes pretty close to assuming that company growth rates are drawn randomly from a normal distribution. See F. M. Scherer, *Industrial Structure and Economic Performance*, 2nd edn., (Chicago, 1980), pp. 145-50, for an illustration of how computer simulations using this assumption can generate plausible trends in an industry's concentration.

11 James A. Brander, 'Intra-Industry Trade in Identical Commodities', *Journal of International Economics*, 11 (1981), pp. 1-14.

12 At full capacity, the average cost of the 300-unit plant is £84.5 (£70 AVC; £14.5 AFC). At two-thirds capacity, AFC is 50 per cent higher at £21.75.

13 $(5 \times £1,650) + (5 \times £2,850) - (10 \times £2,000) = £2,500$.

14 The unit cost of the 400-unit plant is £81 at full capacity (£70 AVC; £11 AFC). At one-half capacity AFC is £22, AC is £92.

15 $(5 \times £1,600) + (5 \times £5,200) - (10 \times £2,000) = £14,000$.

16 Relative to the option of replacing like with like, which yields profits of £2,000 a year, the 300-unit plant loses £350 a year for the first five years of its life and gains £850 a year for the remaining five. The present value of this stream of opportunity costs and benefits is:

$$PV = -350 \left[(1 + i)^5 - 1\right]/i + 850 \left[(1 + i)^5 - 1\right]/i \, (1 + i)^5$$

PV just positive when $i = 0.19$, negative when $i = 0.20$.

The 400-unit plant yields a present value

$$PV = -400 \left[(1 + i)^5 - 1\right]/i + 3200 \left[(1 + i)^5 - 1\right]/i \, (1 + i)^5$$

PV is positive at $i = 0.50$.

17 Whether or not the 400-unit plant justifies itself, at a discount rate of 19 per cent, when a tariff, t, is imposed on the 100 units exported depends on whether:

$$PV = [(200 \times 8) - (200 \times 10)] \ [(1 + i)^5/i - 1]$$
$$+ \ [(300 \times 13) + 100\{94/(1 + t) - 81\} - (200 \times 10)] \ [(1 + i)^5 - 1]/[i(1 + i)^5]$$

is positive. This condition is satisfied provided that $t < 0.31$.

18 Scherer, *Multi-plant Operation*, pp. 118 and 119, table 3.22. The converse was not true: imports did not appear to reduce plant size.

19 The Herfindahl index is expressed as:

$$H = \sum_{i=1}^{n} S_i^2$$

where n is the number of firms in an industry, S_i is the ith firm's share of industry sales. If s_i is the deviation of the share of the ith firm from the industry mean,

$$\text{the variance} = \frac{1}{n-1} \sum_{1}^{n} s_i^2 = \sum_{1}^{n} S_i^2 - \frac{1}{n}\left(\sum_{1}^{n} S_i\right)^2$$

$$= \sum_{1}^{n} S_i^2 - \frac{1}{n}$$

$$\text{since } \sum_{1}^{n} S_i = 1$$

Therefore the Herfindahl index

$$H = \sum_{1}^{n} S_i^2 = \text{variance of market shares} + \frac{1}{n}$$

20 By way of illustration, in an industry composed of r large, equally-sized firms and a large number of small firms, and the Concentration Ratio, CR_r, measures the combined market share of the largest r firms, the Herfindahl index approximates to CR_r^2/r — hence the degree of correlation observed between the two measures of concentration. Scherer, *Industrial Market Structure*, p. 58, reports a correlation of 0.936 between the Herfindahl index and the four-firm concentration ratio for 91 American manufacturing industries.

21 The 150-unit producer's unit cost will decline from £94 at 150 units to £84.5 at 300-units at full capacity. At one-half capacity, the 300-unit plant's unit cost rises to £99 (£70 unit variable cost plus £29 average fixed cost). Therefore the 150-unit plant will earn £9,000 during its life (150-units earning a margin of £6 over 10 years). By expanding, the 150-unit producer earns a margin of only £1 over the five years prior to the withdrawal of the marginal producer (£750 in total); and of £9.5 during the subsequent five years (£94 − £84.5), yielding a profit of £14,250. In total, expansion yields £15,000, £6,000 more than remaining at 150-units.

22 The marginal producers' unit cost was £100; A's was £90. Total cost: £10,000 + £10,000 + £18,000. A's unit cost after trade is £81; A's 400 units cost £32,400.

23 Williamson, *Trade and Economic Growth*, p. 36.

24 To illustrate this difference, Williamson and the Wonnacotts calculated the benefits in terms of the reduction in costs arising from the average increase in the exporting industry's volume. In the example analysed above, the exporting industry's volume increased by 22 per cent. This implies an average cost reduction of 2.2 per cent and a cost saving, on the exporting industry's original volume of 450 units, of 10 units. The approach adopted above focused on the cost savings resulting from the displacement of the 100-unit producer by the 200-unit producer, whose unit cost falls from £90 to £81 and saves 100 × (£100–£81) + 200 × (£90–£81) = £3,700, or 37 units valued at the original pre-trade price of £100, equivalent to 8 per cent of industry's pre-trade volume, compared to the 2.2 per cent implied by the Wonnacott–Williamson approach.

CHAPTER 3

INTRA-COMMUNITY TRADE
AND INDUSTRIAL STRUCTURE

This chapter describes an investigation of the intra-Community trade pattern in the mid-1960s.[1] Its main purpose is to explore the first proposition in the conclusion of the previous chapter — that as the Community's internal tariffs were dismantled and intra-Community trade gathered momentum, those industries which were operating at that time with a scale advantage began to dominate those operating on a smaller scale. Larger scale would imply lower unit costs, which would provide the competitive advantage with which industries with these scale advantages could press into their neighbouring markets. If this proposition is correct one would expect to find an association between an industry's relative scale of operations and its trade performance *vis-à-vis* its Community neighbours. This investigation tests whether such an association existed in the bilateral trade patterns in 1964 between the three major members of the original Community: France, Germany and Italy.

A country's trade performance in each industry *vis-à-vis* a trading partner is defined in this study in terms of its trade balance with its partner, divided by the two partners' bilateral trade, in the products of the industry concerned. For example, if in a particular industry, French exports to and imports from Germany were respectively $60m and $40m, the French industry's trade performance *vis-à-vis* the German industry would be measured as $(60-40)/(60+40) = 0.2$.[2] The object of the enquiry is to test whether trade performance, measured in these terms, can be explained by comparative scale, measured in terms of the comparative size of the representative companies or plants in each pair of competing industries.

In order to isolate and identify these relationships it was necessary to consider the competitive context in 1964. The analysis in the previous chapter argued that in the absence of tariff barriers, competition would develop across frontiers in accordance with the dictates of profit-maximization; but was cross-border competition a reality at that time, particularly in highly concentrated industries? Or was competition still severely restrained by non-tariff barriers and a spheres-of-influence mentality conditioned by a long history of cartelization? The analysis in the last chapter also assumed away comparative advantage within the Community. How reasonable is this assumption? If it is not, the basis of this comparative advantage needs to be identified and its effects isolated from those of comparative industrial structure.

THE COMPETITIVE CONTEXT

The setting for this analysis was a common market in a fledgeling state. The

Treaty of Rome was signed in 1957; the signatories pledged to begin dismantling tariffs levied on imports from each other from 1 January 1958 and to have eliminated them by 1 January 1968. Many of the tariffs imposed in 1957 were substantial, particularly those of France and Italy (30 per cent and 35–40 per cent respectively on cars, 25 per cent on cameras and radios, for example). Trade was slow to respond to these tariff reductions. Intra-Community trade was equivalent to 5 per cent of the Community's manufacturing output in 1960. During the early 1960s trade increased very gradually to only 6.5 per cent of Community production in 1965. By 1980, the corresponding figure (relating to the six original members) had reached 30 per cent.

In the period covered by this chapter, and for some years after, intra-Community trade made little impact on the very high price differentials existing between community markets. In part these were due to discriminatory pricing policies adopted by manufacturers, reinforced by prohibitions on dealers which prevented them from re-exporting from the low-price to the high-price markets. But although it is the restrictive practices designed to snuff out parallel trade which attracted attacks by the commission,[3] it was probably the archaic distribution systems still in operation in much of the Community in the 1960s which contributed more to restraining trade. Whereas Germany adopted a rationalized distribution system in 1967, with specialized dealers, mail order houses, large department stores, and self-service shops, France, Belgium, and Italy still operated traditional, unspecialized, high-margin distribution systems. Thus in 1968, retail prices for radio and TV sets in these countries were 30–50 per cent higher than in Germany.[4]

Archaic distribution systems posed considerable entry barriers in terms of cost of access to a market; and, more relevant to this study, they tended to weaken the link between manufacturing performance and trade. The traditional retail system is slow to pass on to the consumer any cost reductions achieved in manufacturing by rationalization and economies of scale. As a result, the manufacturers' sales are less price-sensitive. In circumstances such as these, profit-maximizing calculations argue in favour of exploiting cost advantages in the form of increased profit margins rather than higher volumes. A lack of economic integration in the Community increases the likelihood that producers would set prices on this basis, suggesting that it would be unrealistic to expect that trade patterns in 1964 would be more than moderately sensitive to international differences in unit costs and to features of industrial structures which gave rise to such unit cost differentials. Moreover, it seems necessary to take explicit account of this kind of rational pricing behaviour when exploring these sensitivities, a subject which is returned to later.

Spheres of Influence and Restraints on Trade

The discussion in the previous chapter suggested that export opportunities within the Community would tend to encourage the expansion of the lower-cost producers at the expense of high-cost producers in both the export and the domestic markets. This assumes that competitors in the Community do not reach tacit understandings to refrain from seriously engaging each other across national frontiers. Was this assumption justified in 1964? There are both historical and theoretical grounds for doubting whether it was. European industry was heavily cartelized before the Second World War and a number of industries such as steel, chemicals, and cement carried over this tradition of anti-competitive behaviour into the post-war period. And even where cartels were absent, it was to be expected that the market leaders in the respective national markets, which had enjoyed a sheltered existence behind tariff barriers before the formation of the Community, would hesitate before locking horns with their counterparts in neighbouring markets once the tariff barriers were removed. Oligopolistic industries would be the most likely of any to exercise this restraint and recognize their respective spheres of influence. Oligopoly theory argues that industries dominated by a few producers will exercise restraints on those forms of competition likely to be most damaging. According to this account, the leading protagonists in an industry are able to recognize and anticipate each other's competitive responses and to reach thereby a *modus vivendi* which yields benefits to the owners of the industry, in the form of higher profits, greater stability in market shares, or a quieter life. If this theory has any relevance to competitive behaviour, it is possible that any restraints which may condition the competitive modes in the domestic markets carry across to the international level. If a neighbouring industry is also highly concentrated, the leaders in both industries will recognize their interdependence and will refrain from making damaging visits into each other's territory. It is a natural extension of oligopoly theory to suggest that intra-industry trade would be lower in relation to industry output when the trading partners' industries are highly concentrated.

Empirical studies of individual industries' competitive behaviour prior to the formation of the Community lend some indirect support for this line of argument. Phlips's pioneering study of integration in the European cement, fertilizer, and photographic film markets in the period up to 1958 concluded that the marketing practices adopted by these industries, which had the effect of isolating national markets, would have the effect of restraining cross-frontier price competition even if tariffs were removed.[5] On the other hand, the previous chapter has advanced a competing hypothesis that concentration actually encourages trade. It was suggested that, provided high industrial concentration did not inhibit competition, concentration would encourage trade because trade originates in part from within-industry unit cost differentials; and that these in turn could be related to the dispersion of company size in an industry, itself a measure of industrial concentration.[6]

As a preliminary piece of ground-clearance work it was decided to test the respective strengths of these hypotheses. The test examined the same bilateral trade flows between France, Germany, and Italy discussed above. It calculated the propensity to trade in each industry — the level of bilateral trade divided by the combined output of each pair of industries — and tested whether this

TABLE 3.1.   *Regression Results: Bilateral Trade and Concentration*

Dependent Variable :	$\dfrac{\text{bilateral trade}}{\text{combined output}}$ × 100			
Constant term	Concentration	Public Purchasing[a]	R^2	F
France–Germany : 1.62	46 industries .0016 (1.44)	−1.79 (1.61)	.076	1.8
France–Italy : 1.18	70 industries .0013* (1.92)	−1.25 (1.55)	.068	2.4*
Germany–Italy : 1.18	44 industries .0035** (2.11)		.096	4.5**

[a] Dummy variable taking value of 1 in three industries: N.I.C.E. 381 (shipbuilding), 382 (railway vehicles), and 386 (aircraft).
* significant at 10 per cent.
** significant at 5 per cent.
The figures in parentheses are t statistics.

propensity to trade was related to the average concentration in the two industries, measured as the average of the eight-firm concentration ratios. The regression results are reported in Table 3.1; the data appear in Appendix 3, and are based upon the *Nomenclature des Industries Etablies dans Les Communautés Euro-péenes* (N.I.C.E.), adopted by the Community's Statistical Office.

In all three trades, the level of bilateral trade was found to be positively related to average concentration with varying degrees of statistical significance, low in the France–Germany trade, 10 per cent in the France–Italy trade, 5 per cent in the Germany–Italy trade. Public purchasing biases in favour of national suppliers were explored with a dummy variable taking values of unity in three transport equipment industries known to be dominated by public purchasing — shipbuilding, railway vehicles and aircraft — and zero elsewhere. The public purchasing variable registered an effect in the expected direction in two cases but of only moderate statistical significance. It would seem, then, that whatever the strengths of the spheres-of-influence mentality, which undoubtedly prevailed in several industries, in so far as it was related to industrial concentration of ownership it was dominated by some other factor.[7] The effect of within-industry cost differentials seems a likely explanation.[8]

Comparative Advantage within the Community

The other preliminary question which the study had to consider was whether the structure-trade performance relationship, which was its prime focus, was operating upon a pattern of intra-Community trade which was intelligible in terms of comparative advantage. Trade theory suggests that countries specialize in industries which make intensive use of the factors of production with which they are

TABLE 3.2. *Bilateral Trade Performance in 1964*

Industry N.I.C.E. classification	Industry description	Trade Performance 1964[a]		
		France / Germany	France / Italy	Germany / Italy
232	Wool	0.5226	0.1515	-0.4523
233	Cotton	0.2633	0.5949	-0.3723
235	Linen and hemp	0.5600	0.8649	-0.7289
236	Other textiles fibres	0.9350	0.0740	-1.0000
237	Hosiery	0.4865	-0.8183	-0.5022
239	Other textiles	0.4232	-0.2593	0.3892
243	Garments	0.2448	-0.6619	-0.8037
244	Mattresses and beds	0.1720	0.1847	0.4345
245	Fur goods	0.7821	-0.4420	-0.2304
251	Saw mills	0.7090	0.9760	0.8651
253	Frames and floors	-0.1856	-0.1562	-0.5612
255	Other wood products	-0.2993	-0.7422	-0.4002
259	Cork products	-0.0899	-0.7640	-0.4477
271	Pulp, paper, and board	0.2008	0.5153	0.1272
272	Paper products	-0.1514	0.4193	0.5021
280	Printing and publishing	-0.3999	-0.6847	0.3044
291	Tanning	0.7130	0.7140	-0.3427
292	Leather products	-0.1902	-0.5550	-0.5727
301	Synthetic rubber	0.2809	-0.3465	-0.5666
302	Plastic materials	-0.2947	-0.3311	-0.4253
303	Synthetic fibres	0.0558	-0.6899	-0.1452
304	Starch, glue, and gelatine	0.5605	0.3831	0.8065
311	Basic chemicals	-0.2773	0.0618	0.2845
312	Industrial and agricultural chemicals	-0.2422	0.2034	0.6941
313	Chemicals for domestic consumption	0.0025	0.2926	0.7795
320	Petroleum	0.9107	-0.8367	-0.5912
331	Baked clay products	-0.6269	-0.4513	-0.0014
332	Glass	0.3334	0.2975	-0.4751
333	Pottery	-0.8327	-0.2009	0.7192

334	Cement	0.8758	0.8967	-0.0625
335	Concrete products	0.2345	-0.9239	-0.8593
339	Stone and non-metallic mineral products	—	-0.6407	—
341	Steel mills	0.0660	0.6989	0.6017
342	Steel tubes	-0.7771	0.3316	0.2368
343	Wire-drawing	-0.3046	0.8258	-0.0919
344	Primary non-ferrous metals	0.1923	0.1188	0.0042
345	Foundries	-0.4019	0.1949	0.3397
352	Second transformation of metals	-0.7760	-0.1300	0.6726
353	Metallic construction	-0.4470	0.5231	0.6468
354	Boiler-works	-0.6099	0.1016	0.7253
355	Metal tools	-0.5423	-0.5842	0.4657
361	Farm equipment	-0.5870	-0.1784	0.7289
362	Office machines	0.1260	-0.3441	-0.1080
363	Machine tools	0.6654	0.6841	-0.2372
364	Textile machinery	-0.6922	-0.2333	0.5561
365	Food products machinery	-0.7375	-0.4913	0.6344
366	Mining and construction machinery	-0.2399	0.0036	0.6268
367	Transmission equipment	-0.2811	0.4447	0.2838
368	Other specific machinery	-0.8706	-0.6312	0.7044
369	Other machinery	-0.5970	-0.3846	0.4545
381	Shipbuilding	-0.5928	-0.2867	-0.5857
382	Railway vehicles	-0.5243	-0.4107	0.7599
383	Motor vehicles	-0.2992	-0.2262	0.0657
385	Motorcycles	0.2474	-0.3084	-0.8598
386	Aircraft	0.7463	0.1259	-0.7467
389	Other transport equipment	-0.3995	-0.2988	-0.3652
391	Measuring equipment	-0.6786	0.3297	0.2845
392	Medical equipment	-0.5844	-0.6207	0.8995
393	Opthalmic and photographic equipment	-0.6235	-0.0515	0.4477
394	Watches and clocks	-0.3764	0.5691	0.5330
395	Jewellery	-0.3229	-0.7381	-0.8581
396	Musical instruments	-0.8384	-0.8106	-0.2784
397	Games, toys, and sports equipment	-0.4380	-0.3984	-0.1985

a The trade performance measures are calculated on the basis explained on page 37.

relatively well endowed. If a factor of production is relatively abundant in a particular country, it will tend to be cheaper in terms of other factors, compared to the situation in countries which are less well-endowed in that factor. Countries with abundant land, export food in exchange for manufactures; or those with abundant unskilled labour specialize in low-technology, labour-intensive manufacturing activities, producing items such as clothing and footware.

Within the industrialized countries of Europe there is no pronounced comparative advantage based on factor proportions but to the extent that comparative advantage does exist, it is more likely to depend on the availability of skills. The relative abundance of skilled labour in Germany, generated by its excellent technical education system, suggests that Germany is likely to specialize in skill-intensive newer-technology industries in the mechanical and electrical engineering sectors, and to export these products in exchange for those of the more mature technologies such as process industries, textiles, and clothing. This expectation is borne out by an impressionistic look at the first and second halves of Table 3.2. In the first 31 industries (N.I.C.E. 232–335) which include the textile sector and a range of process type and materials-based industries, Germany was out-performed by France in 20 out of the 31 industries. But in the second half of the table (N.I.C.E. 341–97), which is largely composed of machine building, other capital goods industries, electronics, and instruments, Germany out-performed France in 25 out of 31 industries. A similar pattern is evident in the Germany–Italy trades. There was evidently a distinct comparative advantage within the Community as between Germany and the other two countries studied here.[9]

PROBLEMS OF DATA, MEASUREMENT, AND MODEL DESIGN

The main data problem was the absence of an industrial classification to reconcile trade classifications and the Community's industrial census classification. Accordingly, a cross-matching of the trade and census classifications for the entire industrial spectrum had to be developed from the ground level. The industrial structure data base was provided by the 1963 industrial census conducted throughout the Community by the Statistical Office of the European Communities and published in 1969. The census was organized around the Community's own three-digit, N.I.C.E. classification system.[10] Five-digit Standard International Trade Classification (S.I.T.C.) categories were allocated to the 3-digit N.I.C.E. industry categories. In a number of cases the S.I.T.C. categories had to be distributed among 2, 3, or even 5 N.I.C.E. categories. A number of industries could not be matched with trade classifications and had to be excluded. In the shoe industry, for example, the census distinguished between shoes manufactured by mass production methods (N.I.C.E. 241) and by hand (N.I.C.E. 242). No such distinction was found in the trade data. The reconciliation is shown in Appendix 4.

The other data problems were associated with measuring the representative plant and firm sizes of each industry. It is not entirely clear from a conceptual viewpoint which dimension of size is most appropriate to this analysis. The discussion in the previous chapter emphasized the *largest* units in an industry (without distinguishing plants and firms) since these appeared to have the strongest incentives (and capacities) to attack neighbouring markets. The measure used for this was that used by Bain[11] — the average size of the largest 20 plants and firms in an industry. But arguably the size of the *representative* firm or plant should also be considered. If an industry has a propensity to build larger plants than its neighbour (larger, that is, in relation to the average plant size differential between the two countries) it should be more competitive.

The choice of the representative unit itself was not straightforward. It was clear that simple averages of company or plant size in an industry would not suffice; they would be dominated by the long tail of small firms which probably did not participate in international trade at all and whose coverage in the census, it was suspected, varied from one country to another. For example, the traditional handicrafts activities are stronger in Italy than in France and Germany. In industries which include such activities (footwear, textiles, furniture) it was noticeable that the number of Italian establishments with less than 10 employees far outnumbered the French and German establishments, even though the overall structures of these industries were in other aspects comparable. But selecting an average of larger companies could introduce biases too. As Scherer[12] observed, a comparison of the mean size of the top 20 plants can be ill-advised when the size of the two industries is widely different. Each industry has its complement of 'cats and dogs' plants which exploit special technologies or serve special market segments. The smaller the industry, the deeper into this tail of 'cats and dogs' plants one would have to reach in order to find 20 plants. It is quite possible that the top-20 measure proposed above suffers from this problem. Although the three countries are broadly similar in economic size, so that this bias is not as great as it might be in comparisons of, say, the USA and Canada, the bias is not negligible.[13] The representative size measure was chosen to avoid this problem; it measured the average size of the largest firms and plants accounting for 60 per cent of industry employment.

The purely statistical problem of calculating the top-20 and top-60 per cent measures from the grouped and incomplete census data was rather greater. This was particularly so in respect to the German data on employment by enterprises, which for disclosure reasons were either suppressed altogether in a number of larger size classes (and in at least one other size class to prevent accurate calculations of the suppressed class's employment by subtraction) in most industries, or made less precise in respect of both plants and enterprises by collapsing neighbouring size classes together.

A study by Phlips[14] on concentration discarded the German data for analytical purposes altogether. It was found possible to work around these difficulties, noting first that the suppressions related to enterprise size rather than plant size; whereas the Phlips study was concerned with ownership and oligopolistic behaviour, this study is concerned more with comparative costs. Because this aspect is related much more strongly to relative plant size, rather than the size of the top four or eight enterprises, suppressed data relating only to the latter was not a problem. Secondly, because of the central role played by the German economy in Community trade it was essential for this study to persevere with the incomplete German data and to extract the maximum value from it. To this end, rather more intensive thought was devoted here than was given in previous studies to develop the interpolation techniques necessary to derive the top-20 and top-60 per cent measures (see Appendix 5).

Part of the missing data problem diminished when it was realized that the employment in the smaller classes, suppressed to prevent accurate calculations of the employment in the larger enterprises, could be assumed without introducing substantial errors. The possible errors introduced by assuming that the class mean of the smaller classes lies at the mid-point of the class boundaries turned out to be small in relation to the size of the employment in the larger classes, which the study was primarily concerned with.

The Specification of the Regression Model

One problem of model design was the capture of comparative advantage using census data. No data on industries' skill composition were available. From a theoretical viewpoint, the average industry wage, which was available, is the best proxy, since inter-industry wage differentials would reflect skill requirements if labour markets were functioning efficiently. They generally do not, of course; skill differentials are frequently compressed by the bargaining powers of the semi-skilled and unskilled; workers in capital-intensive industries have superior bargaining power because of the relative inelasticity of the derived demand for their labour (the highest wages in 1962 in this study were paid by the most capital-intensive industry, petroleum); and in the early stages of the Community, before intra-Community trade had made a significant impact on competitive behaviour, wage levels in many industries could be influenced just as strongly by the absence of competitive behaviour as by skill differentials. Average wages were experimented with in the study as a proxy for skill but without success.

A more promising approach, which side-steps some of these complications, focuses on the distinction between capital-intensive process industries and skilled, labour-intensive industries. A reasonable proxy for the capital-intensity of an industry is its value added per worker, or labour productivity in value terms; if the capital per worker in these industries tends on average to earn its appropriate return, it will be reflected in value added. The highest labour productivity was recorded by the petroleum industry, followed by synthetic fibres, cement, and the chemicals industries. It is true that value added per worker will also be influenced by skill-intensity but this appeared to have been swamped by the effects of capital-intensity. This variable offered a way of making the distinction which was sought, that between mature technologies in which France and Italy were likely to have had a comparative advantage, and newer, generally more labour-intensive, industries in which Germany had and still has a basis for a comparative advantage. Accordingly, value added per worker is averaged across each pair of competing industries; German trade performances are expected to be negatively related to it.

The second problem of model design was to cope with the distortions in competition, which are known to have existed in the early 1960s. The previous discussion suggested that inefficiencies in distribution which were prevalent in the 1960s weakened the link between prices and market shares. In conditions of this kind, there is considerable scope for particular industries to price significantly above costs without incurring grievous damage from imports from partner countries.[15] Since particular industries did price well above costs, and to a greater extent than their counterparts in partner countries, one would expect to see a poor bilateral trade performance, despite the muted state of cross-frontier competition.

The census offers no direct way of measuring these margins,[16] but here again, it offers an indirect approach. It permitted calculations of value added per employee for each industry. Value added per employee is a product of physical labour productivity and the 'price' of value added. Thus the level of the French value added per employee in a particular industry relative to the German equivalent is equal to:

$$\frac{\text{French physical labour productivity}}{\text{German physical labour productivity}} \times \frac{\text{French price levels}}{\text{German price levels.}}$$

If relative labour productivity is included in an equation explaining trade performance, its role will depend on which of these two quotients dominated the variable, and on the extent to which the structural variables (relative plant and firm size) already pick up relative physical labour productivity, as would be expected from the close relationship between relative plant size and physical labour productivity found in the Scherer study. If it is the case that relative prices dominate this variable, and/or relative plant size already reflects relative physical labour productivity, an industry whose value added per employee is high relative to that of its competition, will, paradoxically, tend to have a poorer trade performance. Relative productivity (value added per worker) is, in principle, able to identify a major source of trade distortions.[17]

Tariffs are the more obvious source of trade distortion but were not expected to be a useful contributor to this study. Tariffs on intra-Community trade were still important in 1964, and because harmonization related to percentage reductions, and not to levels, they probably distorted trade balances until they were eliminated. But tariffs themselves are not independent variables. They originate from industries' needs; weak performers tend to put pressure on their governments to negotiate for higher tariffs. Therefore tariffs could hardly figure as an explanation of industries' trade performance.[18]

The final element in the design of the analysis is concerned with the basic question: is the model actually testing what it purports to test? It purports to test the impact of scale advantage on trade performance, but could the direction of causation just as likely run in the opposite direction? The discussion in the previous chapter suggested that industry structure and trade performance are interrelated; trading opportunities encourage the larger companies to expand by displacing smaller competitors in both export and domestic markets. As trade develops, industries which secure positive trade balances will increase in size relative to those which sustain deficits and they may also increase their relative plant size in the process. Plant superiority generates balance of payments surpluses which may in turn reinforce plant size advantage.

It is for consideration, then, whether the interrelation between trade performance and relative plant size can be adequately handled in a simple-equation model, or whether it is necessary to endogenize relative plant size in a simultaneous system. The latter approach was considered but not pursued because there were insufficient independent variables to identify such a system. But in any case it seemed likely that a single-equation approach would be adequate for this particular analysis. The relative strengths of the two causal relationships (from structure to trade performance and from trade performance to structure) depend on the stage at which integration had reached in the Community. In the early stages, intra-Community trade was a modest 5 per cent of industrial output. The snapshot of the trade patterns in 1964, which is studied here, represents the position soon after the European competitors had made their opening lunges into their neighbours' markets from the vantage points determined, it is suggested, by their relative plant sizes in 1962. The bilateral trade balances at that time were too small, at most a few per cent of industry sales, to make significant differences to average plant sizes. Only when trade had accelerated throughout the 1960s would one expect to see noticeable effects of export success in any one market within the Community on the average plant sizes of the exporting country. For this reason, it seems likely that the direction of causation underlying any significant correlation which may emerge between trade performance in 1964 and relative plant size in 1962 ran from plant size to trade performance.

An alternative hypothesis which can be tested is that trade performance and relative plant size are associated, because both variables are joint consequences of some other success factor. Industries which are successful in world markets, for whatever reason, might be expected to succeed also in Community markets; their success provides the room for the construction of larger plants — hence a likelihood of an observed association between trade performance and relative plant size. As a check against this possibility, relative industry size was included as an independent variable alongside relative plant size, to test whether there is an association between relative plant size and trade performance independent of trade performance.

The variables used in the analysis are as follows:

Dependent Variables:

TP_{fg} = French trade performance with respect to Germany,
TP_{fi} = French trade performance with respect to Italy,
TP_{gi} = German trade performance with respect to Italy.

TP is measured in terms of exports, X, whose direction is indicated by the order of the country subscripts, e.g., French exports to Germany are denoted by X_{fg} (an industry subscript to all variables, suppressed for notational simplicity, is to be understood throughout). TP is defined as the bilateral trade balance for each industry, as a proportion of the bilateral trade:

$$TP_{fg} = (X_{fg} - X_{gf})/(X_{fg} + X_{gf})$$
$$TP_{fi} = (X_{fi} - X_{if})/(X_{fi} + X_{if})$$
$$TP_{gi} = (X_{gi} - X_{ig})/(X_{gi} + X_{ig}).$$

Independent variables:

$P_{20fg}, P_{20fi}, P_{20gi}$ = ratios of average plant sizes of the largest 20 plants in each country, measured by employment. The numerator in each case is the average plant size of the largest 20 plants in the country referred to by the first subscript, the denominator is the corresponding average for the country referred to by the second subscript.

$F_{20fg}, F_{20fi}, F_{20gi}$ = ratios of average enterprise sizes of the largest 20 enterprises in each country, subscripts referring as above.

$P_{60fg}, P_{60fi}, P_{60gi}$ = ratios of the average size of the largest plants accounting for 60 per cent of each industry's labour force in each country.

$F_{60fg}, F_{60fi}, F_{60gi}$ = the corresponding ratios for firms.

$IS_{fg}, IS_{fi}, IS_{gi}$ = ratio of industry size, as measured by gross output.

$PY_{fg}, PY_{fi}, PY_{gi}$ = ratios of industry labour productivities, measured by net output per employee in all establishments employing more than ten employees.

$\overline{PY}_{fg}, \overline{PY}_{gi}$ = Mean labour productivities, as measured above, in the two countries indicated, deflated by 10,000.

As a preliminary exercise, Table 3.3 presents a correlation matrix of the main variables for the France–Germany trade analysis, using the top-60 per cent variant of the relative plant and firm size variable. As predicted, French trade performance *vis-à-vis* Germany was positively and significantly correlated with relative plant size, relative industry size, and average labour productivity. The three structural variables P_{60}, F_{60}, and IS were all correlated; the close correlation between P_{60} and F_{60} anticipated multicollinearity problems. The significant correlations between IS, TP, and P_{60} confirmed the need to include IS as an independent variable, to test whether P_{60} exerted any significant influence on TP independently of the effects of IS. The negative correlation between trade

performance and relative productivity, counter-intuitive though it is, was
anticipated.

TABLE 3.3.   *Correlation Matrix of Variables used in France–Germany
Analysis*

Variable	TP_{fg}	P_{60fg}	F_{60fg}	IS_{fg}	PY_{fg}	$\overline{PY}_{fg}$
TP_{fg}	1.00	0.29*	0.18	0.29*	−0.09	0.29*
P_{60fg}		1.00	0.77**	0.54**	0.16	0.08
F_{60fg}			1.00	0.32*	0.26	0.07
IS_{fg}				1.00	0.36**	0.03
PY_{fg}					1.00	0.12

** significant at 1 per cent level.
* significant at 5 per cent level.

The total absence of a simple correlation between relative productivity and
trade performance, coupled with a weak correlation between relative plant size
and relative productivity, suggested that the latter was dominated by differentials
in profit margins, or wage rates, or both, as between French and German industries.
These differentials would have interacted with whatever relationship existed
between relative plant size and trade performance, via scale-related unit cost
differentials. The effect of an industry's superior plant size on its trade advantage
could have been weakened if its market leaders opted to enjoy the economic
rents afforded by their cost advantages; and conversely, an industry with a cost
disadvantage might for a time postpone the damaging consequences for its
trade performance by pricing at below economic cost. In mathematical terms,
the first derivative of trade performance with respect to relative plant size was
itself negatively related to relative labour productivity, now decidedly a proxy
for pricing behaviour, as follows:

$$TP = a_0 + a_1 P$$
where $a_1 = b_0 + b_1 PY$
yielding $TP = a_0 + b_0 P + b_1 P \cdot PY$
where $a_1, b_0 > 0, b_1 < 0.$

These considerations suggested that relative 'productivity' should enter the
model in a multiplicative form with a relative plant size.

EMPIRICAL RESULTS

The various elements of the analysis can be be drawn together in an attempt
to explore the effects of scale on intra-Community trade performance in a
multivariate framework. Regression runs were performed using both the top-20
and the top-60 per cent measures of both dimensions of scale, relative plant
size, and relative firm size; relative labour productivity was included in the
multiplicative form suggested above as a proxy for pricing policies; average

labour productivity was a proxy for capital-intensity, and relative industry size was a proxy for success factors unrelated to industry structure. The previous discussion argued for positive coefficients on the relative scale variables with plant size likely to be the more significant because of the known importance of scale economies in manufacturing. The economies in R and D, finance, and distribution, likely to operate at the level of the firm are less clear cut. If as anticipated, relative labour productivity reflected relative price levels, unrelated to relative levels of physical productivity, its coefficient would be negative. The coefficient on average labour productivity was expected to be positive in French–German trades (where the dependent variable is defined as TP_{fg}) because average labour productivity was a proxy for capital-intensity, in which type of industry France was expected on comparative advantage grounds to perform well *vis-à-vis* Germany. By the same logic the coefficient is expected to be negative in the German–Italian trade remembering that the trade performance variable is defined in terms of German, relative to Italian, trade performance. The coefficient on relative industry size was expected to be positive.

The multiple regression results are shown in Tables 3.4 and 3.5. The first set employed the top-20 plant and firm size variables; the second employed top-60 per cent variants. These results are as encouraging as could reasonably be hoped, given the formidable data problems. The best-fit equations, for the three trade patterns, explained between one-seventh and one-quarter of the inter-industry variations in bilateral trade performance. These are fairly modest proportions but it should be remembered that the analysis was dealing with trade patterns between advanced industrial countries with similar industrial structures and factor endowments, whose bilateral trade was less easily explained by trade theoretic variables than, for example, that of the USA which is strongly influenced by the American lead in technology, or that between advanced and developing countries which is shaped by vast international differences in the availability of human capital. Against an analytical background in which the pattern of intra-Community trade was largely a mystery, the explanatory power of these regressions represents a significant step forward.

The relationships which emerged most strongly and consistently from these results were the positive impact of relative plant size on trade performance, and the negative impact on trade performance of relative productivity, weighted by relative plant size (see regressions 5, 10, 15, 19, 23, and 27). This was a robust relationship, unaffected by choice of firm size variable or the inclusion of other variables. Comparative advantage did not emerge at all clearly in these results though this may have been due to the inadequacies of $\overline{PY}$ as a proxy for capital-intensity. The contribution of average labour productivity ($\overline{PY}$) was of the expected size in both the German trades in Table 3.4 but not at all significant, yet it did prove to be statistically significant, and of the expected sign, in regression 19.

It was predicted that the plant size dimension of scale would operate more

TABLE 3.4.   Trade Performance Regressions: Industry Structures Reflecting Size of Largest 20 Plants and Firms[a]

France–Germany Dependent variable: TP_{fg}

Regression	Constant	P_{20fg}	F_{20fg}	IS_{fg}	$P_{20fg} \cdot PY_{fg}$	$\overline{PY}_{fg}$	R^2
1	−0.405	0.532** (3.04)					0.13
2[b]	−0.409		0.488** (3.42)				0.17
3[b]	−0.369	−0.302 (0.66)	0.707 (1.95)				0.17
4	−0.522	2.11** (2.93)		0.338 (1.70)	−1.857* (2.61)	0.0005 (0.24)	0.22
5	−0.488	1.963** (2.73)			−1.322* (2.05)		0.18

France–Italy Dependent variable: TP_{fi}

Regression	Constant	P_{20fi}	F_{20fi}	IS_{fi}	$P_{20fi} \cdot PY_{fi}$	R^2
6	−0.135	0.456 (1.58)				0.04
7	−0.119		0.031 (1.37)			0.03
8	−0.135	0.558 (0.78)	−0.872 (0.16)			0.04
9	−0.220	0.560** (2.87)		−0.025 (0.94)	−0.326* (2.54)	0.14
10	−0.203	0.498** (2.72)			−0.320* (2.50)	0.13

Germany–Italy Dependent variable TP_{gi}

Regression	Constant	P_{20gi}	F_{20gi}	IS_{gi}	$P_{20gi}\cdot PY_{gi}$	$\overline{PY}_{gi}$	R^2
11	−0.288	0.121** (4.27)					0.22
12[b]	−0.212		0.090** (3.33)				0.16
13[b]	−0.284	0.104* (2.04)	0.014 (0.31)				0.22
14	−0.275	0.344** (3.74)		−0.047 (1.39)	−0.127* (1.99)		0.30
15	−0.275	0.295** (3.45)			−0.137* (2.21)	−0.0009 (0.45)	0.28

[a] 65 industries
[b] 61 industries, due to missing data on German firm size in four industries.
The figures in parentheses are t statistics.
** indicates significance at the 1 per cent level.
* indicates significance at the 5 per cent level.

TABLE 3.5.   *Trade Performance Regressions: Industry Structures Reflecting Top 60 per cent of Employment*

France–Germany Dependent variable: TP_{fg} (59 industries)

Regression	Constant	P_{60fg}	F_{60fg}	IS_{fg}	$P_{60fg} \cdot PY_{fg}$	$\overline{PY}_{fg}$	R^2
16	−0.342	0.401* (2.29)					0.08
17	−0.167		0.070 (1.40)				0.03
18	−0.372	0.513 (1.85)	−0.041 (0.52)				0.09
19	−0.664	1.46* (2.24)		0.269* (1.96)	−1.18* (1.98)	0.0004* (2.37)	0.23

France–Italy Dependent variable: TP_{fi} (63 industries)

Regression	Constant	P_{60fi}	F_{60fi}	IS_{fi}	$P_{60fi} \cdot PY_{fi}$	R^2
20	−0.213	0.075 (1.80)				0.05
21	−0.165		0.034 (1.32)			0.02
22	−0.213	0.081 (1.20)	−0.005 (0.13)			0.05
23	−0.190	0.403* (2.42)	−0.010 (0.22)	0.018 (1.25)	−0.283* (2.12)	0.12

Germany–Italy Dependent variable: TP_{gi} (58 industries)

Regression	Constant	P_{60gi}	F_{60gi}	IS_{gi}	$P_{60gi} \cdot PY_{gi}$	R^2
24	-0.159	0.061* (2.54)				0.10
25	-0.535		0.028 (1.50)			0.04
26	-0.188	0.157* (2.29)		0.037 (1.74)	-0.099 (1.66)	0.18
27	-0.190	0.403* (2.42)	-0.009 (0.22)	0.018 (1.25)	-0.283* (2.12)	0.12

The figures in parentheses are t statistics.
* significant at the 5 per cent level.

strongly than the firm size dimension because economies of scale are more important in production than those which operate at the level of the firm in marketing, R and D and finance. These predictions were born out pretty well by the relative performances of P_{20} and F_{20}, and of P_{60} and F_{60}, in the regressions viewed as a whole, although the collinearity between relative plant size and relative firm size (the correlation coefficient between them was invariably over 60 per cent in each country) prevented a conclusive runoff between P_{20} and F_{20}. Each performed as well as the other when included on their own; P_{20} dominated F_{20} in the Germany–Italy trade (regression 13), and vice versa in the France–Germany trade (regression 3). However, P_{60} emerged much more strongly than F_{60} in all three trades, suggesting that the economies of scale at the dimension of the plant were more influential than those at the level of the firm.

The relative strength of the regressions in Table 3.4 compared to those in Table 3.5 suggested that the relative size of the largest plants was more influential than that of the representative plants. This does not appear to be due to any statistical peculiarities of the measure itself. It was noted earlier that the top-20 measure reached down proportionately further into the size distribution of a smaller industry, and could therefore be picking up some of the influence of relative industry size. However, the IS variable appeared to be no weaker in the P_{20} regressions in Table 3.4 than in the P_{60} regressions in Table 3.5. There was no evidence that P_{20} was feeding off relative industry size. The result confirms the importance attached in Chapter 2 to the relative size of the largest plants in an industry.

CONCLUSIONS

The analysis described in this chapter has attempted to test the first hypothesis derived from the theoretical analysis in the first chapter; this was that in the early state of the Community the balance of trade tended to favour those industries with scale advantages over their competitors. The consistently significant and positive impact of relative plant size, measured particularly in relation to the 20 largest plants, which was identified in statistical explanations of 1964 intra-Community trade patterns, was consistent with this hypothesis. The more significant role of relative plant size, contrasting with the role of relative firm size, suggested that economies of scale in production, rather than in head office functions such as R and D, marketing, and finance, are of greater significance. This also was in line with expectations; whereas economies of scale in production — often rooted in engineering relationships — are well understood and documented, those claimed to exist in respect to the overhead functions are not. These findings have important business implications. They suggest that in so far as business leaders in Britain, for example, were acquiring others in the merger wave of the early 1970s as part of a strategy to 'get in shape' for the entry into Europe, they were for the most part misinformed. The message from these findings is that to be competitive in Europe, companies needed to secure economies of scale in production, through the establishment of minimum efficient-sized plant — an objective not usually furthered by acquisition.

Finally, the analysis underlined the fact that cost advantages did not feed through automatically into superior trade performance. To the extent that industries preferred to enjoy the economic rents afforded by superior cost positions, rather than use their cost advantage to resist imports and secure greater market shares in export markets, the link between cost and trade performance was weakened. Preferences for the former option are understandable in the early stages of integration. When the market acceptability of an industry's product in export markets, and hence its price cross-elasticity, was initially low, due to consumers' lack of familiarity or to the operation of non-tariff barriers, it made more sense for low-cost exporters to operate at high price-cost margins. The expectation would be that once the integration of markets became more complete, price cross-elasticities would increase, the price-cost margins justified by profit-maximization calculations would diminish and the links between unit cost, price, and trade performance would become stronger. These themes are pursued in the three industry studies on cars, trucks, and white goods, which follow.

NOTES

1 An earlier version was presented at the First International Institute of Management Conference on Industrial Structure held at Deidesheim, West Germany in May 1974 and was subsequently published under the title 'Scale Economies in the EEC', *European Economic Review*, 7 (1976), pp. 143-63.

2 This measure was chosen because it is bounded at plus or minus one and is a more suitable measure for an enquiry into the effects of relative scale on trade performance than an absolute measure of trade performance such as trade balances. A potential weakness of the measure is its insensitivity as between highly traded and less traded products. If a country imported nothing from its neighbour in some categories, it would register the maximum trade performance score regardless of whether it exported one unit or millions. However, the fairly broad (3-digit) level of aggregation used in the study ensures that there are few situations of near-zero trade. An analysis on the basis of a truncated sample, which excluded industries which traded relatively little in relation to their outputs, in fact yielded weaker results.

3 In 1972, for example, the Commission prosecuted a system of price discrimination practised in the insulation materials industry by Pittsburg Corning Europe in conjunction with its Belgian and Dutch distributors, which had the effect of compartmentalizing the German market, sustaining prices in Germany at as much as 40 per cent higher than in the Belgian and Dutch markets (General Report on the Activities of the European Communities, 1972, p. 93).

4 *Report on the Activities of the Communities*, 1968, p. 97.

5 Louis Phlips, *De L'Intégration des Marchés* (Louvain, 1962). Phlips noted that photographic film producers were able to separate national markets by granting distributors the monopoly over imports and prohibiting re-exports; the cartelized cement industry had organized a separation of national (and regional) markets which Phlips judged unlikely to be overthrown by opening up national frontiers; and the fertilizer industry

showed a tendency to find a *modus vivendi* which safeguarded control of prices.

6 This connection could explain the association betwen high profitability and concentration. Price levels equate to the unit costs of the highest cost producer; the greater the size advantage of the industry leaders over the marginal producer, the greater their cost advantage and their abnormal profits.

7 Alternative specifications were tried which incorporated two variables which seemed likely proxies for tradability; the inverse of value per tonne; the distance within which 80 per cent by value of shipments by the corresponding industry travelled in the USA. Neither variable proved in any way significant.

8 For a much more complete analysis of intra-industry trade, see Richard Caves, 'Intra-industry Trade and Market Structure in the Industrial Countries', *Oxford Economic Papers*, July 1981, pp. 203–23. Caves's analysis neither confirms nor disconfirms the analysis here. He used different structural variables, measured on the basis of United States industry, to explain multilateral trade flows, rather than bilateral flows, between 13 OECD countries.

9 These themes are developed by Frank Wolter, 'Factor Proportions, Technology, and West German Industry's International Trade Patterns', *Wirtschaftliches Archiv* 113/2, 1977, pp. 250–65. Wolter found that Germany's comparative advantage across 18 sectors in 1972/73 *vis-à-vis* developed countries was positively related to human capital-intensity, as reflected by wage levels, and negatively related to physical capital-intensity.

10 *Résultats définitifs de L'enquête industrielle de 1963*, Etudes et Enquêtes statistiques 2/1969, Office Statistique des Communautés Européennes.

11 J. S. Bain, *International Differences in Industrial Structure* (New Haven, 1966).

12 Scherer, *Multi-plant Operations*, p. 66.

13 To understand the order of his bias, consider a typical French manufacturing industry in 1962 having the following plant size distribution at the upper end:

Number of plants	Plant size (employees)
1	2,000–4,999
4	1,000–1,999
10	500– 999
35	200– 499

The top-20 measure is around 940 for such a distribution (assuming for convenience that firms cluster at the class midpoints). If the German counterpart contained twice as many plants in each size class – a fairly typical situation – the German top-20 measure is near to 1,400. In other words, an industry with the same size distribution but double the size would register a top-20 measure nearly 50 per cent higher.

14 L. Phlips, *Effects of Industrial Concentration: A Cross Sectional Analysis of the Common Market* (Amsterdam, 1971).

15 Price surveys carried out periodically in the 1960s by the Commission revealed large and persisting differences in prices between member countries, differences which had delayed but significant effects on export performance, according to Glejser (H. Glejser, 'Empirical Evidence on Comparative Cost Theory from the European Common Market Experience', *European Economic Review*, 1972, pp. 247–58).

16 Information on industries' pricing margins was insufficiently disaggregated for this analysis. An input–output analysis of Community Countries in 1965 (*Tableaux Entrées-Sorties: Coefficient Directs*: Série speciale 8–1970: Statistical Office of the European Communities) provided a basis for calculating profit margins for a limited number of industries. Unfortunately only 13 of these corresponded directly to the 3-digit NICE industries featuring in this study.

17 Market imperfections did not appear to arise from high industrial concentration; relative labour productivity was not correlated with relative concentration, nor did relative concentration perform at all well in the model in place of relative labour productivity.

18 A relative tariff variable was included in one regression (France–Germany) out of curiosity. The average trade-weighted tariff levied by France on German imports was divided by the trade-weighted German tariff on imports from France. As an explanatory variable it took the 'wrong' sign. French industries actually did worse with higher tariffs, suggesting that tariffs are responses to trade performance. Fortunately for this study, they are only partial responses, otherwise there would have been no trade pattern to explain!

CHAPTER 4

THE EUROPEAN CAR INDUSTRY

The car industry figures more prominently in the public's mind than any other manufacturing industry. In the larger European countries it employs more than any other single, easily identifiable, manufacturing operation; between 4 per cent and 8 per cent of those employed in manufacturing, and as many again in component and materials supply. It attracts considerable Government intervention. Its technology is perhaps the best known and corresponds to the public's idea of what manufacturing is about — complicated and technically impressive, yet anonymous and repetitive. There is also a popular identification with the product itself. The car is the largest manufactured item that the typical household ever purchases, a fact which partly explains the popular interest in the product and in the industry which produces it. As Lord Stokes, former Chairman of British Leyland, once observed ruefully, at the time of the Company's collapse: 'everyone is an expert on the motor industry'. For these reasons alone, no account of industrial developments in the European Community can leave the car industry aside.

There is also an analytical reason for its inclusion as a central exhibit in this study. The car has become an international product and hence it illustrates as well as any the economics of European integration. A number of the car's characteristics contribute to this. In the first place, it is a mature product, in what is, in Europe, largely a replacement market. Its technology is widely disseminated and the car's basic configuration has settled down in a way which optimizes the key parameters of economy, power-to-weight ratio, the ratio of interior to exterior volume, and quality of ride. There was a time in the 1950s and 1960s when the volume producers of Europe produced family cars with idiosyncratic national styles. In the 1970s these styles converged to the point where the economy car from the various European nations looked almost indistinguishable (if one compares, for example, the Volkswagen Polo, the Ford Fiesta, the Renault 5, the Leyland Metro, and the Fiat 128). This convergence in engineering has shifted the competitive emphasis away from unique or novel engineering features or the cultivation of special loyalties to particular marques, towards the provision of fairly undifferentiated motoring packages, with emphasis on value for money. This shift in emphasis focused attention more than before on achieving the lowest unit cost through high volumes. This in turn pushed the industry into a European dimension, as car manufacturers looked to wider markets in order to secure competitive unit cost positions. In short, the development of a universally accepted car design has defined a competitive mode which leads towards an integrated European car industry.

In terms of technical regulations, too, the Community car market has moved a long way towards a more integrated state. Fifty-nine Community directives, relating to technical aspects such as emission controls and noise were approved between 1970 and 1980. However, intra-Community movements of cars are by no means fully liberated. There is as yet no harmonized, European, whole vehicle type approval procedure (WVTA). The directives which would achieve this are blocked, pending a resolution of the so-called Third Country problem, namely, that if WVTA was adopted, no Community member would have a legitimate means of blocking the entry into their market of Japanese cars whose producers had demonstrated compliance with the WVTA to the satisfaction of any other Community member. It would be surprising if the countries with no major vested manufacturing interest in car production, such as the Netherlands or Belgium, with Japanese import shares in excess of 25 per cent, withheld WVTA from Japanese importers. The response of the car-producing countries to the Japanese threat therefore has an inhibiting effect on the completion of the European car market.

TABLE 4.1.   *Motor Industries' Economic Contribution 1970-1974*

	Germany	Britain	France	Italy
Share of manufacturing employment %	8	6	5	4
Share of manufactured exports %	13	10	10	10
Direct employees (000)	600	480	250	200

Source: Interfutures, OECD, 1978.

TABLE 4.2.   *The World's major car[a] producing countries 1950-1977 (000 units)*

	1950	1960	1970	1977
European Community				
Germany	220	1,800	3,500	4,000
France	260	1,200	2,300	3,100
Britain	520	1,400	1,600	1,300
Italy	100	560	1,700	1,400
Belgium				290
Netherlands				50
Community Total	1,100	4,900	9,100	10,100
North America	6,900	7,000	7,500	10,400
Japan	—	170	3,200	5,400
World	8,100	12,500	22,600	30,600

[a]   Including car-derived vans.
Sources: 1950-1970: *'International Overview of Development in the Motor World'*, Daimler–Benz, 1975.
         1977:   'Automobiles Statistiques', *L'Argus de l'Automobile*, June, 1978.

THE INDUSTRY STRUCTURE

The significance of the car industry in the four major Community countries is illustrated in Table 4.1. Table 4.2 provides general scene-setting snapshots of the world's motor industry over 30 years. The four major Community countries produce 97 per cent of the Community's car output. Of the world output of 30 million cars in 1977, and the Community and North America each produced a third; Japan produced half the rest. The North American share fell from 85 per cent in 1950 to 33 per cent in 1977. Within the Community, France and Germany emerged as the major producers, with two-thirds of the Community output; Britain's share of the Community total fell from 50 per cent in 1950 to 17 per cent in 1970, 13 per cent in 1977, putting it on the same footing as Italy.

TABLE 4.3. *Major European Community motor manufacturers in 1977 (000 units)*[a]

| | Location and volumes by country | | | | | |
Company	Germany	France	UK	Italy	Belgium	Total Volumes
Volkswagen[b]	1,600					1,600
Peugeot–Citroën[c]		1,350				1,350
Ford Europe	540		510		290	1,340
Renault		1,260				1,260
Fiat[d]				1,200		1,200
General Motors Europe	920		90			1,010
British Leyland[e]			650	40	50*	740*
Chrysler Europe		480	170			650
Daimler–Benz	410					410
BMW	290					290
Alfa-Romeo				200		200

Note: Other low-volume manufacturers in the EC include Volvo (50,000 units in Netherlands) and Porsche (35,000 units in Germany): the former is part of the main Volvo group which produces 160,000 units in Sweden. The latter has strong design links with the VW Group.
a   Passenger cars plus car-derived vans plus 'Completely Knocked Down' (CKD) kits supplied abroad.
b   Including Audi–NSU.
c   Peugeot–Citroën acquired Chrysler Europe in 1978 to become the largest European car manufacturer (over 2m units p.a.).
d   Including Autobianchi and Lancia.
e   Including Jaguar, Rover, Triumph in the UK, and Innocenti in Italy.
*   Estimated.
Source: *L'Argus de l'Automobile.*

The cast of principal characters in the Community's volume car industry is introduced in Table 4.3. It sorts itself into three groups:[1]

1   Five European volume producers:
     Volkswagen
     Peugeot–Citroën
     Renault

    Fiat
    British Leyland
2 Three United States multinationals:
    General Motors
    Ford
    Chrysler (whose European assets have now been acquired by Peugeot-Citroën)
3 Three high-performance specialists:
    Daimler–Benz
    BMW
    Alfa–Romeo

The European volume producers are nationally based in Europe (except for British Leyland's facilities in Belgium and Italy, now sold) and are in a sense national 'champions' in so far as they tend to have nationalistic orientations and, in some cases, support. Volkswagen originated from the 'people's car' concept of 1934; the Federal Government and the government of Lower Saxony together own 40 per cent of its equity and appoint four of the 21 supervisory directors. Renault is state-owned and operates on a sales-maximization basis subject to a fairly low profitability constraint (subject, however, to realistic allowances for depreciation). The company has always seen itself as technological leader in French engineering and manufactures its own machine tools. Fiat is privately owned but due to its dominant role in Italian engineering it plays *de facto* a national role and has received considerable protection in recognition of this.[2] British Leyland is the only British-owned volume car producer in Britain; it was effectively nationalized in 1975, following a rescue operation which made it clear, witness the preamble to the Ryder Report which defined the 95 per cent state-owned company's objectives, that the company was regarded by the government of the day as an indispensable part of British industry. In their product policies, the national champions have tended to cover the entire product range (Volkswagen is the exception). They have shown in the past an ability to produce models with tremendous survival qualities, based on engineering originality and styling flair, sometimes with too little regard to manufacturing costs. A number of classic products in the motoring landscape have emerged from these companies; the VW Beetle which ran with modifications from 1934 to the 1970s, with a production run of 18 million, longer even than that of the Model T Ford; the Mini which appeared in 1958 and runs still today, and which has provided the entire European industry with the basic design configuration for the small family car; and the 2CV and DS models from Citroën.

    The American producers have pursued very different strategies. All have operated in at least two countries, with no national commitment; they have shown a willingness to switch part of their production between European countries as economics dictate. In general they have pursued profitability as the overriding goal, through tight managerial control on costs. Their model policies have been directed solely at the volume segments of the market with an emphasis on value engineering, value-for-money, and short replacement cycles. The Americans, and particularly Ford, have advanced the logic of rationalization in car production. Common models have been introduced throughout Europe, reducing unit design costs and drawing on common sources of power-train components, castings, and pressings.[3] General Motors' style has always favoured competing subsidiaries, following Alfred Sloan's philosophy, and hence Vauxhall and Opel continued to act independently rather later than Ford in Europe. In 1970, Vauxhall's losses led to the establishment of a European headquarters, in London, and to standardization of models and components. Chrysler opened its European headquarters in 1969. The two models launched in 1970 (the 160 and the 180) were jointly designed by both subsidiaries. There are two dimensions to this process; a geographical dimension in which European models are standardized, permitting centralized production of major items (engine, transmissions, body panels) which will fit equally well in Fords assembled in Cologne or Dagenham, in General Motors' Opels assembled in Saarlouis, or in Vauxhalls assembled in Luton; and an engineering dimension in which the spectrum of motoring performance is encompassed by fewer models, each of which is engineered in such a way that a wide variety of options (horsepower, transmission, trim) can be generated using comparatively few engines, body shells, and other major components.

Lastly, the specialists offer distinct quality advantages which permit the comparatively high unit costs associated with low volumes to be recouped profitably. Survival is less easy than this recipe sounds, as the Delorean fiasco demonstrated. Daimler–Benz need, and achieve, volumes per model which are quite substantial (250,000); less than the 300,000 a year of VW, Renault, and Fiat, but still on a par with some of the less successful volume producers. The very low volume specialists require truly outstanding engineering features for survival (Rolls Royce, Aston Martin, Lotus, Porsche, and Alfa-Romeo) and the litany of defunct producers of quality cars is long and saddening to the car enthusiast.

History is not on the side of the specialist producer or of the smaller volume producer. The degree of concentration in Europe's car industries as measured in terms of car production has increased to high levels, as Table 4.4 indicates. However, this trend has not in general provided the industries' leaders with increased market leadership in their respective national markets. As Table 4.5 shows, the share of imports has risen in all four markets, sufficiently in three of them to outweigh the effects of increased concentration in production on market concentration. The British, Italian, and to a lesser extent the German experience illustrates this. In the British case, for example, the combined market shares of the three leading British producers fell from 74 per cent in 1965 to 49 per cent in 1977 despite increasing their combined share of British car production, from 79 per cent to 92 per cent, over this period. The vast bulk of European imports in 1977 were from the Community itself; 75 per cent of

TABLE 4.4.   *Trends in Concentration in terms of unit output 1955–1977*

	1955	1965	1970	1977
Germany				
Volkswagen	40	45	52	42
General Motors (Opel)	22	25	23	24
Ford	8	11	12	14
Share of 3 largest National Producers	70	81	87	81
France				
Renault	31	35	43	41
Peugeot	16	19	21	43
Citroën	22	28	19	
Chrysler	27	17	16	15
Share of 3 largest National Producers	80	82	83	100
Britain				
British Leyland[a]	39	37	48	49
Ford	27	29	27	31
Chrysler	11	11	13	13
General Motors (Vauxhall)	9	13	11	7
Share of 3 largest National Producers	77	79	88	92
Italy				
Fiat	94	88	88	83
Share of 3 largest National Producers	100	96	97	100

[a]   Companies appear under their 1977 designations but the production share
figures prior to any mergers refer to the largest entity in these companies in
any year e.g. British Leyland figures refer to BMC in 1955 and 1965.
Sources: 1955–1970: Daniel Jones, University of Sussex, mimeographed paper.
        1977:   'Automobile Statistiques', *L'Argus de l'Automobile*, 1978.

German imports, 82 per cent of French, 65 per cent of British, and 97 per cent
of Italian. In purely structural terms, the Community's trade is exerting a
diluting effect on 'market power' in this industry, in so far as market shares
reflect market power, despite the trend towards greater concentration in car
production. In behavioural terms, the diluting effect is even more marked, as
the remainder of this chapter demonstrates.

THE PATTERN OF INTRA-COMMUNITY TRADE IN CARS

Intra-Community trade in cars has expanded very much faster than car production (four times as fast between 1965 and 1977). The Four exchanged half a
million cars in 1965, one and a half million in 1977[4] (Fig. 4.1). As this trade
has expanded, its pattern has changed, from one of bilateral equilibrium, to
one in which distinct winners and losers emerged from a pattern marked by
substantial bilateral surpluses and deficits. In 1965, the Four were all roughly in
balance with each other; by 1970, France had secured substantial surpluses, with
Germany (140,000 units), Italy (50,000 units), and Britain (40,000 units).

TABLE 4.5.   *Trends in Market Shares 1965–1977 (percentage)*

	1965	1970	1977
Germany			
Volkswagen	38	32	30
Opel	22	19	19
Ford	18	15	13
Other German	11	12	15
Imports	11	22	23
Share of 3 largest National Producers	78	66	62
France			
Renault		31	34
Peugeot		21	18
Citroën		18	17
Chrysler		10	9
Imports		20	22
Share of 3 largest National Producers		70	69
Britain			
British Leyland	36	38	24
Ford	26	27	19
Chrysler	12	11	5
Vauxhall	12	10	9
Other British	9	1	–
Imports	5	14	41
Share of 3 largest National Producers	74	76	49
Italy			
Fiat	n/a	n/a	55
Imports	12	28	36
Share of 3 largest National Producers	88	72	64

Sources: As for Table 4.4.

By 1976, the overall pattern had moved further away from bilateral equilibrium; although the French surplus with Germany had eased to 50,000 units its surpluses with both Britain and Italy had risen to 130,000 units. Germany also increased its surplus with Britain, to 100,000 units; Italy had reversed a 1970 deficit with Britain into a 60,000 unit surplus. Thus by 1976 the French car industry had emerged as the clear winner in terms of securing footholds in its neighbours' markets and in defending its own market against them; Germany and Italy were joint runners-up, sustaining deficits with France, maintaining a neutral balance with each other, and surpluses with Britain. Britain was the clear loser, conceding one-third of its market to continental producers and in return gaining trifling exports to France, Germany, and Italy; in 1977, exports were lower in aggregate than they were in 1965.

Expressing these developments in terms of market penetration (Table 4.6), in the mid-1950s, prior to the formation of the Community, interpenetration of European car markets was negligible, with the exception of Italian excursions into the German market using local assembly. High tariffs of 30 per cent and

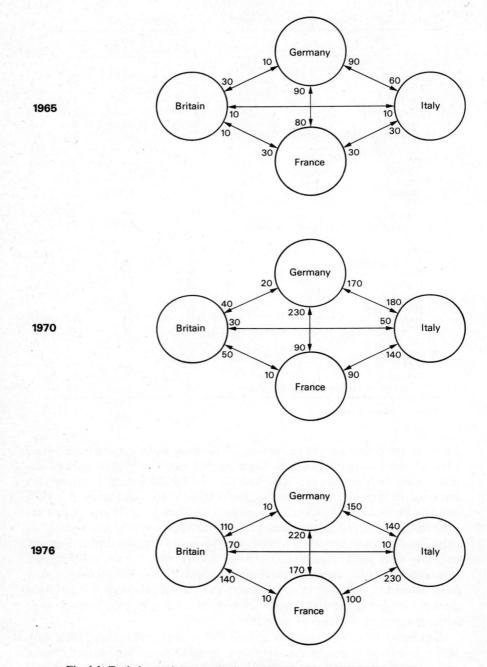

Fig. 4.1. Trade in cars between the Four: 1965, 1970, and 1976 (000 units)
(Import data from respective national trade associations)

TABLE 4.6. *Penetration of Community Car Markets 1955–1976 (percentage shares in terms of unit sales)*

	German Exports			French Exports		
Market	France	Britain	Italy	Germany	Britain	Italy
1955	1.1	1.1	0.8	1.0	0.8	0.3
1960	2.9	2.2	3.4	4.8	4.8	1.6
1965	7.3	2.6	6.7	5.8	1.1	3.7
1970	6.6	3.4	13.3	10.9	4.2	10.2
1976	8.9	7.9	12.2	9.5	10.4	19.4

	British Exports			Italian Exports		
Market	Germany	France	Italy	Germany	France	Britain
1955	1.0	0.7	0.3	3.0	0.1	0.4
1960	0.7	1.0	1.3	7.4	1.3	0.5
1965	0.4	2.6	1.0	5.8	3.1	1.1
1970	0.7	0.5	3.9	8.2	6.8	2.7
1976	0.6	0.7	0.5	6.6	5.5	5.0

Source: As for Table 4.5.

more, imposed by France, Britain, and Italy, contributed to the isolation of those markets at that time (Table 4.7). By 1962 the Community's internal tariffs had been reduced substantially; trade in cars between Germany, France, and Italy began to develop, and import penetration in all three markets reached 5 per cent or so in the 1960s. In contrast, the British market was still strongly protected at that time; its external tariff stood at 28 per cent and it faced comparatively little competition from EFTA countries, of whom only Britain and Sweden produced cars at all. As a result, import penetration remained pretty much at 1950s levels. By the early 1970s the French car industry occupied 12 per cent of the German market and 10 per cent of the Italian markets. Its own market was penetrated further as well, though to a lesser degree than its neighbours'. And once Britain announced its intention to join the Community, and then joined in 1973, its three major partners rapidly doubled their penetration of the British car market. The British car industry was totally unable to reciprocate; its penetration of the major Community markets was no higher than in 1955. During the 1970s the German car industry recovered some of its domestic market from the French, and seized additional ground in the French market; meanwhile the French strengthened their own position in the Italian market.

THE ECONOMICS OF THE INTRA-COMMUNITY CAR TRADE

Once tariff barriers had been dismantled in Europe, it is not difficult to understand the acceleration in growth of the car trade. This growth was assisted by a growing market acceptance of a European car, made possible by the fact that

TABLE 4.7. Tariffs on Imported Cars 1956–1978 (in percentage terms)[a]

	Germany		France		Italy		Britain	
	World	Community countries	World	Community countries	World	Community countries	World	Community countries
1956	17		30		35–45[b]			30
1962	19	10	28	15	38	27		28
1965	20	3	25	9	31	14		26
1970	15	0	15	0	15	0		15
1972	11	0	11	0	11	0		11
1978	11	0	11	0	11	0	11	0

[a] Nearest percentage point.
[b] Italy applied higher tariff rates to small cars, since its own industry specialized in this segment of the market.

Community car buyers drive on similar types of roads, have similar purchasing power, and face similar traffic densities and motoring costs (as compared to, say, North Americans or Africans) and therefore demand the same sort of car.[5] But why did the Community's car trade assume the shape that it did? Why did the French car industry emerge as the most successful, and the British as the least successful? These are the basic questions which the remainder of this chapter seeks to answer.

If a motoring correspondent were to be asked to comment on the trade pattern which emerged he would no doubt focus on the road test reports, aspects of styling and engineering, reliability, the degree of dealer support, and the value for money offered by different producers, as the explanatory factors, since these are, after all, the diet of the educated motoring public. This study looks at none of these considerations. It grants that they are important, but goes behind them to a prior consideration. Let us suppose that one particular country achieves a superior market position through some advantageous combination of the characteristics mentioned above. Given that there is no mystery in volume car production techniques and engineering design among the leading practitioners, the issue reduces to the simple question: how does this successful competitor *afford* to offer superior value for money? The answer which the analysis in Chapter 2 suggests is that the successful industry has secured an advantage in unit manufacturing costs. If, for example, unit costs of car manufacture in France are lower than those of its neighbours, the French car producers will find it profitable to export to neighbouring markets provided that prices in those markets reflect local unit costs. The marketing mix adopted in order to secure these exports will of course reflect judgements about the relative appeal of engineering, advertising, dealer support, and price, but it is not necessary to explore these sensitivities to understand the broad trends in international competitiveness in the car industry. It is sufficient to understand that a competitor's unit cost position determines the amount of effort it can direct profitably into exports, as the formal mathematical statement in Appendix 1 confirms. Thus it is possible to bypass the detailed mechanics of the car business and to develop an explanation of the intra-Community car trade which is solely in terms of relative unit costs, linked to the analysis of industrial structure, scale, and trade performance presented in Chapters 2 and 3. A single-cause theory of this kind does not do justice to the nuances of the industry, of course, but this is not the object of the study. The object is to expose the economic forces which drive European integration along.

The line of attack adopted for this purpose can be summarized as follows. The economics of car production in each of the four countries were represented by their market leaders, which happened also to be the local champions: Volkswagen, Renault, British Leyland, and Fiat. For each of these four producers a price index was constructed, running from 1955 to 1977 for Volkswagen, Renault, and British Leyland, and from 1965 to 1977 for Fiat. These price indices were then adjusted by the profit margins earned by the companies over the period in each of the years considered, to yield unit cost indices. Relative movements in these unit cost indices were then explored to see whether they explained the observed shifts in the intra-Community patterns of trade in cars between the four countries.

The broad details of these calculations are as follows. The price indices were based upon the respective domestic prices (exclusive of VAT and purchase tax) for all models produced in volumes in excess of 20,000 a year. The price indices were chain-linked; taking each pair of successive years, the models which were produced in both years, in the minimum volumes mentioned, were identified. The market value of the model range in the earlier of the two years was calculated at the first and the second years' prices. The main conceptual difficulties faced by this (and any) index is that it cannot cope with improvements in specification (and in this respect, Volkswagen's many improvements in the 'Beetle' went unrecognized, resulting in some overstatement of VW's unit cost increases), or the introduction of new models, which could not get aboard the index until their second year in production (for what would their price in their year of introduction be compared with?). To the extent that new models embody enhanced value-for-money compared to their predecessors, price indices constructed in the way described must fail to capture some important elements of cost reduction. One would imagine that all new models must embody some improvement in value for money, or they would not be introduced at all. In quantitative terms, however, the improvement does not seem to amount to very much, to judge from conversations with the industry on pricing policies that suggested that new models are introduced at a price premium over the models they replace in order to make them 'competitive'. This suggests that the price premiums reflect the quality differences between old and new models and that therefore, new models do not in fact embody significant quality-adjusted price reductions. Sometimes old and new models overlap for a time and need to be distinguished in terms of price and other features as clearly as possible, which argues for price premiums on the new models that fully reflect their quality advantage.[6] These considerations suggest that the price index used here is a reasonable basis for analysis.

The four companies' unit cost indices, deflated by the respective national GDP deflators, are shown in Figure 4.2. Over the period as a whole, Renault emerged as the star performer in terms of cost reduction. In the 1950s, Renault and Volkswagen reduced unit costs sharply and in parallel, by one-fifth in five years. British Leyland's unit cost remained fairly constant overall at this time. Throughout the 1960s Volkswagen's unit costs remained constant, Leyland's and Fiat's (1965–70 only) were reduced at the rate of 1 per cent a year, whereas Renault reduced its unit costs by nearly 3 per cent a year. After 1973, unit costs in the industry rose sharply, partly as a result of reduced levels of capacity utilization following the oil crisis and partly for internal reasons, manifested in increasing levels of industrial unrest, absenteeism, and loss of productivity. The car manufacturers demonstrated differing capacities to cope with these testing conditions; Volkswagen's unit cost rose by 10 per cent in 1974 alone,[7] provoking a financial crisis in the company, after which the management seized a firm grip on unit costs, holding them steady up to 1977. Renault's costs rose by 15 per cent in 1975 but were contained in the two subsequent years. Fiat's rose by a similar degree in 1975 and continued upwards in 1976. But of the four manufacturers, British Leyland was least able to regain a grip on unit costs; over the period 1973-7, Leyland's unit costs rose continuously by a total of 25 per cent in real terms, largely as a result of declining productivity.

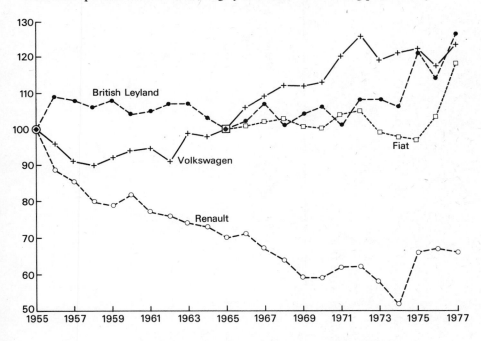

Fig. 4.2. Unit cost indices for major car producers at constant prices, 1955–1977
(Unit costs are expressed in respective national currencies and deflated by respective wholesale prices indices, 1955 = 100 (Fiat: 1965 = 100))

These price indices are, in effect, performance indicators which place each manufacturer in its own context, comparing their cost indices with those of their respective economies. A general observation worth making at this point is that unit costs in manufacturing tend to decline relative to those in the rest (roughly two-thirds) of the economy, mainly because the service industries in the latter have human inputs which are difficult to reduce (and in the public sector unit costs are definitionally constant because 'output' is measured in terms of inputs). And within the manufacturing sector itself, unit costs tend to fall more quickly in the newer industries than in the mature industries, since the latter tend to exhaust opportunities for additional scale economies and new technological breakthroughs. In this overall perspective, the substantial cost

TABLE 4.8.   *Currency Movements and Inflation Rates 1955–1977* (1955 = 100)

	France			Italy		Germany		
	British prices			British prices		British prices		
	French prices			Italian prices		German prices		
	£/Franc	All items	Manufactures	£/Lira	Manufactures	£/DM	All items	Manufactures
1955	100	100	100	n.a.	n.a.	100	100	100
1960	71	86	74	n.a.	n.a.	100	103	92
1965	71	83	73	100	100	105	102	100
1970	74	85	74	117	110	134	110	120
1975	103	102	91	121	108	215	146	158
1977	114	116	107	114	104	290	182	214

reductions in the 1950s, followed by gradual levelling off, is intelligible, but the cost hikes in the mid-1970s are not. The latter reflect something of a crisis in the industry, and falling volumes.

Looking now at the question of international competitiveness, the relevant consideration is whether unit costs have moved relative to each other in terms, not of national price deflators, but in terms of common currencies. There is a good reason to expect that in the medium and long term, relative movements in manufacturers' unit costs when deflated by respective national deflators would translate into corresponding movements in terms of a common currency, namely, that exchange rates move in such a way as to offset relative movements in national inflation rates of trading partners, thereby maintaining balance of payments equilibria. If, for example, British car manufacturers' unit costs rise faster than British unit costs generally, at a time when French manufacturers' costs are keeping in line with the French unit cost index, one would expect that the unit cost of British cars would increase relative to French cars in sterling terms, assuming that movements in the sterling/franc parity had taken care of any differences between British and foreign inflation rates.

Broadly, this assumption about the behaviour of exchange rates finds qualified support in Europe over the last twenty years, as Table 4.8 indicates. The values of the franc and the lira, relative to sterling, move pretty closely in line with the prices of British manufacturers relative to those in France and Italy, maintaining overall competitiveness in the three countries' manufacturing sectors. During a period of over twenty years in which British prices rose fourfold, they rose by 16 per cent relative to French prices; the franc appreciated by 14 per cent to almost exactly offset this. The German experience after 1970 is rather a departure from this pattern; the Deutschmark appreciated after 1965 substantially faster than was required to offset the low German inflation rate, to the extent that by 1977, the price-competitiveness of German exports had declined by 35 per cent compared to the position in 1955. This says a lot for the German ability to improve their non-price dimensions of competitiveness.

The exchange rate mechanism which operated between the four countries is the link between the configuration of cost indices presented in Figure 4.2 (deflated by respective wholesale price deflators) and the same indices appearing in Figure 4.3, converted into sterling and deflated by the British deflator. The two sets of data are broadly similar save for the effects of the French devaluation in 1958, which accentuated the already sharp decline in relative costs of French cars, and the real-terms appreciation of the Deutschmark in the 1970s, which made German cars increasingly expensive relative to other European cars.

Relative Costs

Thus far, nothing has been said about relative costs of car manufacture in the four countries at any particular time. Table 4.9 provides such a comparison. The data suggests that in 1975 Britain was the most expensive place to manufacture cars in the four countries and France was the cheapest. This snapshot

of the position in 1975 can be used to anchor the unit cost indices presented
in Figure 4.3 so as to reveal the evolving configurations of comparative unit
costs for the entire twenty-year period, shown in Table 4.10.

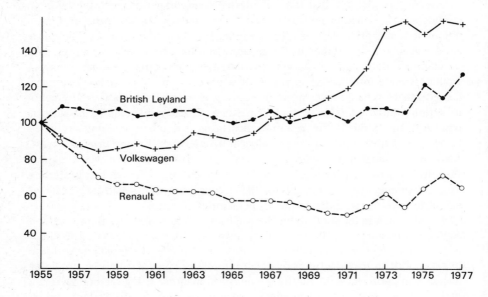

Fig. 4.3. Unit cost indices at constant prices on a common currency basis, 1955–1977
(Unit costs are converted to Sterling and deflated by the British wholesale price index)

Table 4.10 starkly exposes some very contrasting experiences. For the first
ten years of the period, Volkswagen's unit costs were considerably lower than
those of the others; only half of Renault's in 1955 and around 80 per cent of
British Leyland's over the decade. This must have owed something to the learning
curve effects of single-mindedly producing one model and a lot to the under-
valuation of the Deutschmark throughout this period. The steady appreciation
of the mark after 1970 combined with the incremental costs of diversifying
the product range, pulled Volkswagen's costs above those of Renault and towards
those of Leyland and Fiat. Renault began the period with a considerable cost
disadvantage (60 per cent with respect to Leyland, 100 per cent with respect
to Volkswagen), which it rapidly reduced, aided by the franc devaluation in
1958. Thereafter, Renault progressed towards its lowest-cost position by consistently controlling costs more successfully than French industry in general,
through scale and rationalization. An interesting general feature of the pattern
in Table 4.10 is the way the Law of One Price has begun to exert itself. In the
early years, which saw very restricted trade in cars, unit costs and therefore
prices, differed considerably between neighbouring countries. As intra-
Community trade opened up, these differences tended to narrow, but not

TABLE 4.9. *Unit Costs of Car Manufacture: 1975*
          (Britain = 100)

Britain	France	Germany	Italy
100	89[a]	93[b]	91[c]

[a] Derived from *The Future of the British Car Industry*, Central Policy Review
     Staff (CPRS), HMSO, 1975, p. 93.
[b] Derived from a comparison between French and German labour productivities
     and wage costs. According to the CPRS report (p. 80), productivity was 7 per
     cent higher in the German car industry than in the French, in 1973. According
     to Jones's provisional estimates (Daniel T. Jones, 'The European Motor
     Industry and Government Intervention', Paper prepared for a working group
     of the Adjustment Project and the EEC Commission, 12/13 Nov. 1979, Table
     9) French productivity had drawn level with the German productivity by
     1976 (at 7.9 equivalent motor vehicles per employee). The cost of labour to
     the employer was 50 per cent higher in the German car industry in 1975
     (CPRS report, p. 80). Reckoning that direct and indirect labour account for
     13 per cent of the unit cost of a car, the Jones estimates suggest that, other
     factors aside, cars cost 4.5–5.0 per cent more to manufacture in Germany.
     Other factors (unit capital costs) tend to be scale-related and probably do not
     significantly affect this comparison, given the comparable scales of the French
     and German industries.
[c] Jones put Italian productivity in 1976 at 6.9, 87 per cent of the German level
     (the British productivity was only 5.5). Since Italian wage costs were 72 per
     cent of German levels in 1975 (CPRS, p. 80), those figures imply a 2 per cent
     cost advantage for the Italians, equal to 20 per cent of the wage costs. Accord-
     ing to figures quoted by Sig. Agnelli (*Autocar*, 24 June 1978), implying an
     Italian advantage of 10 per cent on wage costs three years later, a 1 per cent
     cost advantage over the Germans is indicated.

disappear. But this convergence is not an irreversible process, as the British car
price differentials after 1978 demonstrate (see below).

If the relative costs which obtained in 1975 are compared with the trade
pattern which had developed by 1976 it will be noticed that there is a striking
correspondence between the two configurations. The French industry's unit
costs were the lowest; it also achieved the best trade performance. The German
and Italian industries both operated with unit costs 5 per cent higher than those
of the French and were joint runners-up on trade performance. The British car
industry's costs were the highest of all, and the British trade performance
was by far the worst. This consistency between the four industries' relative

TABLE 4.10. *Comparative Unit Costs of Car Manufacture 1955–1977*[a]
           (Britain = 100 in each year)

	France	Germany	Italy
1955	160	77	n/a
1960	105	65	n/a
1965	91	70	99
1970	79	87	102
1975	89	93	91
1977	82	98	108

[a] Based on Table 4.9 and the unit cost indices for British Leyland, Renault,
     Volkswagen, and Fiat.

performance in manufacturing and in trade is consistent with the proposition that the relative cost position is the underlying determinant of competitive ability in markets which have become more integrated in terms of product acceptability and ease of entry. This contrasts with the situation in the late 1950s when there was no noticeable correspondence between relative costs and trade performance. The substantial cost advantages enjoyed by the Germans and British at that time, particularly with respect to the French, yielded negligible exports into the French market; the British and German shares of the French market remained at or below 1 per cent in the 1955–1960 period. Conversely, the French and Italians, despite their cost disadvantages, achieved rather greater penetration in the German market (5 per cent and 10 per cent respectively in the late 1950s).

Entry barriers were considerable at that time. Prior to the formation of the Community, the French tariff on cars was 30 per cent, the Italian 35–45 per cent. Both countries imposed quotas until the end of 1961; once removed, imports rose rapidly; car imports to France rose from 25,000 in 1960 to 150,000 in 1965. Local assembly was used as a recourse to get round these barriers, notably by the French and Italians. Fiat had an arrangement with NSU to assemble in Germany; Renault with Alfa-Romeo in Italy. Once the Community dismantled the entanglements on trade these arrangements were terminated; but because of Britain's exclusion from the Community, BMC continued its assembly arrangements with Innocenti. The tariffs imposed by the British between 1955 and 1965 were just sufficient to compensate for the German cost advantage in 1955 (British cars cost 28 per cent more than German cars to build, the tariff was 30 per cent; see Tables 4.7 and 4.10) but was insufficient in 1965 (the British cost advantage had increased to 40 per cent whereas the tariff had been reduced to 26 per cent). The German penetration of the British market rose from 1 per cent in 1955 to 3 per cent in 1965. In this trade, at least, trade patterns appeared to be responding in a fairly muted way to the underlying economics, modified as these were by tariffs.

The cross-sectional analysis of intra-Community trade in Chapter 3 suggested another factor, on the supply side rather than the demand side, which tended to limit trade at that time, namely, that domestic prices did not systematically reflect unit costs. In the early 1960s competitors with scale-related cost advantages preferred to exploit this advantage by earning higher margins even though this attracted some imports into their domestic markets and inhibited their exports. The logic of profit maximization argues in favour of this approach, more so than in the conditions of the 1970s, when price sensitivities had sharpened. Some support for this deduction is provided by the European car industry in the 1960s, for when Volkswagen's cost advantage was so substantial in the period between 1955 and 1960, the company's profit margins (pre-tax profits as a percentage of sales) averaged 15 per cent and in one boom year, 1959, reached 25 per cent. As Volkswagen's cost advantage eroded, so too did its margins, averaging around 10 per cent in the 1960s, 5 per cent in the 1970s.

There is then a contrast between the less mature and the more mature stages of the European car market; between the early 1960s when cost advantage yielded substantial profit margins but little in the way of impact in neighbouring markets, and the 1970s when cost advantage translated more directly into advantageous positions in neighbouring markets. The transition between these two stages – the process of integration – can be explored more systematically by analysing the bilateral trade in cars between France and Germany. These two countries were chosen because they are the two car-producing founder members for whom continuous statistics on prices and costs are available over the twenty year period. The propositions to be tested are that the relative trade performance of the two car industries in this bilateral trade depends on their relative unit costs, and that this relationship became increasingly sensitive as the European car market became integrated. In other words, the sensitivity of trade balances to changes in relative unit costs increased in direct relationship with relative significance of the two countries' bilateral trade in cars.

In statistical terms, the dependent variable is the relative trade performance of the two industries, defined as:

$$TP_{fg} = \frac{\text{The French industry's market share of the German car market}}{\text{The German industry's market share of the French car market.}}$$

The two independent variables are *relative unit cost*, defined in common currency terms, as

$$RC_{fg} = \frac{\text{Unit costs of Renault}}{\text{Unit costs of Volkswagen}} \quad (1955 = 100)$$

and *market integration*, defined as

$$MI_{fg} = \text{(French share of the German market} + \text{German share of the French market)}/2 \text{ (per cent)}$$

The propositions to be tested are that trade advantage was negatively related to relative costs, the more so as market integration increased:

$$TP_{fg} = a + b\,RC_{fg}$$

where $\quad b = c + d\,MI_{fg}$

$$\text{and } b < 0, c < 0, d < 0$$

such that $\quad TP_{fg} = a + c\,RC_{fg} + d\,RC_{fg}{\cdot}MI_{fg}.$

The results appear in Table 4.11. They provide a striking confirmation of the propositions advanced above. The coefficients of both relative costs and the multiplicative term were negative as predicted and were both highly significant statistically. The equation explained almost half the variations in the relative trade performance of the French and German car industries in their bilateral trade; the Durbin–Watson statistic indicates that there was no autocorrelation problem. The magnitudes of the coefficients are plausible; they imply that the elasticity of relative trade performance with respect to relative costs over the period was −1.7. The overall coefficient with respect to relative costs ($c + d\,MI_{fg}$) doubled over the period from −0.022 to −.044. These findings are evidence of an increasingly well-functioning European car market over the twenty-year period.

TABLE 4.11. *Regression Results : Trade Performance, Relative Costs and Integration : France and Germany 1955-1976*

Dependent variable	Constant	RC_{fg}	$RC_{fg} \cdot MI_{fg}$	R^2	Durbin–Watson Statistic
TP_{fg}	3.36	−.019* (3.92)	−.0025* (3.31)	0.46	1.83

t ratios in parentheses.
* significant at the 1 per cent level.
The data appear at Appendix 7.

These findings do not by any means imply the universal applicability of the Law of One Price in the European car market by the late 1970s, but in view of their strong econometric support of a trend towards a unified European car market, it is surprising that prices in Britain moved so far out of line from continental levels after 1978. According to the Institute of Fiscal Studies report,[8] in 1981 average discounted car prices net of tax were 38.5 per cent higher in Britain than in Belgium. The report produced four explanations of the differential: first, that Japanese imports were 'voluntarily restrained' to 11 per cent of the British market, a factor which must have encouraged the Japanese to ration by price; second, slow adaptation of car prices to the rise in the real sterling exchange rate between 1978 and 1981; third, nationalistic buying preferences of British corporate car buyers; fourth, 'all but total' control by manufacturers over dealers, which prevented the arbitrage which would eliminate the differentials. The report ruled out collusion between car producers on the grounds that the characteristics of the market do not allow this. The analysis of trade and concentration in the previous chapter supports this conclusion; concentrated industries such as the car industry exhibited a greater propensity to trade than the average. The factors mentioned above, singly or taken together, do not wholly explain a differential as high as 40 per cent; sterling appreciation does not imply higher oil prices in Britain than elsewhere; constraints on the Japanese need not inhibit European producers from seeking to expand their British market shares by pricing at continental levels; and controls by producers over their established dealers need not in themselves deter the entry of new 'unauthorized' dealers willing to take delivery of cars in, say, Belgium and ship them to the British market, as individual car buyers have been doing.

The most likely reason why 'unauthorized' dealers do not practise arbitrage is that they would have difficulty in obtaining Type Approval information from manufacturers in order to license and register imported cars. But the fundamental source of the price differential is that continental producers have been content to cream off excess profits from the British car buyer, rather than compete for increased market shares.

What light does the foregoing analysis shed on this? The discussion in Chapter 2 argued that aggression in export markets is conditioned by the prospects of displacing high-cost producers in that market. The real appreciation of sterling after 1978 accentuated the existing cost disadvantage of the British producers and would, according to the logic and empirical evidence discussed above, have increased the attractiveness of aggressive moves into the British market. This appears to have occurred; continental producers' share of the British market rose from 23 per cent in 1976 to 44 per cent in 1981. Two factors in particular may have operated in the opposite direction to moderate this trend, giving rise to the price differentials referred to. First, continental producers may have reasoned that because a large part of the British manufacturing industry was uncompetitive at the 1980 exchange rate, sterling must before long depreciate. Second, the willingness of the present British Government to continue the policy of their predecessors of supporting British Leyland's investment programme, despite the company's continuing losses, must have influenced continental producers' expectations about the likelihood of securing BL's share of the British market by aggressive pricing. By 1981, BL held 19 per cent of the British market, equivalent to 43 per cent of the 45 per cent share of the market retained by domestically produced cars. There would have been even less likelihood of continental producers displacing the Japanese from their 11 per cent market share, because this share is constrained by a voluntary agreement. The Japanese car producers, with the lowest-cost position in the world, would have no problem in matching any conceivable price reduction that the continental producers might offer. Thus in 1981, the continental producers were in a position of already holding 44 per cent of the market and knowing that over one-half the remainder was unattainable, in the expectation that BL's 19 per cent share was to a significant extent underwritten by the Government and that the Japanese car producers' 11 per cent share was secured by their unassailable cost advantage. These considerations, taken in conjunction with views about the unsustainable level of sterling, could explain why continental producers preferred to cash their cost advantage, and make windfall profits in the British market, rather than pursue more aggressive pricing policies.

To sum up, the fact that in the five years from 1976 to 1981, continental producers increased their share of the British market from 23 per cent to 44 per cent during a period in which the British producers' cost disadvantage widened, is further evidence of a reasonably functioning European car market. But the emergence of price differentials as high as 38 per cent reflects the present limitations of the Community; the lack of a harmonized vehicle type approval which would facilitate the arbitrage which is so clearly absent in the car market, and the determination of governments to moderate the verdicts of the market when a national champion and major employer is threatened.

Structural Effects

What were the structural aspects of these trade patterns? The discussion in Chapter 2 concluded that industrial structures would change as a result of market leaders displacing (or absorbing) smaller producers during the process of, or soon after, developing export positions. The probability of aggressive moves by market leaders towards smaller producers is increased by trade opportunities. And to the extent that market leaders expand faster than their smaller competitors through exporting, their unit costs will fall relative to those of smaller producers, increasing the latter's vulnerability.

The structural changes which have taken place in the motor industry within the 1955–1972 period are consistent with this hypothesis. Table 4.4 showed changes in the share of national output accounted for by the largest three producers in each country between 1955 and 1977. Italy is least interesting since Fiat has accounted for nearly the entire post-war Italian car production, but the other three countries show rising concentration in this period. The interesting feature of these changes is that the substantial increases in concentration occurred not when an industry was on the defensive but when it was making aggressive moves. The increase in German concentration occurred between 1955 and 1970, when Volkswagen's unit costs (see Table 4.10) were the lowest in the Community and the German car industry's trade performance was at its best. The increase in British concentration occurred between 1965 and 1970 when BMC's unit costs were low and its trade prospects looked excellent. During the 1970s these industries moved on to the defensive; German concentration fell and so would have British concentration, had not government intervention supported British Leyland and Chrysler. The growth in French concentration between 1970 and 1977, after remaining static between 1955 and 1970, also coincided with a growing cost advantage and export success. The comparative export performance of individual French manufacturers contributed directly to this structural change. French car exports to Britain escalated rapidly between 1970 and 1977. The export of 130,000 cars to Britain in 1976 represented an increment of production of 6 per cent for Renault, of 4 per cent for Citroën and Peugeot, and of 2 per cent for Chrysler. At the same time Renault increased its share of the French market from 31 per cent to 34 per cent at the expense of Chrysler and Citroën (see Table 4.5).

The discussion so far has indicated the role played by cost differences in determining the present shape of the European car trade and hence, of the European car industry. But why did relative unit costs in the four countries change as they did? Changes in effective exchange rates have been important within limited periods but by and large these movements have been due to delayed responses to contrived situations, such as the overvalued franc in the 1950s, and the undervalued Deutschmark in the 1960s. As Table 4.8 indicates, in relation to sterling the franc effectively appreciated by only 6 per cent, the lira by only 10 per cent, and the Deutschmark by 35 per cent over a span of

22 years. In the long term, relative costs have reflected car manufacturers' ability to control costs relative to other industries in their respective economies.

ORIGINS OF UNIT COST DIFFERENCES

The study looks now at the obvious source of cost differences, namely, scale. Economies of scale are a well worn subject in the car industry. The original contribution attempted here concerns their demonstrable impact on costs, and their competitive relevance. For whereas the industry's own estimates of scale economies have frequently been reported in the literature there have been few attempts to test these estimates statistically, and to demonstrate their relevance in terms of competitiveness. The discussion begins by unpicking some technological considerations, then tests their implications using the cost indices derived for the leading European manufacturers, and concludes by assessing the role of scale in the competitive configurations which have already emerged.

The Manufacturing Technology

A schematic presentation of the production sequence is shown in Figure 4.4, drawn from the CPRS study. The details of the processes have been described elsewhere. The general observation to make is that, moving through the production sequence, operations become less susceptible to automation, less capital and more labour intensive; they operate with progressively smaller production runs; and most importantly, they offer fewer opportunities for securing economies of scale. In the press shop, for example, body panels are formed by passing sheet steel through a sequence of presses which successively deform the metal with the aid of matching dies. Both the presses and the dies are expensive, as is the automated handling between the presses. Production runs of up to 15,000 identical panels are not uncommon. High volume generates scale economies by reducing the frequency of changing the dies, increasing the possibilities of automating the handling between presses, and reducing working capital requirements. Similar considerations apply to foundry and forging, and to a slightly lesser extent, to machining engine blocks and transmission components and to body-welding. However, at the final assembly end, the scope for automation is much less, save for welding bodies. The sheer number of different parts, the fiddly operational tasks they entail, and the degree of differentiation achieved on a modern assembly line (each car differs in some specifications from those before and after it on the line) imply a comparatively labour-intensive operation.

These basic differences in process characteristics explain the plant structure of car manufacturing whereby the upstream operations are uncoupled from assembly operations, and concentrated in specialized plants serving the whole group; and the assembly operations, with limited scale requirements, can be dispersed to serve different markets. Some published estimates of minimum scale requirements for the major operations are reported in Table 4.12. The Table indicates that scale requirements diminish as the car or its components

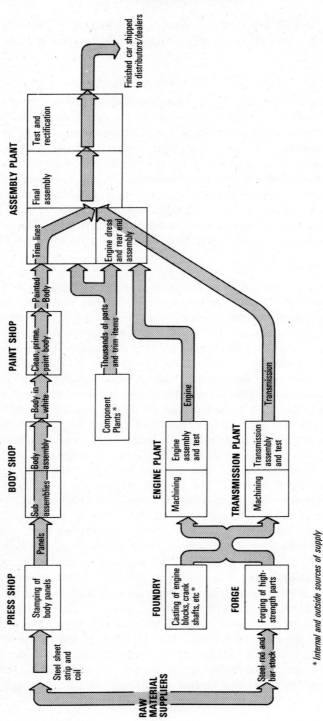

Fig. 4.4. Automobile production: sequence of operations
Source: CPRS, *The Future of the British Car Industry* (HMSO: London, 1975)

travel downstream and that final assembly exhausts available scale economies
in plants producing 200,000–300,000 cars a year. These figures refer to a single
basic model type (but embracing 2-door and 4-door variants, and options in
respect of engine, transmission, colour, and trim). There is less apparent consensus in the literature on minimum scales at the upstream end.[9] This is due
partly to changes in technology between the various reports; advances in forging
and foundry technology have raised minimum scales from 200,000 to 2m.;
and partly to error. It seems prudent to accept the Euro-Economics figure since
it must closely reflect current best-practice techniques.

TABLE 4.12. *Estimates of Minimum Efficient Scales*
(000 units p.a.)

Source of estimates	Operations			
	Foundry and Forge	Pressing	Engine and transmission	Final assembly
Pratten[a]	1000	500	250	300
Rhys[b]	200	2000	1000	200
White[c]	'small'	400	260	200
Ford UK[d]	2000			300
McGee[e]		2000		
Euro-Economics[f]	2000	2000	1000	250

[a] C. F. Pratten, *Economies of Scale in Manufacturing Industry* (Cambridge, 1971).
[b] D. G. Rhys, *The Motor Industry: An Economic Survey* (London, 1972).
[c] L. J. White, *The Automobile Industry Since 1945* (Cambridge, Mass., 1971).
[d] Evidence to the House of Commons Expenditure Committee Session 1974–75, Minutes of Evidence taken before the Trade and Industry Sub-Committee, Vol. I.
[e] John S. McGee, 'Economies of Size in Auto Body Manufacture', *Journal of Law and Economics*, Vol. XVI (2), October, 1973.
[f] *Euro-Economics*, 'The European Car Industry – The Problem of Structure and Overcapacity', March, 1975.

The optimally organized car manufacturer would, according to the Euro-
Economics conclusions, produce 2m. cars using one foundry, one forge, one
press shop, two engine and transmission plants, and eight assembly plants or
lines. No European manufacturer achieves this volume though the majors achieve
50–80 per cent of it. What then are the cost penalties incurred by operating at
lower-than-optimum volumes? Again, a number of estimates have been reported
(see below) but they do not always relate to the current view of efficient scales,[10]
nor do they all explain the production considerations underlying the estimates
as much as one would wish. Neither do the comments which follow, but they
go some way towards deriving estimates of scale economies, related to current
thinking on efficient scales, based on operational considerations. For illustrative
purposes they focus on the press operation, as representative of the capital-
intensive end of car manufacture, and assembly.[11]

The volume car body is a welded assembly of panels which accounts for 10 per cent of the ex-works cost of a car. The panels (roof, bonnet, boot, and sidewalls) are cut ('blanked') from coiled steel and shaped through passage under a series of presses (usually 4–7) which compress the blanks between pairs of mated cast-iron dies (strictly speaking, the upper half is the punch, the lower is the die). The presses are linked in series partly because the desired panel shape may be too complex for a single die to impart and partly because the sheet metal will wrinkle or tear if subjected to single, large deformations. The presses themselves are highly durable, capable of functioning effectively for thirty years, whereas dies are model-specific but capable of outlasting the model in many cases, encouraging attempts to prolong their useful life by using common panels on several models. The transfer of the panels between the presses can be performed manually, semi-automatically (automatic unloading, manual loading), or completely automatically. Major press lines operate at a work rate of 7–18 per minute for medium-sized panels (doors, instrument panels, spoilers) and 4–10 per minute for larger panels (roofs, sidewalls, bonnets).[12]

The cost-volume relationship derives then from three factors; the model-specific nature of the dies which cost around £20m. for a volume car, at 1978 prices;[13] the economies available from automating (as the footnotes to Table 4.13 explain, unit labour costs fall but unit capital costs do not increase); and the economies available from operating a batch process (which, except in the limiting 2m. a year case, press operations in the car industry will tend to be) with lower down-time and with fewer finished stocks as volumes increase. These considerations are developed in Table 4.13 for the three illustrative cases (100,000, 500,000, and 2m. a year). The cost reductions are dramatic; in terms of the value added in pressing (i.e. excluding steel costs), the shift from 100,000 to 500,000 reduces unit pressing costs by over 50 per cent; the shift to 2m. reduces them by a further 40 per cent. There is every reason to expect that similar considerations apply in forging, in the foundry, and to a lesser extent, and to smaller volumes, in machining.

Turning now to final assembly, the optimal scale of an assembly line is reckoned to be 250,000 a year, based on the operating parameters that the working year contains 46 productive weeks, each of 80 effective hours on a two-shift basis. Line speeds of 60–80 an hour yield theoretical annual outputs of 220,000–290,000 cars, modified to allow for down-time to 200,000–250,000.[14] The cost penalties associated with less than the optimal scale of 250,000 per model are lower in assembly than in the other manufacturing operations. Sub-optimal outputs force one of several options on managements; operating only one shift per day, operating the line at lower speeds, or running more than one model down the same assembly line. The first two options reduce the capacity utilization of the assembly plant, raising unit overhead costs; the third reduces capacity utilization to some degree and also raises direct labour costs through disturbing the balance of the line. The objective in designing assembly lines is to subdivide work into small elements, grouping them together at successive

TABLE 4.13. *Unit Costs and Scale in Press Operations*
(£1978)

Cost category	I Four models X 100,000 a year	II Four models X 500, 000 a year	III One model X 2 million a year
Labour	45	26	12
Non-Labour Overheads	20	10	6
Depreciation:			
Dies	16	6	3
Presses	15	7	6
Interest charges:			
Dies	12	2	1
Presses	38	19	15
Total unit pressing cost	146	70	43
Total unit pressing cost (Case I = 100)	100	48	29

Notes on estimation

Labour: Case I derived from CPRS report, p. 93, converted to 1978 prices. The £45 is assumed to be composed of £18 for direct manning of presses, £15 for indirect, and £12 for change-overs of dies; the latter figure is derived from McGee, p. 261, quoting a European manufacturer. In case II, it is assumed that direct manning costs are reduced by two-thirds as a result of moving to automated press lines (see Franz Schneider, Karl Maier, and Heinz Molt, 'A New Concept in Press Line Automation in the Motor Industry', *Production Engineer*, Nov. 1976), and unit change-over costs are halved by increases in production run lengths. In case III, change-overs are eliminated altogether, and the simplified production scheduling that this implies reduces indirect labour.

Depreciation: A press shop for a four-model range is reckoned to cost £150m. and lasts for 25 years, implying a unit depreciation cost of £1.5m. per model per year. It is assumed that press capacity increases less than proportionately with volume because die change-overs are fewer and capacity utilization increases, from 40 per cent in Case I, to 80 per cent in II, to 100 per cent in III. It appears that automation does not raise unit depreciation costs, rather the reverse; Schneider, Maier, and Molt indicate that a modern automated system (in their example, that developed by Schuler of Goeppingen) costs between 70 per cent and 80 per cent as much as conventional press lines of equivalent capacity. The authors also expect manning requirements to fall from eighteen (nine men on each of two conventional lines) to only three on an automated line with double the capacity of a conventional line.

A set of dies is assumed to cost £20m., so, following McGee's estimates, a manufacturer with a four-model range designs in sufficient commonality in his body panels to reduce his requirements to the equivalent of only 2.5 die sets, a saving of 40 per cent. In case I, dies are depreciated over 8 years, yielding depreciation costs of £2.5m. per die set, and £1.6m. per model. In case II it is assumed that the manufacturer uses his scale advantage to halve model lives from 8 to 4 years; hence his unit depreciation costs for dies are not 20 per cent of those in case I, as the fivefold model volume alone would imply, but 40 per cent. In case III, the manufacturer is assumed to change models every two years. This, combined with the fact that the case II manufacturer has opportunities to economize across the model range, implies a less than proportional advantage for the case III manufacturer in unit die costs.

Interest Costs: These assume a 10 per cent rate of interest; thus the case I interest costs, on 2.5 die sets costing £50m. amounts to £5m. annually, £1.25m. per model, £12.50 per car at volumes of 100,000 a year.

Non-labour overheads: These generally work out at 50 per cent of labour costs in car manufacture but are probably less in press operations because of the comparative simplicity of the operation. In case III these costs are reduced considerably, because costs of storing finished panels and working capital interest charges are eliminated by coupling the press directly to final assembly schedules.

work stations in such a way that the operators at each station can complete their tasks in the same time, thus minimizing redundancy on the line.[15] Each model would ideally require a different line balance. Therefore to run two models on the same line would require either periodic reorganizing of the line (changing the layout of tools and material supplies), or compromising the line balance to some extent. A line's output could fall by 8 per cent when two models are run down it. This alone raises unit assembly costs by 8 per cent. The additional complications in managing greater part numbers and production scheduling would probably increase this cost penalty to 10 per cent.

TABLE 4.14. *Cost-Volume Relationships: Full Range Car Manufacture*

	Percentage contribution to ex-works costs[a]	I Four models X 100,000	II Four models X 250,000	III Four models X 500,000
Press, foundry, and forge[b]	16	100	71	48
Machining[c]	9	100	75	60
Assembly of power train, body, and final assembly[d]	25	100	90	90
Bought-in materials and components[e]	50	100	90	90
Total	100	100	86	80

[a] These cost breakdowns refer to the 4 X 100,000 car manufacturer and are derived from the CPRS study and other sources.
[b] Derived from Table 4.13.
[c] Derived from the cost–volume relationship derived in Chapter 5, according to which unit machining costs decline by 20 per cent with each doubling of volume.
[d] Based on the estimated 10 per cent cost penalty of assembling two models on one line; scale economies are exhausted at 250,000 units (see Table 4.13).
[e] The manufacturer's bargaining position makes most of the scale economies in component manufacture available to him. It has been assumed that the scale economies are at least as great as those in car assembly up to 250,000 units.

It is now possible to construct an overall picture of the cost–volume relationship in car manufacture; this is presented in Table 4.14. It is based on unit cost indices for the four major items of cost, weighted by the contribution of each to the total ex-works cost of a volume car. The cost–volume relationship for pressing (Table 4.13) is taken to represent those for forging and casting; for machining, the discussion in Chapter 5 is drawn upon. Components are difficult to analyse because of their variety and wider markets in engineering industries. Because they themselves are mostly manufactured items it was felt reasonable to assume that their cost–volume relationship lay somewhere between those for car assembly and for the capital-intensive upstream operations, probably lying towards the former because smaller items can in general be manufactured on an automated basis at lower volumes. However, the fact that many components are not manufacturer-specific and are marketed across the industry, and even across the engineering sector, must modify the cost–volume relationship with respect to the individual manufacturer. These considerations argue for scale economies in component supply no greater than those in final assembly, i.e. 10 per cent as total volume increases from 400,000 to 1 million, and none beyond this volume.

The conclusion of this analysis is that, compared to the 4 × 100,000 manufacturer, the 4 × 250,000 manufacturer has a unit cost advantage of 14 per cent; the 4 × 500,000 manufacturer has a cost advantage of 20 per cent. In other words, every doubling of volume reduces unit costs by around 10 per cent. This figure is broadly consistent with published estimates.[16] Rhys[17] cited a manufacturer's estimate that unit costs fall by 23 per cent as total volume rises from 100,000 to 500,000, implying a 10 per cent cost reduction with each doubling of volume. Pratten's estimates[18] suggest the same figure over the range 250,000 to 500,000, but only half this figure above this volume. A second estimate quoted by Rhys refers to fixed costs, which fell by 60 per cent as annual model volume rose from 300,000 to 750,000. Reckoning that fixed costs accounted for 25 per cent of the 300,000 volume per model car, these figures suggest a reduction in unit costs of 15 per cent over this range, suggesting a cost reduction of 12 per cent with doubling of volume. A higher figure is suggested by Ford's observation that the Cortina produced in 1970 would have cost £170 more had volumes been one-third as great as they were.[19] Given the prices of that period, this estimate implies a 14 per cent cost reduction with every doubling of volume.

To sum up: the manufacturing technology employed in car manufacture implies that unit costs decline by 10 per cent with every doubling of volume, right up to two million cars a year. This figure finds support from industry estimates cited in the literature in the lower ranges.

Empirical Evidence of Scale Economies

These estimates of scale economies will now be compared with evidence on the actual movement in unit costs of the major manufacturers over the last twenty years, considered in relation to movements in volume. One of the many difficulties in reconciling theoretical estimates with observed practice, is that the former assume that manufacturers operate plant at designed levels of output whereas the data on performance take manufacturers as they are, sometimes at full capacity, at other times not. This is a serious difficulty because given the cost structure of the business, short-term variations in the level of capacity utilization can be expected to have an influence on unit costs which could swamp the predicted effects of scale. Thus, for example, short term variations in capacity utilization of 25 per cent would raise or lower unit costs by 6 per cent and 10 per cent respectively, given that fixed costs account for 30 per cent of total costs. This impact is equivalent to that of a decade's growth in volume.

It is therefore necessary to separate short-term and long-term effects of scale in order to have a chance of isolating the latter. Four companies were chosen for analysis: British Leyland, Volkswagen, Renault, and Ford UK.[20] Capacity utilization estimates were made for each company, on the basis of departures from trends in peak production levels.

Before presenting the results of this exercise, it is worth commenting on the expected values of the volume and capacity utilization coefficients. The 10 per cent cost reduction per doubling of volume is the expected central figure for long-term scale effects; it was calculated on the assumption that cost reductions in components played a minor role, because the component supplying industry supplied a wider market, compared with which the volume increases of one car manufacturer might be comparatively slight. This is true of Britain and Germany, which have had an extensive engineering infrastructure; it has not been true of France, and this consideration prepares one for a more marked volume effect in Renault, recalling that in Table 4.13, in-house scale effects had three times as much impact as bought-in scale effects on the overall cost reduction. The other consideration is that total volume and model volume were assumed to move together; where they do not, overall scale effects will be different. For example, a profileration of models which leads to reduced model volumes would depress the overall scale effect; pruning the range would enhance it. Scale effects achieved in practice could therefore be as low as 5 per cent, as high as 20 per cent, implying cost-volume elasticities ranging from -0.07 to -0.32.

Theoretically, the elasticity with respect to capacity utilization should be -0.3, given that fixed costs acount for 30 per cent of costs. But several factors conspire to erode this. In periods when capacity utilization increases, manufacturers face substantial wage claims, partly because they have more to lose from shut-downs in boom conditions; boom conditions may also call for premiums for multiple-shift working and overtime and the use of marginal, less efficient capacity. These factors will reduce the capacity utilization elasticity or nullify it altogether. And so it proved in the preliminary runs of the analysis. The capacity utilization variable exerted no statistically significant effect on unit costs in the current year, suggesting that the short-run adjustment costs of increased utilization offset the effects of spreading fixed overheads over greater volumes. Once adjustments have been made, however, one would expect the latter effect to dominate, and with this consideration in mind, the capacity utilization variable was introduced lagged one year:

$$\text{Unit cost}_t = \text{Constant} . \text{Volume}_t^{\alpha} . \text{Capacity utilization}_{t-1}^{\beta} .$$

The results appear in Table 4.15 and are encouraging in that in all four regressions the volume coefficient is negative and significant at the 1 per cent level. The volume elasticity ranges from -0.06 to -0.32, implying that every doubling of volume produced cost reductions of 4 per cent at Volkswagen, 6 per cent at Ford, 12 per cent at British Leyland, and 20 per cent at Renault.

TABLE 4.15. *Unit Costs, Volume and Capacity Utilization*

Company	Constant Term	Volume$_t$	Capacity Utilization$_{t-1}$	R^2	DW
British Leyland 1956–1977	2.0	−0.19* (6.94)	−0.10 (1.61)	0.77	1.14
Ford of Britain 1956–1977	1.94	−0.09* (3.45)	−0.12* (2.77)	0.55	2.18
Renault 1956–1977	1.7	−0.32* (8.87)	0.16 (0.99)	0.82	0.88
Volkswagen 1956–1976	1.9	−0.06* (2.98)	−0.13 (1.50)	0.41	0.86

t ratios in parentheses.
* significant at 1 per cent.

The average of these figures is 10 per cent, coinciding with the engineering estimate arrived at above. There is therefore a reassuring agreement, at the broad level, between the study's theoretical and empirical estimates of economies of scale in car manufacture. Renault's high cost–volume response requires comment since it is roughly twice as high as the others'. The most likely explanation, anticipated above, is that in the 1950s and 1960s when the bulk of Renault's (real terms) cost reductions were achieved, the French engineering base was comparatively narrow, compared to the British and German engineering industries. For this reason, Renault developed its own machine tools and automated equipment. The expansion in British and German car volumes is likely to have had a less decisive effect on scale in their respective engineering sectors than was the case with the expansion of the French car industry; since the bought-in element of costs is as high as or higher than the value added element,[21] this could explain why Renault's cost–volume response is over twice as high as the average response of the other three manufacturers.

Capacity utilization has a predicted negative effect on costs in three of the cases (British Leyland, Ford, and Volkswagen); its coefficients are significant to varying degrees in all three and cluster closely together around −0.11 to −0.13. As expected this is well below the theoretical −0.3 figure. The overall fit of the equations is encouraging though the Durbin–Watson statistic indicates auto-correlation in the Renault and Volkswagen equations; the coefficients will not be biased but their statistical significance is likely to be overstated — a problem possibly in the Volkswagen equation but not in the Renault equation. Taken together, the results are as good as could be expected from a two-dimensional analysis which takes no account of a number of factors known to be influential, such as industrial relations, wage pressures, and the degree of plant and product rationalizations.

Various attempts were made to find fuller explanations of unit cost movements. Two sets of variables were explored: wages and productivity; and other dimensions of scale. The car industry's wage levels are usually well above the manufacturing average but have declined in some countries since 1970.[22] The variability in the differential suggested the inclusion of motor industry wage indices as an independent variable. Similarly, the comment that there has been a growing and general disenchantment in the industry's labour force, manifested in disputes, absenteeism, and high labour turnover, suggested that variations in labour productivity, independent of scale and utilization, may have contributed to changes in unit costs. Neither the wage variable nor the labour productivity variable performed consistently or in line with their predicted effects. The wage variable had a strong significant positive effect on Volkswagen's unit costs but this was surprising since wages in the German motor industry have shown less tendency to change, relative to the manufacturing average, than those in the other three countries. The productivity variable showed a weak, negative effect in the British Leyland and Ford equations, but not in Renault's or Volkswagen's. These two variables added little or nothing to an overall improvement in the model.

TABLE 4.16. *Regression Results: Unit Costs and Volume 1955–1977*

	Constant	Volume	Average Model Volume	R^2	DW
Ford of Britain					
1	5.12	−0.095** (3.25)		0.33	2.14
2	4.68		−0.026 (1.69)	0.12	1.89
3	5.41	−0.180** (3.26)	0.045 (1.78)	0.43	2.39
British Leyland					
4	5.41	−0.154** (4.16)		0.45	0.56
5	5.09		−0.111** (3.20)	0.33	0.71
6	5.46	−0.207* (2.23)	0.078 (0.62)	0.46	0.51
Renault					
7	6.17	−0.312** (9.96)		0.83	0.58
8	5.54		−0.255* (2.14)	0.18	0.33
9	6.09	−0.319** (8.64)	0.023 (0.35)	0.83	0.54

t   ratios in parentheses.
** significant at 1 per cent.
*   significant at 5 per cent.

The more interesting set of variables, closer to the theme of this study, concern other dimensions of scale; average model volume and plant size. The argument for model volume is that many overhead costs are model-specific. The engineering costs, tooling, and dies for a new model can amount to £300m. Spreading these over greater volumes reduces unit costs pretty well in line with the 10 per cent cost–volume relationship already discussed. This cannot be the whole story since some fixed costs can be shared by other models. In pressings McGee reckoned that four models could be accommodated by only 2.5 sets of dies and in capital-intensive operations in the foundry, forge, and press shop, economic utilization of automated equipment depends on the combined volumes of several models.[23] In a straight run-off between the two scale variables, shown in Table 4.16, volume emerges as the clear winner. In the Ford and British Leyland sets of equations, annual volume performed best in the single variable equations, and also when run alongside model volume. Model volume looked plausible on its own but reversed its sign when included with volume.

Plant size was not included in this time series analysis in the way that it appears to deserve, in view of the fact that the cross-sectional analysis in Chapter 3 was built around it. Plant size is a valuable measure of scale in cross-sectional analysis because it is available from censuses of production, but its availability at intervals of many years makes it unsuitable for time series work. More importantly, representative plant size is not the most helpful scale dimension once one gets close to the car industry. It was noted earlier that economies of scale in this industry require a configuration of capacities (ranging from 250,000 to 2m. units) in forging, casting, pressing, machining, and assembly. Comparisons of representative plant sizes, in terms of employment rather than capacities, might well fail to do justice to the differing scale requirements of these activities, and to the extents to which manufacturers had fulfilled them. With that reservation, plant size differences are of some interest.

In 1975 the largest car assembly plants in Europe in terms of employment were Fiat's plant at Mirafiori and Volkswagen's plant at Wolfsburg, each of which employed nearly 50,000 in 1975 (Wolfsburg employed 59,000 in 1970). The two major plants in France (Renault's at Billancourt and Peugeot's at Sochaux) employed over 30,000; the two major plants in Britain employed less than 30,000 (Ford at Dagenham and British Leyland at Longbridge). Nine of the twelve major European manufacturers employed between one-half and two-thirds of their employees at one location. The exceptions were Renault, Chrysler (France), and British Leyland. The British representative plant size is the smallest in the European car industry. A detailed study by Jones and Prais[24] based on census statistics, put the British median plant size at 2,300 employees in 1970; the German equivalent was over three times greater, at 7,600 employees. The German productivity advantage, calculated by the authors to be 43 per cent in 1976, stretched the German plant size advantage to nearly sixfold in terms of output.[25] In assembly alone, the German advantage was only double in terms of employment (12,000 compared to 6,500). The authors argue that plant size is a critical (but not sufficient) element of success in this industry, noting that the growth in the German plant size advantage moved hand in hand with a growing German productivity advantage. British plant sizes remained low by international standards, despite the car mergers of the 1950s and 1960s, which failed to change the physical structure of the indigenous British car-making capacity within the rambling agglomeration of British Leyland.

The relatively small size of British car plants was also partly due to the en-couragement given and pressures exerted by regional policies in the 1960s to open plants in Merseyside and Scotland (the majority of which have failed to perform even up to the standards of the British car industry). But Jones and Prais draw attention to the unmanageability of large car plants in Britain, reflec-ting a general tendency for larger plants in Britain to be more strike-prone than smaller plants. Fiat's difficulties in the 1970s with an increasingly militant workforce at Turin led to greater decentralization, assisted by computer-based production scheduling systems, towards plants in the South which are located in isolation rather than in a complex of the Mirafiori type. These observations caution against recommending that car manufacturers expand plant size to eliminate the cost disadvantage noted above; the economies which are technically available in car manufacture seem more achievable in some countries than in others.

Scale and International Cost Differences

It was observed earlier that the configuration of relative costs (in 1975) corres-ponds very closely with relative trade performance in the Community (in 1976). Scale has been demonstrated to be the main influence on the unit costs of the major manufacturers over time; we would also expect that scale differences between the major manufacturers could explain unit cost differences at a point in time. Looking again at the 1975 position in Table 4.17 the volumes of the four national champions are shown, and their relative costs are estimated on the basis of the 10 percent cost reduction per doubling of volume relationship

TABLE 4.17. *Scale-related Unit Cost Differences: 1975*

	Britain	France	Germany	Italy
Volume of leading national manufacturer, 1975[a] (000)	610	1,300	935	1,010
Predicted Unit Cost[b] (Britain = 100)	100	89	95	91
Actual Unit Cost[c] (Britain = 100)	100	89	93	91

[a] From respective national manufacturers associations: SMMT, CSCA, VDA, ANFIA.
[b] On basis of the derived relationship between unit cost and volume, according to which unit costs decline by 10 per cent with successive doublings of volume.
[c] See Table 4.9.

which has been derived and tested. The estimated configuration of unit costs corresponds very closely to the actual unit costs calculated earlier (see Table 4.9).

Total company volume emerges as the most useful dimension of scale in this industry, best able to elucidate scale economies, to explain unit cost movements over time, and to explain recent international patterns of costs. The fuller picture must include the other dimensions too. Germany's lowest-cost position in the 1955–65 period probably owed something to volume per model, since Volkswagen produced virtually only one model until the early 1960s in annual volumes of over 700,000 in an exceptionally large plant at Wolfsburg. The proliferation of models after 1960 reduced Volkswagen's model volume (see Table 4.18) and must have contributed to its increased unit costs relative to other competitors. By the mid-1970s, the major producers' model volumes were broadly proportional to their total volumes (five models accounted for around 80 per cent of each manufacturer's total volumes); plant size played some part too. It seems clear that part of the British cost disadvantage is attributable to low plant size (lower even than might be expected given the volumes of British manufacturers).[26]

CONCLUSIONS

Prior to the formation of the Community, the isolation of national car markets, through tariffs, quotas, and idiosyncratic designs tolerated wide international differences in unit costs of car manufacture. As trade opened up within the Community, these unit cost differences (some of which reversed in time) began to shape the intra-Community trade pattern in predictable ways, with the lowest-cost country dominant, the highest-cost country on the retreat. As trade developed, international unit cost differences tended to become at the same time narrower but more decisive, with the notable exception of the British case after 1978.

Scale factors were the major determinants of unit costs. Engineering considerations suggested that unit costs decline by 10 per cent with every doubling in volume, up to a volume of two million cars a year. An empirical analysis of the movements in the leading European car manufacturers' unit costs over a twenty year period showed that these movements were broadly consistent with this cost–volume relationship, which also explained international cost differences in the mid-1970s. Thus, in the Community's most important industry, scale was shown to be a major determinant of unit costs, which in turn were shown to feed through strongly into trade performance within the Community. In the process, larger, low-cost producers tended to expand at the expense of smaller, high-cost producers; and within the organizational boundaries of the producers themselves, plant rationalizations and single-sourcing of major engineered items have led in effect to the displacement of smaller units by larger. National industrial policies and constraints have tended to inhibit this process; even the largest European producers fall well short of the two million minimum economic scale.

TABLE 4.18. *Total Volume[a] and Average Model Volume[b] (000) for Leading Manufacturers 1955–1975*

	Renault		Volkswagen		British Leyland		Fiat	
	Volume	Average Model Volume	Volume	Average Model Volume	Volume	Average Model Volume	Volume	Average Model Volume
1955	180	140	290	280	470	70	230	n/a
1960	490	380	760	730	650	90	510	n/a
1965	510	200	1,230	500	870	120	990	240
1970	1,050	210	1,270	320	790	160	1,390	350
1975	1,300	270	940	190	610	120	1,130	220

[a] Volumes exclusive of CKD Kits.
[b] Defined as the average volumes of those highest-volume models which accounted for 80 per cent of each manufacturer's total volume in each year.
Sources: Respective motor manufacturers' trade associations.

None the less, the developments analysed in this cha
of the previous chapters; they illustrate, too, the econom
the founding fathers' conception of the Community, a
but for the development of a more, if not completely, ir
would not have been the same impetus towards scale and l

NOTES

1 This characterization draws on D. F. Channon's case study 'The European Automobile Industry', *British Business Policy: A Casebook*, ed. John M. Stopford (London, 1975).

2 Italy concluded a bilateral agreement with Japan which pre-dated the Treaty of Rome, limiting imports of Japanese cars to 2,200 a year.

3 Until 1966, Ford in Europe operated as two independent entities in Britain and Germany with their own product ranges, designers, components, and suppliers. Ford of Europe was established in 1967 (based at Warley, UK) to fit these two companies into an overall European plan, whereafter common models were introduced, beginning with the Transit van, followed by the Capri (1969), the Cortina/Taunus (1970), and the Granada (1972), designed jointly and assembled in both Britain and Germany (*Engineering Today*, 26 June 1978).

4 The Four produced 40 per cent more cars in 1977 than in 1965 (9,800,000 compared to 6,900,000), and traded 180 per cent more (1,350,000 compared to 480,000).

5 There are, however, national differences in respect to the *size* of car favoured by the respective domestic markets, according to a study by R. D. Hocking, 'Trade in Motor Cars between the Major European Producers', *The Economic Journal*, Sept. 1980, pp. 504–19. Hocking noted that relative to the European norm, French and Italian demand patterns were orientated towards small, utility, cars; British demand favoured medium cars, and German demand favoured large cars. He then demonstrated that in their trade with each other, these four countries specialized in the type of car favoured by their respective domestic consumers. This interesting observation is not in conflict with the argument advanced here that designs have converged in Europe; nor does it say anything about overall trade balances in cars within Europe.

6 The use of quality-adjusted prices offers one way around this problem (Keith Cowling and John Cubbin, 'Price, Quality and Advertising Competition, An Econometric Investigation of the United Kingdom Car Market', *Economica*, Nov. 1971, pp. 378–94) but was not adopted here because the range of characteristics within the high-volume models which dominate the cost indices was found to be too narrow (and nebulous) to be related to price econometrically.

7 This was partly due to the impact of increased engineering costs, necessitated by the need to develop a new range to replace the ancient Beetle and the three models which competed with it (the VW 411, the Audi 100, and the NSU K70), two of which had in effect been acquired through mergers but not integrated into a coherent model range. Thus in the four years prior to 1974, VW spent DM 2.5 billion developing the model range, or roughly £100 for each car produced in that period.

8 M. A. Ashworth, J. A. Kay and T. A. E. Sharpe, *Differentials between Car Prices in the United Kingdom and Belgium* (The Institute of Fiscal Studies, 1982). According to the authors (p. 36), these differentials resulted in a direct loss to the UK national income, via excess payments to foreign manufacturers or wholly-owned subsidiaries of foreign companies, of £1 billion, equivalent to one-half per cent of national income in 1981.

9 According to McGee, White was 'seriously mistaken' in citing 400,000 units a year as the efficient scale in pressing, in the belief that 400,000 is the limit for die life. McGee failed to find any case in which a manufacturer replaced dies because they were worn out, and found many in use after several million pressings.

10 Pratten's detailed estimates refer to scales well below the two million level.

11 McGee provides the most informative account (see below), of press operations, and from

ves estimates of unit die costs, though not unit pressing costs.

y smaller parts, such as mounting brackets, are produced on small, high-speed, automated presses with speeds of up to several hundred a minute.

13 McGee reported costs of $16–20 million at 1972 prices, equivalent to £16–20m. at 1978 prices. The CPRS study cites a figure of £15m. at 1975 prices, equivalent to £23 million at 1978 prices.

14 This reflects European practice; American line speeds are generally higher and have reached 120 an hour.

15 Balancing losses generally work out at a low percentage, certainly less than 10 per cent. In other words, a low percentage of the total operators' available time is not utilized because some work stations have less work to perform (measured by work study engineers in minutes of standard work) than others and the latter determine the speed of the line.

16 This discussion has assumed that volume per model is proportional to total volume; this is generally true though there are exceptions. Specialists such as Daimler–Benz, Volvo, and Saab concentrate on one or two models. Some volume producers have proliferated models (British Leyland). The considerations discussed in this section suggest that the 1 × 250,000 producers will have a slight cost advantage (of say 2–3 per cent) over the 4 × 100,000 producer because, although the scale economies available to the former in the capital-intensive operations can be achieved by the latter if he engineers in the degree of commonality envisaged by McGee, the 1 × 250,000 manufacturer will secure a 10 per cent cost advantage in the assembly operations.

17 D. G. Rhys, 'European Mass-producing Car Makers and Minimum Efficient Scale: A Note', *Journal of Industrial Economics*, June 1977, pp. 313–32.

18 C. F. Pratten, *Economies of Scale*, p. 142.

19 Quoted in *Engineering Today*, 26 June 1978. Set against the ex-works cost of a 1970 Cortina (£570, equal to 82 per cent of the retail price of £744), this cost saving represented 23 per cent of the hypothetical costs of the one-third scale manufacturer, implying a 14 per cent cost reduction with each doubling of volume.

20 Fiat was excluded because price and profit margin data were unavailable prior to 1965.

21 75 per cent, according to Table 4.14.

22 The motor industry's wage differential for males' hourly earnings has declined since 1970:

	France (percentage)	Germany (percentage)	Britain (percentage)	Italy (percentage)
1970	17	12	23	23
1973	2	11	18	9
1975	−2	16	9	−1

Sources: Department of Employment Gazette; Eurostat: Average Hourly Earnings, 1976.

23 Comparing the unit fixed costs of two models, each in production for eight years, one at 100,000 a year, the other at 400,000 a year, the unit fixed costs of the latter are around £100, compared to the former's £400. The total unit cost of the 400,000 a year model is therefore around 20 per cent lower than that of the 100,000 a year model.

24 D. T. Jones and S. J. Prais, 'Plant Size and Productivity in the Motor Industry: Some International Comparisons', *NIESR*, Sept. 1977.

25

	Median plant size (employees)		Productivity[b] (equivalent units per employee)	
	Germany	Britain	Germany	Britain
1960	4,900[a]	2,700[a]	5.2	5.0
1970	7,600	2,400[a]	7.5	5.6

[a] Interpolated from chart 2, page 9a.
[b] Table 4, page 14a: 1960 figures are averages of 1955 and 1965 figures.

26 The CPRS study attributed two-thirds of the British manufacturer's 11 per cent cost

penalty in 1975 to scale factors (p. 93); of this one-third was due to low model volumes, one-third to low plant sizes, and one-third to excessive overmanning (excessive, that is, in the sense that it could not be offset by low British wage levels).

CHAPTER 5

THE EUROPEAN TRUCK INDUSTRY

Do the conclusions of the car study apply only to consumer goods industries, or do they read across to capital goods sectors? This chapter looks at the heavy end of the vehicle industry to find out. It restricts itself to on-the-road commercial vehicles with gross vehicle weights in excess of 4 tonnes, referred to hereafter simply as 'trucks'. It does not concern itself with commercial vans, either of the car-derived type or light delivery types such as the British Leyland Sherpa and Ford Transits; it also excludes specialized vehicles such as fire engines, refuse disposal vehicles, and various off-the-road types for military and civil engineering uses.

Trucks and cars are manufactured by and large by the same companies using very similar manufacturing technologies, but whereas the car is a consumer durable, the truck is a piece of capital equipment, costing over three times as much as a car, built for more intensive use over a lifetime mileage roughly three times greater than the car's. Whereas the car is sold as a predetermined package of fairly restricted options, the truck tends to be tailored to individual customers' requirements, as capital items often tend to be. Partly for this reason and because of the investment in spares necessary to operate a fleet of vehicles, customer loyalty is very strong. The truck in use tends to be hedged about with rather more restrictions than the modern car, due to its greater weight and impact on the environment. All these factors taken together — the truck's relative complexity, the loyalty of its customers, and the restrictions which surround its use — tend to make the truck industry more impervious to the European-wide economic pressures than the car industry. The interest of this chapter resides in the analysis of the extent and the way in which the pressures of European competition have reshaped a captial goods industry, of which the truck industry is in many ways representative.

THE PRODUCT

The product itself falls mainly into two categories, rigid trucks and articulated trucks ('rigids' and 'artics' in the trade). The former are single chassis vehicles with up to four axles which are delivered by the truck producer to body builders which erect platforms or closed bodies to customers' specifications. Articulated trucks are simply tractor units, with two or three axles, which attach to trailers or semi-trailers; most heavy duty vehicles are of this type. Trucks' weight designations refer to the gross vehicle weight (GVW) which they are deemed capable of handling by road licensing authorities. The pay load increases as a proportion of gross vehicle weight as the latter increases; a 32 tonne gross vehicle weight

truck will carry a pay load of around 25 tonnes. A rough classification of trucks
by weight which finds favour in the trade is as follows:

Light	4–6 tonnes rigid type
Light/Medium	6–16 tonnes rigid type
Medium/Heavy	16–24 tonnes rigid type
	21–28 tonnes articulated
Heavy	Over 28 tonnes articulated.

Rigid types extend only to 24 tonnes GVW. Articulated types take over as
loads increase because their superior manœuvrability makes heavy loads manageable in urban road systems and because of the increased utilization which the
design facilitates by allowing the tractor unit to detach itself from its load on
delivery and to hitch up immediately to a prepared return load. This last advantage
has become more important as the heavy truck has become a more capital-
intensive item of equipment. In Britain, two-thirds of fleets have two or more
semi-trailers per tractor unit.

The truck has the marketing features of any capital good and which distinguish
this industry from the car industry. Buyers are relatively few and are technically
far more qualified than car buyers. The marketing approach adopted in the
industry reflects this difference; whereas cars are pulled through the market by
media advertising directed at the public at large, trucks are pushed through
by dealers' representatives, who focus on the known, key individuals in the
market — transport managers of large companies with their own fleets and
managing directors of haulage companies. The former dominate the demand for
lighter trucks, which are used mainly for short-haul distribution; the latter
dominate the demand for the heavier, long-haul trucks.

TABLE 5.1.   *Ranking of Factors Influencing Truck Buyers' Decisions*

	Factor influencing buyers' decisions	Light	Light/ Medium	Medium/ Heavy	Heavy
1	Experience with manufacturer	1	1	2	2
2	Standardization of fleet	3	2	1	4
3	Suitability	2	3	3	8
4	Price	4	4	5	3
5	Delivery time	6=	4=	4	5
6	Dealer service	6=	6	6	6
7	Reliability	5	7	7	1
8	Spares availability	–	8	8	7

Source: A manufacturer's survey of a European truck market, 1977.

The features of the truck which determine buyers' choices are set out and
ranked in Table 5.1, derived from a survey of 2,000 buyers in a European
truck market. Standardization of the fleet ranks second overall after 'experience'.
Truck buyers usually operate several vehicles, unlike the typical farmer or
car owner. There is therefore an economy and convenience in fleet operators

standardizing on one manufacturer's product range; unless a fleet operator decides to replace his entire fleet at once, this feature tends to lock the buyer into their favoured manufacturer. These considerations imply strong buyer loyalties and this is borne out by evidence from the same survey, which indicated that the proportion of buyers intending to place their next purchase with their existing supplier ran at 85-95 per cent for the light and light/medium ranges, falling to 75-90 per cent for the medium/heavy category, tailing off sharply to less than 50 per cent in the heavy category. About a quarter of the buyers surveyed reported that they would not even consider alternative suppliers at all. Loyalties were very strong in Germany, to judge from a study by Dorward;[1] but as will become clear, this was probably due to technical barriers to entry into the German market and to Daimler-Benz's competitive advantages.

Two other observations are worth making on buyer attitudes. In the heavy category, reliability is the most influential factor, even though this ranks only seventh in the two medium categories. This reflects the paramount need to maintain the fullest vehicle utilization of the capital intensive heavy truck, indicated by its greater usage; heavy trucks are operated over greater mileages over their working lives (250,000 miles compared to 100,000-150,000 miles for the lowest weight categories) and more usefully while on the road (heavy trucks carry full loads for a higher proportion of their working hours than lighter trucks). Since 'reliability' was ranked as more important than what one might term the two loyalty factors — 'experience' and fleet standardization (in the premium category), this segment of the market was more open to new entry than the others, provided that the new entrant already has credentials, as has been illustrated by Volvo, which has taken one-third of the British heavy segment.

Accepting the loyalty factors, which are a fact of life in this industry, this study is more concerned with those factors which can be used most effectively to induce switching from existing to alternative suppliers since these will have most bearing on any changes in competitive positions. Outside this heavy segment of the market these factors are, in order of reported importance: 'suitability', price, delivery, and dealer service. In other words, the key to securing markets rests upon the ability to meet customers' specifications, at reasonable prices, with rapid delivery, and with the prospect of good dealer support for the truck when in operation. It is therefore these factors which the study focuses on in trying to analyse competitive configurations in the European truck industry, in order to discover whether these forces, with the limited leverage allowed them by the strong buyer loyalties and the technical barriers to entry, have in time percolated through to the market and reshaped the industry's structure.

THE INDUSTRY

In the late 1970s the European truck industry was producing over half a million trucks a year. Britain was traditionally Europe's leading truck producer; in 1960 its output was twice the German, three times the French, and four times the

Italian output. The British lead has been attributed to the preponderant use of road transport and the weight restrictions dictated by the British road system. Continental countries used proportionately more rail than road and in some cases, inland waterways played an important part (e.g. 25 per cent of tonne miles in Germany). The large number of trucks in use in Britain owed something to the fact that they were smaller on average. Continental road systems and high wage levels encouraged the use of heavy trucks whereas British weight restrictions actively discouraged them. In the 1970s the maximum vehicle weight in Britain was 32 tonnes; the limit was 38 tonnes in Belgium, France, and Germany, 44 tonnes in Italy, and 50 tonnes in Holland. In the 1970s, British truck production declined against the rising European trend; by 1977, Britain produced less than half as many trucks as Germany, and roughly twice as many as France, Italy, and Sweden (see Table 5.2). It also redirected its export efforts, again against the trend, away from traditional third world markets, where British exports were being rolled back by the Japanese advance in Asian markets, towards Europe.

Over the last twenty years the European truck industry has been concentrated into fourteen major producers, swept into eleven groupings. There are four major national groupings: Daimler-Benz, IVECO (Fiat, Magirus-Deutz, and Unic), Leyland, and Renault (Berliet and Saviem). The three American multi-national car manufacturers have also an involvement, through operations in Britain; Ford, General Motors (through Bedford), and Chrysler (through acquisition of the Rootes Group, now sold to Peugeot-Citroën). The other four major producers (M.A.N., Volvo, Scania, and Daf) are independent heavy-truck specialists, as are three minor survivors in this category in Britain, Seddon–Atkinson, Foden, and ERF. The size, composition, and location of their major assembly plants are shown in Table 5.2. Three topographical features of the industry are worth noting. First, it is dominated by Daimler–Benz, which has an assembly plant at Woerth which produces twice as many trucks as any other assembly plant in Europe. Second, there is one genuinely pan-European company, IVECO, embracing companies in three major Community countries, with a major assembly plant in each. Third, Britain's position as the second largest European truck producer is largely due to decisions by the American multinationals to locate their European truck manufacture in Britain, attracted, probably, by the strength of Britain's engineering infrastructure and the access Britain once offered to Commonwealth markets. A feature of the industry which is not apparent from this snapshot is that the British and French national champions, Leyland and Renault, are less cohesive than they appear on paper. In operational terms, Leyland was for a long time an archipelago of six truck producers loosely federated together; and the two halves of Renault's operation, Saviem and Berliet, were not, in 1980, fully integrated, marketing in the main separate marques based on distinct engineering and production systems. The first public appearance of models common to both companies was not until the autumn of 1978 (the Berliet GB 131 and the Saviem HR 15).

TABLE 5.2.   *Truck Production by Country and Company, 1977*
(trucks of 4 tonnes GVW and over)

Germany	Britain	France	Italy	Sweden	Holland
Daimler–Benz	Ford	Berliet	Fiat	Volvo	Daf
Woerth	Langley	Vénissieux	Turin	Tuve	Eindhoven
100,000	42,000	20,000	50,000	25,000	14,000
Düsseldorf	Bedford	Saviem		Saab Scania	
30,000	Dunstable	Blainville		Sodertalje	
	35,000	20,000		20,000	
M.A.N.	Leyland	Unic			
Augsburg	Leyland, Bathgate	Trappes			
19,000	25,000	17,000			
Magirus–Deutz	Chrysler				
Ulm	Dunstable				
17,000	9,000				
165,000	110,000	60,000	50,000	45,000	14,000

Source: Chambre Syndicate des Constructeurs d'Automobiles.

This structure emerged in the last twenty years, largely as a consequence of domestic mergers in the 1960s and international mergers and co-operative agreements in the 1970s. In the decade after the Second World War, the industry looked pretty much like the car industry immediately after the First World War. A host of small companies which had pioneered the industry prior to the First World War still survived as independent entities. This was particularly true of the British truck industry, which had led truck production in Europe. In the 1940s twenty or so small companies coexisted alongside the five volume producers, which were all divisions of the major car producers — Bedford, Ford, Austin, Nuffield, and Rootes. In Italy, OM and Lancia still survived, having begun truck manufacture in 1908 and 1912 respectively. The small company was a specialist producer, prepared to design and build a combination of wheel base, engine, gear box, axle ratios, positioning of various fitments such as petrol tank, instruments, and accessories, specific to a particular customer's requirements. For reasons discussed later, this breed has largely been seen off by the high-volume competition. In Britain, by 1968 no less than nine specialists were absorbed, together with Austin and Morris (Nuffield) into the Leyland organization (AEC, Albion, Crossley, Daimler, Guy, Maudslay, Scammell, and Thorneycroft). Thorneycroft and Maudslay were subsequently sold off and out of truck production. In 1970, two remaining independents merged to form Seddon–Atkinson. Thus by the 1970s the British truck industry had coalesced around just four major producers, and three American companies (Ford, Bedford, and Chrysler) and Leyland, and three specialists, Seddon–Atkinson (now owned by International Harvester), Foden, and ERF, the latter each producing around 2,000 heavy trucks in 1976.

In the German industry, there were fewer independents surviving into the 1960s, and the more significant of those which did were absorbed by Daimler–Benz and M.A.N. M.A.N. first acquired 50 per cent of Büssing, Germany's oldest truck producer, in 1969 and subsequently absorbed it totally after 1971. Daimler–Benz took over Krupp's truck operation in 1968, apparently to secure the latter's distribution facilities. Krupp was a heavy truck specialist which ran into financial difficulties from 1964 onwards and tried without success to find a way out of them via co-operative arrangements with various foreign companies looking for an entrée into the German market. In 1969 Daimler–Benz followed this by acquiring Germany's second largest truck producer, Hanomag–Henschel. In the 1970s the sole remaining independents were Faun and Kaelbe, each producing only a few hundred units in 1976.

In France and Italy, the tradition of independent truck manufacture was much weaker and is now almost terminated completely. In 1970, Fiat absorbed Lancia, OM, and the French producer, UNIC, and in effect acquired the German producer, Magirus–Deutz in 1975 to form IVECO. Only Alfa-Romeo remains outside this grouping. In France, the merger in 1955 of Renault's truck interests with those of Somua formed Saviem, controlled since 1959 by Renault. Berliet, the other major French truck producer, was a family firm until its acquisition by

Citroën in 1967; it was later acquired by Renault in 1975. Of the four remaining independents, Hotchkiss, which produced 800 or so trucks in 1964, disappeared in 1970, Bernard was acquired by Mack of the USA, Willeme was acquired in 1968 by Leyland and subsequently faded away, and Sovam survived, producing miniscule volumes (100–200) of light trucks.

But, rapid though this process of concentration in the national truck industries was, it was unable by itself to secure the economies foreseen by the industries' leaders. In the late 1960s and throughout the 1970s, leading producers began reaching towards each other, frequently across national boundaries, to find co-operative arrangements which would secure a competitive base. The more significant of these linkages were as follows:

1. The Club of Four: a company was established in 1971 (now disbanded) by Daf, Magirus–Deutz, Saviem, and Volvo to design and co-ordinate production of a light truck (6.6 tonnes GVW) which appeared in 1975, largely in response to the perceived threat from the British volume truck producers, expected to materialize following Britain's entry into the EEC. The components of this range were standardized and contributed by members of the Club on a specialized basis; assembly was carried out at members' own plants and marketing was done independently, without territorial restrictions.

2. M.A.N. and Volkswagen: in 1976 the companies agreed to develop a light truck range (6–9 tonnes GVW) to enable both companies to enter a new segment of the market (in 1979) which lay between their existing product ranges; Volkswagen supplied cabs, M.A.N. supplied chassis.

3. Daimler-Benz and M.A.N.: the companies had agreed to exchange engines (over 150 hp) and heavy axles since 1972. The two companies also jointly own a subsidiary (Motoren and Turbinen Union Muenchen) which performs development work on gas turbines and high speed diesels.

4. Sofim: Renault (Saviem) and IVECO (Alfa-Romeo) jointly own a subsidiary, established in 1974, to manufacture 40–100 hp high-speed diesel engines in Italy, which came on stream in 1978.

5. M.A.N. and Saviem: in 1968 the companies agreed to exchange Saviem's cabs for M.A.N.'s engines.

6. Daimler-Benz and IVECO: the companies had hoped to jointly develop an automatic truck transmission; the proposal ran into opposition from the German Cartel Office.

Vertical Integration and the Role of the Specialists

As the cost structure shown in Table 5.3 indicates, assembly accounts for only 10 per cent of the ex-works cost of a typical truck, and is usually carried out in plants dedicated to truck assembly with major items supplied from special-purpose feeder plants producing engines, axles, transmissions, and pressings.

TABLE 5.3.   *A Cost Breakdown of Truck Manufacture*

Item	Percentage of total ex-works cost
Cab	14
Engine	20
Gearbox	10
Axles	7
Chassis	4
Line Assembled Components (seats, trim, tyres, instrumentation, brakes, etc.)	35
Final Assembly	10
	100

Source: Various manufacturers.

This sourcing pattern is illustrated in Table 5.4 for the leading companies in each country, though there are exceptions to this; Bedford produce their own engines, axles, and cabs, and assemble their trucks, all at the same site at Dunstable; Leyland plants are also integrated to various degrees.

TABLE 5.4.   *Sourcing Patterns: Selected Companies*

	Daimler–Benz	Berliet	Ford	IVECO
Engines	Mannheim	Vénissieux	Dagenham	Ulm/Turin/ Brescia/ Bourbon Lancy
Axles	Kassel	St Priest	Swansea	Milan
Transmissions	Gaggenau	St Étienne	Swansea	Brescia
Pressings cabs	Woerth	Vénissieux	Southampton	Brescia
Final assembly	Woerth	Vénissieux	Langley	Turin/Ulm/ Trappes

This natural division between component manufacturer and final assembly has offered the truck industry two routes for its development; either to develop these activities separately or to integrate vertically. In the two countries where an active engineering infrastructure existed (Britain and Germany) the former route was followed; where this infra-structure was absent (France and Italy), truck producers were perforce obliged to integrate vertically. The former arrangement has an industrial logic to it; since the economies of scale have been so much more important in component manufacture than in final assembly it was natural that the two activities should be carried out independently, particularly as component producers supplied other sectors also, such as tractors and construction equipment, and as a consequence, component supply is concentrated in the hands of fewer companies than truck production. Thus in Britain, the manufacture of engines is dominated by Cummins, Rolls Royce, Perkins, and Gardner, that of gear boxes by Turner and David Brown, that of transmissions by Eaton, and that of axles by GKN and Rockwell. In Germany, ZF dominates transmission manufacture, and Fichtel & Sachs and Borg–Warner clutch manufacture.

Vertical separation allows the small assemblers to obtain the benefit of the economies of scale available in the component sector. It allowed three small scale specialists (Seddon–Atkinson, Foden, and ERF) to survive in Britain and assisted Leyland itself, since the latter was formed from several small companies. The independent specialists have pushed the buying-in philosophy to its logical extreme and themselves account for little more than the 10 per cent of the total value of the truck represented by assembly. Although unable to achieve the (fairly modest) economies in assembly, the specialist was once able to offset this disadvantage by offering a premium product, adeptly combining the best engineering available from the supply sectors, for example, using configurations built around the much-in-demand Gardner engine.[2] Foden stated that it expected to be able to charge prices 5 per cent above those of its main competitors.[3]

This strategy which served the small producer so well in the restricted markets of the 1960s became increasingly vulnerable in the wider markets of the 1970s. It rested more than on any other factor on the superiority and availability of independents' engines over those of the large scale truck producers. There are indications that the latter's engines are regarded as being among the best (Volvo and Daimler–Benz, in particular, especially in terms of power-to-weight ratios). Moreover, it is to be expected that truck producers will look for any opportunity to increase (profitable) valued added. High volume producers are already doing so, using the co-operative arrangements outlined above to achieve the necessary scale. Daimler–Benz has already moved into engines, is producing a rear axle with M.A.N. and is reported to be even displacing ZF in transmissions. In Britain, the leading truck producers naturally prefer to offer their own engineering where it can compete, and increasingly the supply infrastructure can no longer provide its traditional competitive advantage to its customers. The CPRS study on the British car industry observed that the price advantage offered by the British component industry was more than offset by poor quality and delivery.[4] In truck manufacture, uncertainties in component delivery are a major management concern. In any case, to the extent that the British component sector is capable of providing its customers with a competitive advantage, why would British component suppliers restrict this benefit to its UK customers as the European market develops? The indications are that the major component suppliers are looking to the European market as a whole[5] and are likely, by extending their markets, to generalize whatever competitive advantages they can offer their customers.

These developments have been putting increasing pressure on the base of the small specialist producer. Vertical integration by the majors is tending to undermine the scale advantage traditionally enjoyed by the component supplier, *vis-à-vis* its customers, exposing the specialist in two ways. The cost of its components could increase relative to those of the majors; and their availability may also deteriorate if, as is likely, component suppliers become less disposed to tool up for specialists' requirements and schedule them as a priority, because of their search for volume business in a wider European market.

Non Tariff Barriers

The European dimension took longer to make an impression on the various national truck industries than was the case in the car industry. Intra-Community trade developed later and at a slower pace, with the result that by the late 1970s, after the Community's first 20 years, import penetration in three of its major truck markets was at the modest 10–20 per cent level, compared to 20–35 per cent in cars. The strong buyer loyalties which have already been referred to contributed to this isolation; so too did technical and tariff barriers. The French truck industry was traditionally nervous about the competitive threats posed by the low-cost British truck industry and was influential in securing the exclusion of trucks from the Kennedy round. Thus in the late 1960s and early 1970s, British truck producers faced an external Community tariff of 22 per cent.[6] Within the Community itself, however, a commonly agreed basic truck configuration had emerged by the 1960s, making trade possible. The diesel engine had displaced the petrol engine and the search for the maximum ratio of payload to gross vehicle weight had led to the displacement of bonneted by forward-control cabs. There was also a general consensus on noise limitation, braking systems, and power-to-weight ratios.

National idiosyncrasies and regulations, however, still tended to inhibit trade. Britain was typically the most liberal in its arrangements. Its 'custom and use' regulations merely specify general design characteristics, rather than precise dimensions of components, which do not have the force of law; they merely leave the manufacturer open to legal action in the event of accidents arising from their contravention. Italy, on the other hand, has a number of exacting requirements, for example, a minimum rate of acceleration in top gear over certain speed ranges. The Italian market is probably the most difficult to enter. One producer reported that the Italian authorities insist on 30–40 safety specifications which take 1–2 years to satisfy because inspectors insist on testing importers' compliance on a serial basis, requiring the importer to satisfy each specification before testing the next. The general verdict of the completion of the European market is that it is a long way off; non-tariff barriers remain in several markets and it will be of interest to see below whether and to what extent these barriers have withstood the economic forces within the European truck industry which have been exerting themselves against them.

COMPETITIVE PERFORMANCE IN THE EUROPEAN MARKETS

These general observations on the industry's character and structure set the scene for an analysis of the principal issue addressed in this chapter, namely: to what extent is it possible to explain why particular industries and companies

TABLE 5.5.   *Market Structures 1977*[a]
            (percentage shares)

	Germany		France		Britain[b]		Italy	
Domestic producers	Daimler–Benz	67	Renault	47	Ford	26	Fiat	87
	M.A.N.	12	Unic	7[c]	Leyland	19		
	Magirus	11			Bedford	17		
					Chrysler	8		
Foreign producers	Fiat	4	Daimler–Benz	16	Seddon	5	Renault	3.5
	Ford	2	Fiat	11	ERF	4	Daimler–Benz	2.5
	Scania	1	Volvo	5	Foden	1	Scania	1.5
	Daf	1	Daf	2	Volvo	6	Ford	1
			Ford	2	Daimler–Benz	3		
			Magirus	1.5	Daf	2		
			Scania	1.5	Fiat	2		
			M.A.N.	1	Scania	2		
			Bedford	1	Magirus	1		
Import Penetration	11		46		18		9	

[a]   Trucks of over 3.5 tonnes gross vehicle weight in France, Britain, and Italy; over 4 tonnes in Germany.
[b]   1978 figures.
[c]   Estimated on the basis that Unic exported 9150 trucks in 1976, selling 4850 in the domestic market.
Sources: industry estimates.

were relatively successful in European markets?

Table 5.5 outlines the competitive position in Europe in 1977-8. It shows that the German truck industry was the most successful in terms of defending its domestic market (11 per cent import penetration), followed by Italy (13 per cent), and Britain 18 per cent. The French truck industry was the casualty in this scene; imports took 46 per cent of the French truck market in 1977. It is significant that the two markets least penetrated by imports, Germany and Italy, were each dominated by one company, Daimler–Benz and Fiat respectively, and that it is these two companies which were mainly responsible for imports into the French market (16 per cent and 10 per cent respectively). The other major success was Volvo, with shares of 5-6 per cent in Britain and France, which reflects shares of over one-third in the heavy trucks segment in which Volvo concentrates. The British producers as a whole failed to translate their traditional strength into worthwhile bridgeheads in continental markets. The only British producer with a significant European showing was Ford, with

1-2 per cent shares in the other three markets. In order to explore this landscape, a framework for analysing competitiveness in this industry is now developed.

In view of the relative complexity of the truck and its market, competition in the European truck industry cannot be analysed as if the truck were a commodity product as it was possible to do with reasonable success in respect of competition in the car industry. The truck has to meet diverse and functionally specific demands, and consequently it is less homogeneous than the car and takes longer to build, with lead times from ordering to delivery of three to six months, compared to the car's lead time of one to six weeks. Three major dimensions of competitiveness were identified earlier:

1 *Product suitability*: offering reliable quality products with a sufficiently wide range of options.

2 *Price*: achieving unit manufacturing costs which are low enough to offer attractive prices on a profitable basis.

3 *Delivery*: offering acceptable customer lead times and reliable delivery dates.

Product Quality

The truck's essential function is to harness power to payload. The simplest, robust assessments of the product focus on its reliability, since the cost and inconvenience of down-time are so important. Subsidiary to this dominant requirement are aspects of the product's engineering, reflected in its capacity to meet several objectives:

Capacity to achieve good overall journey times through flexibility ('high torque rise'), achieved with the minimal amount of gear-changing, driver fatigue, and transmission losses.

Fuel economy achieved through engine design and through matching engine performance with gearbox and axle differential ratios in a way which accommodates variations in the load and the journey characteristics.

Driver comfort, which is a function of cab design, the responsiveness of the controls, and 'drivability' (high torque rise).[7]

Comparisons in this field are apt to be invidious but an observation which would command general assent in the truck market in the late 1970s, to which this study refers, is that the quality of German and Swedish trucks was outstanding. The Swedish product is directed at the heavy category whereas Daimler–Benz operates across the entire range and is therefore more relevant to this study. In the light/medium range, Mercedes trucks were rated highest for quality in Britain, by a wide margin. This is apparent in the details of the product. Because of its scale, Daimler–Benz could afford to tool up more costly and more effective engineering solutions to problems at no unit cost penalty, using pressings where smaller manufacturers might use fabrications, and forgings where the latter might use castings. It is also reflected in superior fuel economy, as one would expect, in view of the observations made above on the objectives underlying engine and transmission design. Superior fuel economy contributed (and no doubt also reflected) the long distance role in which Mercedes trucks are used by British buyers. The German quality advantage was the major reason why imported trucks from Britain and Italy found it almost impossible to secure a foothold in the German market.[8] Entry was no easier through direct investment. Two major American producers − Ford in the period 1956–60, and International Harvester in the period 1965–6 − attempted this without success.

MANUFACTURING POLICIES FOR PRODUCT OPTIONS AND DELIVERY PERFORMANCE[9]

The approach adopted to product options is a major manufacturing policy decision in this and any capital goods industry. It is essential, of course, to cater for individual customer requirements in order to obtain business; the aspect that is of interest concerns the engineering policies which support this objective. Two contrasting policies were evident in the truck industry, which led to very different performance characteristics, due to complicated interactions between the market and the manufacturing system. The traditional approach was to engineer a significant proportion of customer orders, within an overall design framework. This implies a tailoring of the product to individual customer specifications ('customizing'), drawing upon engineering staff to design specific features and to arrange for their compatability with all the other features of the truck. This approach was pursued by many of the now defunct specialist producers and still, in 1977, informed the operations of some surviving specialists, and a significant proportion of the British truck output, particularly that of Leyland, which at that time, still comprised distinct ranges of the original companies which merged to form that company. The alternative policy is to offer planned variety, by restricting customer choice at the outset, designing a range of product options which can be assembled from a core of common and compatible components − an approach which has been described as 'the building box system' (Baukastensystem) in Germany or 'Meccano Set' in Britain. This policy rests upon a value engineering approach to the product, whereby the marginal value of each feature and component (and hence its contribution to a truck's saleable value) is related to its marginal cost. Using this logic and pruning down the component list and the varieties offered, high-volume producers are able to concentrate on a pre-determined package of product options. In Europe, Daimler–Benz has developed this approach further than any other; in Britain, Ford could be said to be the leading exponent, following techniques applied so successfully in its car operations.

The customizing approach clearly comes closer than the planned variety policy to providing the customer with what he wants, but at a cost. Part of this extra cost, due to the additional engineering work, is obvious, but the major

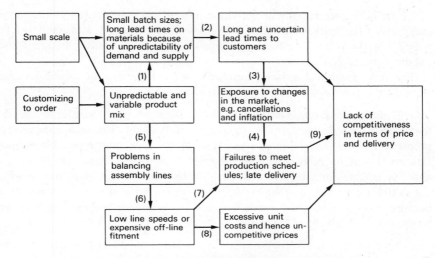

Fig. 5.1. Consequences of small scale and customizing to order

part, arising from adverse system effects of building greater variety into a manufacturing system, is less obvious. Figures 5.1 and 5.2 illustrate the system effects
of these two engineering philosophies, allied to the effects of the scale associated
with each. The central point to emerge from this analysis is that the objective
of giving a customer what he wants competes with the two other main objectives:
achieving low unit costs and hence prices, and offering prompt and reliable
delivery. Tracing the effects rippling out from the customizing approach in
Figure 5.1 suggests that this policy implies a unit cost penalty and delivery dates

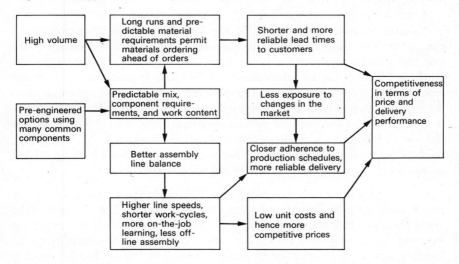

Fig. 5.2. Consequences of high volume and pre-engineered options

which are both long and unreliable. The combined effect of these penalties could easily offset the market appeal of customization. In contrast, a planned variety policy has the opposite effect; it reduces unit costs and facilitates rapid and reliable delivery dates.

The linkages in the system, numbered for convenience in Figure 5.1, are elaborated below:

1. Without standardization of parts it is difficult to predict material requirements until orders are actually received in full detail. Unless a company is prepared to hold colossal stocks to cater for the near-infinite possible permutations, it will be constrained by suppliers' lead times. These may be longer and less reliable for the customizing and/or low-volume manufacturer than for competitors prepared to order in higher quantities per part or per sub-assembly because small and irregular batch sizes are less economic and are hence apt to be shunted to the back of the queue.

2. Supplier lead times, particularly for the items on the critical path, such as frame members or springs, feed through into the total lead time.

3. A long and possibly uncertain lead time in the market exposes the manufacturer to the risks of inflation. Price increases within the lead time provide cover against these risks but at a cost; customers are free to cancel orders, leaving the manufacturer with material stocks, some of which will have little alternative use in the immediate production programme.

4. Because of the order-specific nature of the materials ordered, a cancellation leaves a hole in the production schedule which cannot easily be filled in time, causing shortfalls in the build programme.

5. Assembly lines depend for their efficiency on achieving fairly constant work loads at each work station on the line, in order to avoid bottle-neck operations. Few truck manufacturers can achieve this because of variety of the mix and reckon to operate separate lines, one for heavy, high work-content trucks and another for the lighter vehicles. Even so, the variations in work-content from one truck to another on the same line remain because most manufacturers do not want to batch up orders for similar vehicles and run them down the line in series; it would lengthen the delivery date and would require rebalancing the line for each batch — a tedious business. Inevitably, a sequence of heavy/light/medium trucks is arrived at which allows line operators to work back up the line on easier jobs to recover the time expended on the heavier ones.

6. If the mix is variable, this sequence will be broken and the balance thrown out, causing lower line speed and a loss of effective work. The problem will be compounded by lack of opportunities for learning by repetition — one important advantage of assembly-line work. To avoid the worst effects of variability on the line, recourse is made to off-line fitment — virtually a one-off facility which is expensive to operate as a consequence.

7. Variability leads to short-falls in production. It is not intuitively obvious why this should be so, if the work content is accurately predicted and allowed for in the manufacturing programme, based as it should be on matching work content with available effective hours. But the hidden cost (and delay) has the effect on the rest of the system of an extra dimension of variability, a process somewhat akin to the retarding effect of the marginal motorist on the other road users in a city road system.

8. The unit cost penalty of lack of line balance is hard to quantify; one producer spoke of an anticipated reduction in assembly time of 50 per cent on moving to a new line on which the line balance could be improved.

9. If delivery dates are calculated from schedules, slippage must entail late delivery; planning and scheduling in some companies are based on schedules which are rarely achieved. The lack of integrity in this procedure is readily grasped by suppliers, who discount schedules accordingly; the message must also get through to customers.

The very different implications of these two contrasting product philosphies is substantially confirmed by a comparison of delivery performance of nine European companies, summarized in Table 5.6. It appears that:

1. At any given scale, there is a trade-off between customization and delivery performance. Pre-engineering the product options appears to be the key to achieving quick and reliable delivery dates; the greater the degree of customization the worse the delivery performance.

2. Larger scale enables a producer to achieve superior combinations of customization and delivery performance. Low volume producers do not offer their customers as many options as their larger competitors, and even so, can only achieve the delivery performance of those larger producers which do.

These observations are at odds with the stereotype of the large producer as an inflexible juggernaut, the product of bureaucratic arthritis and the technological imperatives of mass production. The reality is that, in this industry at least, it is the small producer which is the less flexible. An illustration of this is provided in Table 5.7 which compares the range of options in the two- and three-axle rigid category offered by four British producers, and their respective capacities to generate these options from the basic ingredients available to them (wheelbases, engines, and gearboxes). The table indicates that Ford, the 'meccano set' producer, offered more models and more options than either the two 'customizers', Leyland or Bedford, and it did so with fewer basic building blocks — engines, gearboxes, and wheel bases. On the basis of the final column in Table 5.7, which admittedly leaves out much of the engineering which Leyland and Bedford built around their basic options, Ford could be said to have generated options in a more economical fashion. The low-volume producer, ERF, not only offered fewer options but it did so with scarcely any economy in the use of its

TABLE 5.6. *Product Policy and Delivery Performance*

Volume	Company	Product policy	Customer lead time	Delivery reliability
High	A	Pre-engineered options with high interchange-ability of components	2–3 months, with flexibility in 60 per cent of orders; in basics (engines, chassis, etc.) up to six weeks; in details up to 18 days before scheduled assembly date	Very high
Medium/High	B	Pre-engineered options, substantial component interchangeability	3 months	High
	C	A substantial degree of customization	3–6 months	Modest
Medium/Low	D	Pre-engineered options	3 months, very limited flexibility	High
	E	Pre-engineered options		High
	F	Very high degree of customization	5–6 months	Low
Low	G	Pre-engineered options	6–7 months	not known
	H	Modest customization	6 months	not known
	I	Modest customization	4 months	Low

building blocks, which number almost as many as the options offered.

There was a time when small specialist producers were able to compete with high-volume producers on the basis of offering greater choice. It now appears from this analysis that by engineering a high degree of component interchangeability between model options, the high-volume producer has reversed this competitive situation and is now in a position to offer a wide range of options, quick and reliable delivery, and flexibility on specifications even within these short lead times. These are profound changes which derive from a technological development which has overtaken this and other manufacturing industries in recent years, namely, the introduction of computer software, which has led to quantum jumps in production controllers' ability to co-ordinate highly complex manufacturing operations, thereby eliminating the diseconomies of scale which were once associated with the co-ordination function.

TABLE 5.7.   *Illustration of Options and Complexity: Two- and Three-Axle Rigids*[a]

	Number of models	Options offered[b]	Number of different wheelbases	Number of different engines	Number of different gearboxes	Options offered ingredients available[c]
Ford	27	161	22	8	9	4
Leyland	20	148	31	10	10	3
Bedford	13	69	23	6	11	1½
ERF	3	13	7	2	2	1

a   British market: Source: *Commercial Motor*, 1977.
b   Options are defined as distinct combinations of wheelbase, engine, and gearbox.
c   'Ingredients' refer to the combined total of different wheelbases, engines, and gearboxes used in the range.

The observations made above can be appreciated better by considering the data processing demands of the industry and the problems of handling them within a timetable which is acceptable to the market. A representative, traditional, production timetable for a complex engineering product such as a truck might typically involve a total lead time of six months. The time actually required to assemble and test a truck is only two weeks; the remaining five-and-a-half months are spent calculating material requirements and procuring them. In the first stage, a customer's specification is examined from the point of view of its internal compatability. The laborious second stage entails a breakdown of the specification into sub-assemblies and ultimately into the smallest components. Punched cards have traditionally been used for this to reduce the clerical drudgery involved, but do not eliminate it since the material requirements for each truck have to be aggregated and transferred manually into the paperwork system — stock cards for each item and procurement documents (works order cards for in-house items, purchase requisitions for bought-in items). Later, as the assembly date approaches, components have to be marshalled into kits and into a production programme, allowing appropriate assembly lead times for sub-assemblies, such as cabs, engines, electrical harnesses, and hydraulic systems.

The attempted match between the product specification embodied in the assembly programme and the material being procured to satisfy them is vulnerable to random factors. Customers change or cancel orders; suppliers fail to deliver on time. The producer is then compelled to take delivery and pay for materials with no immediate prospect of being used, and to try to build something with them; and to promote other orders into the gaps in the programme created by cancellations and delayed orders. There is inevitably a lot of groping around in the paperwork system right up to final assembly, in an attempt to discover what orders can be built from the parts likely to be available. Given the sheer number of components involved in a truck operation (50,000–200,000) this groping process is very demanding and haphazard if manual methods are used. Thus the production control area is vulnerable to disturbances, which cause gaps in production programmes and slippage in delivery dates.

Even when all goes well, which is rare, traditional methods imply customer lead times which are unacceptable to the market. The long procurement time of four months is the obvious place to reduce them; this can be done by stocking materials, particularly those with the longest delivery time, and reordering periodically on the basis of expected usage, rather than ordering on the basis of known orders. But one constraint on this policy has been the data processing capacity. In order to replenish stocks at intervals, at acceptable cost, and in quantities which provide adequate cover, it is necessary to make stock control calculations which are even more laborious than calculations of the material requirements of additional orders, since they need to be related to several other elements — existing stock levels, the economic batch quantity for the component concerned, the usage already committed up to the period when new orders are to be completed, and the expected delivery of components within that period. These calculations are compromised when revisions are made to production programmes and suppliers' schedules. The task of manually updating all the paperwork is so demanding that either the system is allowed to rumble on regardless, producing too much of some and too little of other components, or informal changes are made in the schedules (e.g. borrowing bits from one order to complete another), an expedient which causes confusion later on. In short, data-processing constraints can make it difficult to reduce customer lead times by moving from the simpler, direct ordering system to the stock-control based methods, and to achieve a match between material requirements and the materials available to cope with the unforeseen changes in the market and in the materials supply systems.

Computer-based methods have broken through in both these respects; computers can perform stock control calculations so quickly that material ordering can be performed on this basis, reducing customer lead times. They are also more accurate than manual methods since they recalculate requirements very quickly to take account of the latest changes, whereas manual methods rely on updating existing calculations on a cumulative basis, in order to reduce the labour involved. An additional advantage of the computer's speed is that a printing of the documents for production can be delayed until the last minute, allowing late changes to be accommodated. Lastly, it is much easier using the computer to interrogate the system in order to find out whether particular trucks can be built on specific dates. As one manager in a manually operated system expressed it: 'A computer cannot tell you what you can build if you ask it, but it can tell you what you cannot build. Without a computer, we cannot even find out what we cannot build.'

The Daimler–Benz assembly plant at Woerth illustrates the changes achieved through using computers in truck assembly. The computing capacity available at Woerth since 1975 enables the management to cope with enormous variety, of these dimensions: 125 basic vehicle types and 2,380 designs, incorporating 78 types of cab, 2,000 engines, 1,600 axles, and 275 transmissions, from which 10m. combinations are possible – a figure equal to a hundred times the annual capacity of the plant. The computer is used to test the engineering validity of customers' specifications in terms of design and conformity to vehicle regulations, to order materials (70,000 part numbers for the Woerth plant), to co-ordinate all supplying plants, and to marshal components into a production programme. This system offers customers a three months lead time and considerable flexibility within that period, compared to the six months lead time with less flexibility which is traditional in this type of industry. A month's production programme is fixed eight weeks in advance. Within the first two of these eight weeks, customers can change the basic specifications (type and design). At this point customers are informed of their probable delivery dates. During the next four weeks, changes in detail can be made. Demand for this facility is high, particularly in the European market; despite the short lead time of three months, revisions are made to 60 per cent of orders. A key ingredient in this flexibility is the standardization of parts which facilitates the match of materials available to specifications required. At 18 days out from assembly the computer takes control of scheduling, co-ordinating all Daimler–Benz plants and those of its outside suppliers on the same time scale, geared to common job numbers. Manual intervention is possible up to within 10 days of final assembly but this is a 'two-key' emergency arrangement. Nothing is physically assembled until seven days out, when work on major sub-assemblies is released. Final assembly takes only four to seven hours, depending on the line. The sequence is decided 8–10 hours before a truck goes down the line; sub-assemblies and components are drawn from buffer stocks, on the instructions of teleprinters at each of 30 work stations along the line.

Computer-based methods have made scale and complexity manageable, and have brought manufacture closer to the market by compressing all stages in the production timetable, reducing customer lead time to half the traditional norm, and increasing the ability to match order specifications and material availability so as to allow greater response to market changes and opportunities. These methods have brought the traditional advantages of the small firm within the reach of the large, and in so doing have opened up the way for significant changes in the configuration of the European truck industry.

ECONOMIES OF SCALE IN TRUCK MANUFACTURE

The manufacturing technology and organization of the truck industry are very similar to those of the car industry, in the sense that the same kind of sub-assemblies are delivered from feeder plants into a final assembly operation. The major differences between the two systems are qualitative; truck components are heavier than those of the car and the truck manufacturer has to accommodate a much wider range of basic specifications (wheelbase, engine, and transmission). These differences impact most visibly on to the assembly operations; the sheer weight of truck components requires larger teams at each work station (5–7 rather than 2–3), on the assembly line, implying longer work-cycle times and hence lower line speeds. The variability in work-content between one truck and another reinforces this effect and also contributes to reducing the line speed, which in effect determines the minimum efficient scale in assembly, which is much lower than in car assembly (100,000 units compared to 250,000).

According to Rhys's[10] estimates, based on the experience of a British manu-facturer, unit costs fall by 13 per cent between 3,000 units a year and 15,000 units, and by a further 14 per cent as volume rises to between 30,000 and 50,000 units a year. It is necessary to extend this analysis to higher volumes, given that in 1977 Daimler–Benz produced 100,000 trucks of over six tonnes, and a further 30,000 between four and six tonnes, and Fiat produced over 60,000 trucks. The available literature is ambiguous on this question. Extrapolation of the Rhys figures suggests a 14 per cent cost reduction between 50,000 and 100,000. But Albach[11] suggests a much lower cost reduction. He puts the minimum efficient scale at 100,000–120,000 units a year, on the basis that a full product range requires 40 model-types, each of which needs to be produced in annual quantities of 2,500–3,000. He relates the scale advantages to the spreading of model-dependent fixed costs, reckoned to be 5–6 per cent of total costs at volumes of 1,500 per model-type, or 60,000 a year with a 40-model range. According to this line of argument, doubling volumes to 120,000 a year would reduce unit costs by ony 2–3 per cent — very much less than the 14 per cent figure which an extrapolation of Rhys's estimates suggests.

As in car manufacture, the scale economies in truck manufacture are least in the labour-intensive final assembly, and greatest in the capital-intensive operations — the foundry, the forge, the press shop, and machining. A look at two of these activities, assembly and machining, suggests some of the factors at work, and their importance.

According to one management view, a truck assembly line can be operated most efficiently on a cycle-time of 5–6 minutes, implying a line speed of 10–12 trucks an hour, and an output of 750 per week on a two-shift basis, yielding 35,000 trucks a year from one line, when operated 46 weeks a year. Heavier trucks (for example, those over 14 tons GVW) would require a longer cycle, lighter trucks would require a shorter one. This variability in work content across the weight range requires two assembly lines to achieve a satisfactory line balance. An optimal assembly operation therefore produces 70,000 built-up trucks a year. In addition, a European assembly plant typically produces half as much again in CKD form, bringing the total to 90,000–100,000 trucks a year. The cycle time in assembly appears to be inversely related to volume. Daimler–Benz use a cycle of 5–6 minutes, medium-sized producers (35,000 units a year) use 8–10 minutes, and small producers (20,000 units a year) use 20 minutes. In part these differences reflect nothing more than the fact that some smaller producers produce heavier trucks; they may also reflect different approaches to organizing the line, involving more or fewer men in each work station on the line. But, abstracting from these factors, faster line speed tends to imply greater operator efficiency since it involves more repetition, and hence learning-by-doing, a less complicated work-content for each operator, and better line balance, since the smaller the work-content, the easier it is to organize roughly equal chunks of work at each work station. Thus, the greater line speed of the larger producers probably implies greater operator efficiency and less redundancy on the line.

Whereas it is possible to achieve optimal scales of operation in truck assembly in Europe (e.g. Daimler–Benz's 100,000 unit plant at Woerth), this is not remotely possible in engines, transmissions, and pressings, remembering the minimum efficient scales for these items in car manufacture. One response to this constraint has been to standardize components, or critical dimensions, across the range. It is possible, for example, to standardize the bores and distances between cylinders when machining engine blocks; this permits two or more engine blocks to proceed down the same transfer line with little or no resetting between batches. One manufacturer observed that standardizing engine parameters permitted the five engines required to cover its horsepower range to be machined on only three lines, reducing capital costs by 40 per cent and unit costs by 6 per cent, if capital and interest charges account for 15 per cent of total engine costs.

Daimler–Benz achieves a considerable degree of standardization. All engines in the 400 series in the 160–530 hp range have both a common bore and cylinder spacing and 80 per cent of these parts are interchangeable. A further 10 per cent require the same machine tools with minor resetting. The range uses only 1000 different parts, compared to the 6000 of its predecessor. There are inevitably some engineering compromises inherent in this standardization. For example, the ideal requirements for V- and in-line engines diverge, yet both have to be accommodated in the same configuration of cylinder bore and spacing. V-engines tend to have greater spacing between the cylinders than in-line engines, to accommodate two con-rods for each crankpin. In-line engines tend generally to have a shorter stroke and larger bore than V-engines. As a result, providing a common bore and cylinder spacing for both engine-types tends to imply a design which incorporates wider spacing and smaller bore than is ideal for the

TABLE 5.8. *Machining Requirements and Scale in Engine Manufacture*

Volume	Degree of standardization	Number of engines	Average volume per engine	Common parts (per cent)	Average component volume	Usage of machinery systems (percentage)		
						General purpose	Semi-automated	Fully-automated
100,000	High	4	25,000	80	85,000	0	20	80
35,000	Medium	4	9,000	50	22,000	50	50	–
20,000	Low	4	5,000	20	8,000	80	20	–

in-line engine, and the converse for the V-engine. But, despite these suboptimalities, it appears that the manufacturing economies and the ease of production scheduling, both afforded by standardization which allows the entire Daimler-Benz truck range to be constructed from only six times the number of parts required for each vehicle, dominate the volume truck's engineering.

In machining operations, the effects of scale are compounded considerably by standardization, permitting the use of automated machining systems, with dramatically reduced manning requirements. Table 5.8 illustrates these effects; if the high-volume producer uses the same number of basic engines as the smaller producer but designs in a higher proportion of commonality, its average component volume could be greater than that of the medium-volume producer by a factor of four, and greater than that of the low-volume producer by a factor of ten. These differences are reflected in the machining systems appropriate to each producer's volumes. The high-volume producer might machine 80 per cent of its requirements on fully-automated systems, whereas the low-volume producer would find it economic to machine 80 per cent of its requirements on general-purpose equipment. To translate these differences in machining loadings into unit cost comparisons, comments from the industry suggest that successive moves from general-purpose machines to semi-automated, and then to fully-automated machines would reduce unit machining costs by 25 per cent and 40 per cent respectively. On the basis of these estimates, the unit machining costs in engine manufacture of the medium- and high-volume producers would be respectively 7 per cent and 33 per cent lower than those of the low-volume producer.

Comparable economies are achieved in machining rear axles. As a result of co-operative arrangements one producer estimated that labour costs had fallen by 30 per cent after doubling axle volumes from 40,000 to 80,000 units a year, implying a reduction in unit machining costs of around 20 per cent. This achievement corresponds exactly with Bonner's[12] theoretical estimate that within the range of 30,000–120,000 units a year, unit machining costs of rear truck axles could be reduced according to the relationship:

$$\text{Unit Cost} = \text{Constant Terms} \times \text{Volume}^{-0.322}.$$

which implies unit cost reductions of roughly 20 per cent with every doubling of volume — as indeed proved to be the case.

In cab production, a low-volume manufacturer can be expected to employ a manually-operated press shop for the cab panels, with two operators loading, and a further two unloading each of seven or so presses in line — a total of 20–25 operators. Medium/high volume permits an automated line to be used, reducing the manning requirement to only three. Automating cab assembly reduces assembly manning requirements by 75 per cent. In chassis building there are also opportunities for standardization and hence economies. Daimler-Benz standardizes the chassis profile of the front and rear ends and the cross members, and drills and punches holes to a common pattern. Wheelbase variation is achieved by inserting extension pieces in the middle section.[13] IVECO is also standardizing its chassis throughout the range, producing them all at Turin. There are inevitably some engineering compromises in this process too. Some trucks will be over-engineered for their loads; some chassis members will be unnecessarily strong for some trucks, or will have unnecessary holes drilled in them.

TABLE 5.9.   *Economies of Scale in Truck Manufacture*
(Unit cost of a 20,000 unit producer = 100)

	Units per year		
	20,000	35,000	100,000
Foundry, forge, press, and machining	25	19	15
Assembly operations	25	22	20
Components and materials	50	50	49
Unit Manufacturing Cost	100	91	84

Drawing these observations together, the cost structure of truck manufacture probably responds to scale as shown in Table 5.9, with a 16 per cent cost advantage to the 100,000 unit producer over the 20,000 unit producer. If these estimates of the economies of scale in truck manufacture are broadly correct we would expect to find them reflected in the pattern of individual company performance in the industry; those producers with scale disadvantages could expect to struggle on the margin of survival or be absorbed into larger groupings and those with scale advantages could expect, on the basis of the estimated scale economies, to earn comfortable and predictable margins. A comparison of company performance is set out in Table 5.10. It confirms these expectations; of the eight producers manufacturing on a scale of 20,000 a year or less, four made net losses in 1977. On the other hand, the three high volume producers, Daimler–Benz, Fiat, and Ford looked relatively profitable; two of them earned net margins of over 10 per cent, and all three earned gross margins of over 14 per cent.[14] Scale clearly pays. Moreover it pays to a degree which is broadly consistent with the estimated unit cost degression of 16 per cent as volume rises from 20,000 to over 100,000 units a year. The three producers in the 17,000–20,000 range that produced a product range similar to that of Daimler–Benz — Saviem, Unic, and Chrysler — all made losses whereas Daimler–Benz earned over 10 per cent (the other small producers were heavy truck specialists).

Viewing Table 5.10 as a whole, there is an obvious scale-related gradient in profitability with one noticeable national pattern superimposed on it; the French producers suffer in comparison with other producers in the same volume bracket and this is discussed below. The other interesting feature of the table is the inverse relationship between scale and stocks. This relates directly to the discussion of manufacturing philosophies and the scale-related drive towards

TABLE 5.10. *Scale and Profitability 1977*

Company	Volume[a]	Net profit[b] margin (percentage)	Gross profit[c] margin (percentage)	Stock levels in terms of weeks' sales
Daimler–Benz[d]	130,000	10.6	14.5	6
Fiat	51,000	5.4	14.9	13
Ford UK[d]	42,000	10.9	14.3	n/a
Leyland	25,000	6.5	7.9	17
Scania[d]	20,000	2.8	7.4	18
Berliet	20,000	−1.8	4.5	23
Saviem	20,000	−4.5	2.6	21
M.A.N.	19,000	4.3	8.0	22
Unic	17,000	−1.5	3.9	22
Magirus	17,000	2.1	5.3	20
Daf	14,000	4.0	9.7	21
Chrysler UK	9,000	negative	n/a	n/a

[a]   Chambre Syndicale des Constructeurs d'Automobiles.
[b]   Pre-tax profits, net of interest payments, as a percentage of sales.
[c]   Gross operating profits (inclusive of depreciation), as a percentage of sales.
     Financial data taken from 'The Automobile Industry: Financial Performance
     Indicators No. 11', *Euroeconomics*, Feb. 1979.
[d]   Financial data refer to car and truck activities.

standardization and compressed delivery lead times, both of which tend to
reduce requirements of parts, work-in-progress, and finished stocks. Thus Daimler–
Benz's stocks are equivalent to only six weeks' sales, a level which is on a par
with German car manufacturers.[15] Of course, this figure partly reflects the fact
that Daimler–Benz is also a car manufacturer, but the significant point is that
although trucks account for half the company's sales, the figure is no higher than
that of the average car producer. The Fiat figure, which refers only to trucks,
is also impressive compared to the typical figure of 20–23 weeks for the low-
volume producer.

INTERNATIONAL COST DIFFERENCES

The role played by scale in determining differences in companies' profitability
suggests also that this factor had an important bearing on international cost
differences, which in turn shaped the intra-Community pattern of trade in
trucks. An attempt to compare unit costs in Germany, Britain, and France is
set out in Table 5.11, taking account of relative wage costs and unit labour
requirements, and standardizing for the product mix and vertical integration
of the three operations used as the basis for comparisons. All three plants
were assembly operations and while assembly accounts for only 10 per cent of
total ex-works costs, they represented the overall positions reasonably closely.[16]
On this basis, the British unit costs in 1976 were 3 per cent lower than the
German level, and the French unit costs were 30 per cent higher.

Table 5.12 considers how the relative cost position might have looked had
the producers in all three countries faced common hourly labour costs and

TABLE 5.11. *Unit Costs in Final Assembly: Germany, Britain, and France, 1976*
(Germany = 100)

	Germany	Britain	France
Hourly paid labour requirement per unit of output[a]	100	160	320
Hourly labour costs[b]	100	55	67
Unit labour cost	100	88	215
Unit assembly costs[c]	100	97	130

[a] 'Output' for the purposes of this comparison is the assembly content at each of the three plants used in the exercise. The assembly content depends on three factors: the proportions of fully assembled and CKD (completely knocked down) kits; the composition of the product mix by weight-category; and the degree to which sub-assemblies (notably cabs) are assembled in the plants under comparison. To standardize for these three dimensions the following rules of thumb were adopted:

Value added content: differences between the plants centred on cab assembly. The French plant pressed its own panels and assembled cabs, the German plant merely assembled cabs, the British plant was supplied with assembled cabs from another plant. The German plant was used as the base; employment at the French plant was adjusted downwards to allow for the press shop labour force necessary for cab panels, reckoned to be one-third of the total cab assembly labour force, in turn reckoned to amount to 20 per cent of the total final assembly labour force. The British labour force was adjusted upwards by this amount, to allow for assembly outside the plant.

CKD: it was assumed that CKD requires one-third as much final assembly labour as fully built-up trucks. The British plant performed its CKD at a separate plant, the German and French plants in-house.

Product mix: The weight composition of all the plants is known. It was found that truck prices and gross vehicle weights are nearly proportional in Germany and Britain, and it was therefore assumed that assembly content is also proportional to gross vehicle weights.

[b] Hourly labour costs include employers' contributions and are taken from the CPRS Study on the Motor Industry (p. 78), referring to 1 Sept. 1975.

[c] Based on the assumption that capital investment per unit of output is roughly comparable in the three operations and that the labour content in German ex-works costs is 28 per cent (from the appropriate company report, 1977).

assesses the contribution of the scale factor to these hypothetical differences. The scale factor accounted for half of the British producer's cost disadvantage (calculated on the assumption of common factor prices), and one-third of the French producer's disadvantage. These figures are consistent with what else was known of the companies' operations. In saying that scale difference accounted for 30 percentage points of the 60 per cent additional unit labour requirements required by the British producer, compared to the German producer, one is attributing the other 30 per cent to managerial/workforce factors. This proved to be the case; the British producer's direct labour requirements were around 30 per cent above the theoretical work standard set by the job estimators in the plant; this compares to near-zero at the German plant. This exactly accounts for the difference in unit labour requirement which is not accounted for by the scale factor. Managerial difficulties accounted for rather more (two-thirds) of the French cost disadvantage because the producer concerned had compounded its scale disadvantage by allowing its product range to elaborate itself excessively, generating precisely those difficulties outlined earlier — short production runs, excessive work in progress, lack of commonality in components — all contributing to very low labour productivity.

TABLE 5.12. *The Scale Factor and International Cost Differences, 1976* (Germany = 100)

	Germany	Britain	France
Unit labour requirement per unit of output[a]	100	160	320
Relative unit costs if all three producers had paid same hourly wage rates[b]	100	117	162
Unit costs corresponding to respective scales of operation of the three producers	100	108	120
Percentage contribution to cost difference of scale disadvantage *vis-à-vis* German producer		50	32

[a] See Table 5.11.
[b] Using German share of labour costs (28 per cent) as basis for the calculation.

What are the implications of these cost configurations? Did they feed through into the market-place and explain the pattern of trade indicated by the market shares shown in Table 5.5? The cost comparisons presented above suggest that France was the high-price market and that it attracted imports for this reason. Even while denying itself profits, or even taking a loss, the French truck industry was compelled to set prices which reflected its own costs in order to survive; and since these costs were higher than its neighbours', the levels of truck prices in the French market were attractive to the latter.

Comparisons of the prices set by the respective industry leaders in the British, French, and German truck markets in the late 1970s bear out this supposition. Table 5.13 compares prices for medium trucks in the French market in 1979. It appeared that Daimler–Benz's policy was to match the prices of the French market leader, Berliet; while Ford's policy was to undercut Berliet's price by 10 per cent or so, as it could afford to do. Daimler–Benz's prices represented attractive value for money, since Daimler–Benz offered both the quality advantages noted earlier and the assurance of an excellent distributor network over the European road network — an important consideration in the heavier, long-haul categories — at the same price as Berliet; Ford offered comparable quality at a lower price. The successful entry of both companies into the French market (see Table 5.5) is explicable in terms of demand-side considerations.

On the supply side the questions to be answered are: first, are the price

TABLE 5.13. *Price Comparisons: French Market February 1979*

Weight Category	Model	Weight (tonnes)	Horsepower	Price (francs)	Price per Horsepower (francs)
12–13 tonnes	Berliet 881 KB	13.0	120	113,700	950
	950 KB	13.6	120	119,600	1000
	130 B 13	13.0	133	118,700	890
	150 B 13	13.0	149	125,000	840
	Mercedes 1213 R	13.3	130	118,100	910
	1217 R	13.3	168	129,500	770
	Ford D1211	12.5	115	93,300	810
	D1311	13.5	115	97,900	850
	D1314 R	13.5	144	116,700	810
16–17 tonnes	Berliet GC191	16.5	185	164.400	890
	Mercedes 1617 R	17.5	168	161,000	960
	Ford D1614	16.25	138	117,900	850
	D1618	16.25	171	129,800	760
19 tonnes	Berliet GR280	19.0	266	218,900	820
	Mercedes 1919	19.0	192	195,000	1020
	1926	19.0	256	232,400	910
	Ford H3824	19.0	243	208,600	860

Average prices per horsepower: Berliet 900 f.
                                         Mercedes 910 f.
                                         Ford   820 f.
Source: *Le Poids Lourd*, Apr. 1979.

configurations in Tables 5.13 and 5.15 consistent with what is known about relative costs and profit margins? and second, did they provide the incentives to the producers to make the moves into the European truck markets shown in Table 5.5? Table 5.14 compares the prices of representative Ford trucks

TABLE 5.14. *International Price Comparison: Same Product; Different Markets: Ford Models in Britain and France*

Model[a]	UK price[b] £	UK price in francs	French price[c] (francs)	French price / UK price
D 1111	7840	67,000	90,700	1.35
D 1114	8636	74,000	97,000	1.31
D 1211	7886	67,400	93,300	1.38
D 1311	8474	72,400	97,900	1.35
D 1414	9880	84,400	110,400	1.30
D 1614	11394	97,400	117,900	1.21
			Average price ratio	1.32

[a] Basic models, shortest wheelbase version available, truck models throughout.
[b] Prices effective from 4 Oct. 1978, including delivery, exclusive of VAT.
[c] Valid at 1 Feb. 1979, quoted in *Le Poids Lourd*, Apr. 1979. Exchange rate at Oct. 1978: 8.54 f. to £.

in the British and French markets. It suggests that Ford obtained 32 per cent more in the French market than in the British market, for an equivalent truck in 1978/79. This exactly corresponds to the unit cost differential between France and Britain estimated in Table 5.11 and suggests that price levels in the two countries reflected the relative costs of the local market leader.

TABLE 5.15. *Price Comparisons of French and German Trucks 1976* (recommended prices in respective domestic markets, exclusive of VAT)

	Model	Price[b] (DM)	Price German model / Price French model
Medium	Berliet GLR 200 Daimler–Benz L1519	77,600 60,150	0.80
Heavy	Berliet TR280 Daimler–Benz 1626S	96,500 87,450	0.90

[a] Comparability even in terms of basic specifications (hp, GVW, and wheelbase) is not easy to achieve. The Daimler–Benz L1519, like the Berliet GLR is a bonneted, platform truck. Its dimensions are smaller (GVW 14.8 tonnes, compared to the GLR 200's 16.0 tonnes), wheelbase shorter (4.2m v 5.04m), but more powerful (192 hp compared to 155 hp). The Berliet TR280 and Daimler–Benz 1625 are both forward control tractor units of 280 hp and 256 hp respectively.

[b] 1976 exchange rate of 1.89 f./DM, average over the year. French prices were obtained from an industry source. German prices from Hans W. Schwacke, *Marktbericht für LKW*, 1/76E Internationale Marktbeobachtung GmbH, Frankfurt am Main.

Table 5.15 compares French and German truck prices in 1976. The comparisons relate to the respective domestic prices recommended for equivalent trucks by Berliet and Daimler–Benz. German prices were 10–20 per cent lower than the French; the German cost advantage was greater in the medium range than in the heavy, reflecting the pronounced volume advantage of Daimler–Benz in the medium range. The average price differential of around 15 per cent between France and Germany is consistent with the preceding analysis of the comparative economics and profitability of French and German truck production. It is possible to work backwards from the price levels, noting that the distributor's margin for heavier trucks was 25 per cent and that the profit margins of Daimler–Benz and Berliet were respectively 10 per cent and zero, to derive estimates of the relative cost of manufacture, as is shown in Table 5.16.

This calculation is consistent with the analysis of manufacturing costs outlined in Table 5.11, which concluded that French unit costs were 30 per cent higher than the German level. These economics explain why Berliet had ceased to contend for sales in Germany by 1979 and why Daimler–Benz was in a position both to attack the French market on a profitable basis and to resist raids on its own market by importers. Within the German market itself, Daimler–Benz was able to use its superior cost position to apply discretionary pressure on

distributors which showed signs of wavering, thereby securing the exceptionally high levels of customer loyalty reported earlier.[17]

TABLE 5.16. *France–Germany: Relative Cost of Manufacture*

	France	Germany
Domestic retail price levels	100	85
less 25 per cent distribution margin, is equal to: Domestic wholesale price levels	75	64
less profit margins (0 per cent, 10 per cent), is equal to: Unit manufacturing cost	75	57
Unit manufacturing cost (Germany = 100)	132	100

By and large, then, the pattern of trade in 1977 makes sense when inter-
preted in these terms. The only anomalous feature was Renault's penetration
of the Italian market (3.5 per cent market share in 1977). In view of its dis-
advantageous cost position, how could Renault afford to secure a share larger
than that of Daimler–Benz (2.5 per cent)? The reasons were, first, that the
Italian market was unusually protected by technical barriers; relative cost
positions were not therefore a major factor in explaining market entry. Second,
it happened that Saviem established early connections in Italy through an
agreement to supply Alfa-Romeo with engines and components. And third,
Saviem also suffered less of a cost disadvantage than Berliet, having achieved a
respectable scale of 20,000, 4–6 tonne trucks a year at its Blainville factory.

CONCLUSIONS

It was remarked at the outset of the chapter that the truck industry illustrated
features of the producer equipment industries which would add distinct dimensions to a study of competitive modes in Europe. This expectation has been
borne out in the analysis. The truck industry traditionally offered its customers
bespoke engineering of a personal kind, particularly at the heavy end of the
weight range. The customer loyalty inherent in this arrangement, combined
with high tariffs and idiosyncratic national regulations bearing on the truck's
weight and engineering, locked truck producers into their national markets in
the 1950s and 1960s; exports tended to be achieved in Third World markets
rather than in Europe. The European dimension encouraged the industry to
break out from this configuration, towards higher volumes and a manufacturing
philosophy more akin to that of the car manufacturer which offers pre-engineered
options, rapid delivery, and greater economy. The companies which were the
first to embrace this philosophy (Daimler–Benz, Ford, and Fiat) prospered at
the expense of those which had persisted with the traditional approach (Leyland,
Saviem, and Berliet).

The pattern of developments in the industry is also consistent with the theoretical picture of intra-Community trade outlined in Chapter 2, which suggested that scale factors underlie this trade and at the same time are enhanced by it; that companies with scale advantages would tend to dominate those without them, and that in the process, the larger companies in the exporting industry would increase their volumes proportionately more than their smaller competitors. In this process, it was suggested, the smaller, high-cost producers in the exporting industry tend to be eliminated, along with the high-cost producers in the importing country. Scale is the basis of the competitive positions of Daimler–Benz, Fiat, and Ford; in terms of options, delivery performance, and price. Exporting also tended to enhance the scale of the larger company relative to the smaller. Thus, for example, in 1977 German exports to the vulnerable French market allowed Daimler–Benz to increase its volume by 7.5 per cent, Magirus–Deutz by 5 per cent, and M.A.N. by 3 per cent. These exports must have displaced capacity in France, whose unit costs were some 30 per cent higher than those in Germany, and doubtless contributed to the pressures on Berliet and Saviem to rationalize their ranges and production arrangements. Moreover, it seems likely, but by no means conclusively demonstrable, that Daimler–Benz's drive to achieve its competitive volumes encouraged the company to absorb or eliminate the high-cost German producers Hanomag–Henschel, Krupp, and Büssing. In short, European competition has had a substantial bearing on the shape of the truck industry, on the level and form of competition which it adopted, and on its efficiency in the use of resources.

NOTES

1 Neil Dorward, 'Market Structure and Buyer Loyalty: A Case Study of the West German Truck Market', *Journal of Industrial Economics*, XXVI, No. 2, Dec. 1977, pp. 115–35. Dorward examined market shares of the five leading German truck producers in 35 registration districts in Germany and estimated the degree of buyer loyalty using first-order Markov processes. Market share and buyer loyalty were found to be positively correlated:

Company	Market Share (1971) (per cent)	Buyer Loyalty (per cent)
Daimler–Benz	58	100
M.A.N.	17	89
KHD	14	83
Henschel	5	80
Büssing	3.5	72

2 This philosophy was expounded by D. G. Rhys, 'Heavy Commercial Vehicles: The Survival of the Small Firm', *Journal of Industrial Economies*, 3, July 1972, pp. 230–52.
3 Evidence of Mr W. L. Foden to the Trade and Industry Sub-committee, 19 Feb. 1975.
4 CPRS, *The Future of the British Car Industry*, p. 93.
5 As illustrated by Guest, Keen, and Nettlefold's blocked bid for the German component producer, Sachs.
6 The Community's common external tariff is still 20 per cent, compared to the 11 per

cent tariff on cars, helping to explain why Third Country imports accounted for less than 1 per cent of the European truck market in 1977.

7 An engine delivers its maximum torque at a speed below its maximum. This is a useful feature since when the vehicle encounters an obstacle or incline, its torque increases as the speed drops, thus enabling it to recover speed rapidly without gear changing. The rate of increase ('torque rise') in torque is a measure of this desirable feature.

8 One producer estimated that trucks destined for the German market each required 20 hours of additional labour to render them acceptable simply in terms of their final preparation.

9 I have drawn on two excellent works on production management in discussing this topic: D. K. Corke, *Production Control in Engineering* (London, 1977) and T. A. J. Nicholson, *Managing Operations: A Casebook* (London, 1978).

10 D. G. Rhys, *Heavy Commercial Vehicles*, p. 238.

11 Horst Albach, 'Notwendigkeit der Konzentration in der Nutzfahrzeugindustrie in nationaler und internationaler Sicht', Frankfurter Gespräch der List Gesellschaft, 10–12 May 1969.

12 A. Bonner, 'Zukunft und Entwicklung der Betriebe im Zwang der Kostengesetze', *Werkstattstechnik*, 56, 1966, Heft 2, pp. 80–9.

13 Peter Walters, 'International Operations in the European Commercial Vehicle Industry', Working paper 77/1 Oslo Institute of Business Administration, 1977.

14 The net margin measure corresponds more closely to the unit cost comparison since it takes in depreciation costs; the gross margin measure does not, but it is less susceptible to differences in international accounting conventions.

15 The corresponding figures for Volkswagen, Opel, and BMW were 6.8, 5.3, and 4.7 in 1977.

16 Relative labour productivities in the companies as a whole reflected those estimated in more detail in assembly operations.

17 These discretionary policies were reputed to include: offering long-term haulage contracts to a buyer who had switched to a competitor, on condition that he revert to buying Mercedes trucks; and offering to sell Mercedes trucks to owners of imported trucks, sweetening the deal by offering to buy their used imported trucks at list prices (*Truck*, May 1979).

CHAPTER 6

THE EUROPEAN WHITE GOODS INDUSTRY

The white goods industry offers an opportunity to assess the impact of the Europeanization of an industry in the household itself. White goods comprise the larger, self-standing domestic electrical appliances — refrigerators, washing-machines, driers, and dishwashers. Generally speaking, households purchase these capital items in the order just mentioned; as Table 6.1 indicates, by 1972 the refrigerator was a feature of most European homes, the washing-machine was installed by the majority, dishwashers only by a small minority.

TABLE 6.1. *Household ownership of white goods 1972*
(percentage)

	Refrigerators	Washing-machines	Dishwashers
Germany	98	73	5
France	86	58	4
Italy	85	63	10
Britain	70	64	2

Source: Guilio Sandri, 'Elektrotechnische Gebrauchsindustrie in der EG: Elektrische Haushaltsgeräte', *Eurocooperation*, June/Sept. 1974.

This study looks first at the by now ancient story of the European refrigerator industry, which underwent its major changes in the late 1950s and 1960s, and then moves on to the washing-machine segment of the industry, whose structural change and competitive patterns are more recent.

REFRIGERATORS

In terms of demonstrable consumer benefits stemming directly from international trade, the refrigerator story is perhaps one of the more encouraging in the Community's history. The refrigerator is an unusually tradable product. Its basic configuration is well established. Most look pretty much alike and hence attract little buyer loyalty. They require hardly any servicing; quality and after-sales are therefore relatively unimportant. For these reasons, the refrigerator sells mainly on price. Intra-Community trade developed rapidly and precipitated structural changes in all the national industries, which permitted substantial price reductions to be made. Prior to the expansion of this trade, each of the four countries supported a number of small refrigerator manufacturers, who operated for the most part on a high-cost, batch basis, with annual volumes of less than 100,000 units — a level far too low to permit the use of automated equipment such as coil-fed, automated press-lines, automatic spot-welding equipment, vertically integrated plastic moulding technology, polyurethane foam equipment, or conveyorization. The product itself was bulky and expensive to make. Substantial wholesale and retail margins, maintained in Britain by Resale Price Maintenance up to 1964, compounded the effect of these high costs on retail prices.

In the late 1950s, the Italian industry broke loose from this configuration by installing large-scale, automated plants to produce narrow ranges of standardized, small volume refrigerators. They reduced their prices in line with the dramatic reductions in unit costs achieved by this quantum jump in scale and drove aggressively into their neighbours' markets, using the new, low-margin mail order chains to bypass the traditional high-margin retailers. By the early 1960s[1] the Italians had captured over 40 per cent of the German and British markets and two-thirds of the French market. Their output rose from 500,000 in 1958 to 2.8m. in 1966, and to 5.4m. in 1972.

TABLE 6.2.   *Production and Trade in Refrigerators, 1972*

	Italy	Germany	Britain	France
Production	5,400,000	1,700,000	1,100,000	500,000
Exports	3,900,000	470,000	190,000	50,000
Imports	200,000	870,000	580,000	890,000
Imports/Consumption (percentage)	2	40	42	65

Source: Guilio Sandri, 'Elektrotechnische Gebrauchsindustrie'.

Why was it the Italians who achieved this breakthrough and how did they do it? Their aggressive style may have been due to their lack of pedigree in the consumer durable business. In contrast to the other major European white goods producers, which evolved largely from established electrical concerns, the Italian industry started from scratch. In the early 1950s, the only important white goods manufacturer in Italy was FIAT, operating under licence from Westinghouse. From 1954 onwards, unknown family firms mushroomed and clawed their way very competitively, growing by reinvestment rather than through mergers, for the most part retaining their close-knit family style of management. Between 1954 and 1960, the number of producers in Italy increased by 45; by 1964 most had succumbed to the competition, and the industry had concentrated considerably.[2] The leading refrigerator producer, Ignis, was producing at the rate of 1m. units a year in 1966 at Varese, accounting for one-third of the total Italian refrigerator production; Zanussi was producing at 700,000 units a year at Pordenone, accounting for a further 25 per cent.

In technical terms their success stemmed from an early recognition that changes in refrigerator technology, allied to large European markets, opened the way to large-scale automated methods. Refrigerator manufacture is basically a cabinet-making operation since the heart of the product, the compressor unit,

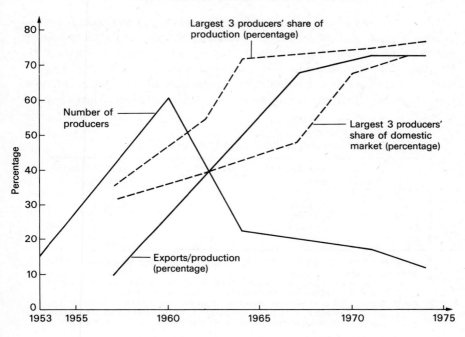

Fig. 6.1. Italian refrigerator industry: exports and structural change

is purchased from independent specialists. The 1950-vintage refrigerator was much bulkier and heavier compared with its slimmer equivalent of today and much more labour-intensive to manufacture. These features were necessitated by the large quantity of fibreglass which had to be incorporated between the inner and outer panels and by the weight of the compressor unit then available. These two features — the volume of the fibreglass and the weight of the compressor — in turn called for a substantial iron frame, since the fibreglass insulation offered no rigidity to support the inner panels. The emergence of cheap, efficient, and light hermetically-sealed compressor units from companies such as Danfos, Aspera, and Sterne both opened the way for and encouraged a corresponding economy in cabinet design and manufacture. These duly came in the form of a technology which replaced fibreglass insulation with rigid vacuum polystyrene liners and interstitial polyurethane foam. This technology permitted thinner cabinet walls and doors with fewer welded stress members. They also opened the way for flow-line production with its economies in work-in-progress and labour requirements. Scale was necessary to exploit these new technologies: 100,000 units a year was reckoned to be the break-even point for the polystyrene moulding equipment; 200,000 units a year for the polyurethane foam equipment. At 500,000 units a year it became economic to make the compressor and at 1m. units to make all components in house; few producers outside Italy achieved these volumes.[3]

Ignis, in particular, under Giovanni Borghi's inspiration, was a major innovator in designing for efficient production, pioneering foaming insulation techniques and their use to provide rigidity in the box without fasteners and press-work. Its annual volume in the mid-1960s of over one million units permitted a greater level of integration than was possible elsewhere in Italy and Europe; compressors, magnetic door gaskets, injection moulding, and thermostats were all manufactured in-house.

TABLE 6.3.   *Comparative Plant Size: Refrigerators, 1967*

	Average of Top 50 per cent[a] (units)	Midpoint plant[b] (units)
Italy	850,000	620,000
Germany	570,000	370,000
France	290,000	200,000
Britain	170,000	120,000

[a] Average of the smallest number of plants accounting for 50 per cent of the industry's output.
[b] The size of the smallest plant to be found in Top 50 per cent, i.e. 50 per cent of the industry's output was manufactured in larger plants than this.
Sources: Italy: Valeriano Balloni, *Industria degli Elettrodomestici*, Table IV 2.2, p. 69. Germany, France, and Britain: F. M. Scherer et al., The Economics of Multi-plant Operation, Appendix tables 3.3, 3.5, and 3.6.

The comparative plant size in the mid-1960s is shown in Table 6.3. Even though the Italian industry was highly fragmented in 1960, by 1967 it had the largest average plant size in Europe, half as great again as that of the German industry, triple that of the French industry and five times that of the British industry. The Italians' scale advantage over the British and French competition implied a distinct but not an overwhelming competitive advantage. According to the calculations in the Scherer study,[4] the minimum efficient scale in refrigerator production for a 1965-vintage plant was 800,000 units a year[5] — the typical Italian level in 1967 — and the cost penalty implied by a scale of production of only one-third of this level (e.g. at the typical French scale of production) was estimated to be only 6.5 per cent. Italian costs were reckoned by a leading French producer to be 15 per cent lower than French costs in 1968.[6] Plant scale differences accounted for 40 per cent of this difference; the remainder was probably due to differences in plant organization and greater variety in each location in the French industry. The British cost disadvantage *vis-à-vis* the Italians in 1968 was 15 per cent. On the basis of Scherer's cost–volume relationship, the British cost disadvantage associated with plants of a scale one-fifth of the Italians' would have been at least 10 per cent; the smaller lot sizes due to the more fragmented product-mix in British plants would have accounted for most of the remaining 5 per cent. The Italian lead in design and weight-reduction must have contributed as well, in view of the fact that during the 1960s, the weight of a typical refrigerator fell by one-third.

The Impact of Trade on Importing Countries

The Italians' initial entry points into their neighbouring markets were the mail order chains, selling mainly on price. Some of the local competition which had been displaced by these invasions rolled with the punch as it were, and began importing cheap Italian refrigerators to complement their own range, using their own labels ('vendor branding'). In Britain, Hoover began importing Zanussi products in 1965; even Hotpoint, the successor to British Domestic Appliances, which had rationalized in response to Italian competition in the 1960s, eventually did the same in 1976. On the Continent, defensive responses extended even further; AEG acquired a 20 per cent stake in Zanussi in 1972 while Philips had acquired Ignis in 1970.

It is not surprising that the Italians made the greatest in-roads into France, their large, high-cost Community neighbour. They concentrated on smaller refrigerators for low-income families. The French refrigerator was typically a larger, luxury item, accommodating the French habit of storing everything in the refrigerator. The Italians drove the French up the size range; whereas in 1964 French production was split roughly 50:50 between box sizes less than and greater than 160 litres, by 1968 these proportions had shifted to 20:80.

TABLE 6.4. *Structural Changes in the French Refrigerator Industry 1965–1970*[a]

1965		1970	
Company	Volume (000 units)	Company	Volume (000 units)
Thomson–Houston	150 ⎤ merged 1966		
Hotchkiss–Brandt	135 ⎦		
Whirlpool Royal	110 acquired by Claret[b] 1966	merged 1968 Thomson–Brandt	540
Frigeavia	75		
Frigidaire (General Motors)	50	withdrew 1967	
Arthur Martin	40	Arthur Martin withdrew 1972	70

[a] The table refers to domestic refrigerators; other producers specialize in specialized types, e.g. absorption refrigerators, office refrigerators.
[b] Claret entered the refrigerator market through this merger, being already the supplier of three-quarters of the industry's compressors. When it was acquired by Thomson–Brandt, the Claret plant at Romilly was closed down.
Sources: Francine Bougeon-Maasson.

Prices in the French market dropped by 25–40 per cent in this period. Under the pressure of this competition the structure of the French industry was transformed in only five years, as Table 6.4 indicates. A spate of mergers occurred between 1965 and 1970 from which Thomson–Brandt emerged as the sole French producer of domestic refrigerators, with one optimally-sized plant producing 750,000 units a year at Lesquin. These defensive moves by the French industry managed to retain 45 per cent of the French market for the surviving French producer.

The British industry suffered less damage and underwent less structural change than the French, shielded to some extent by an external tariff of 15 per cent in 1960 (falling to 12 per cent by 1965, 9¼ per cent by 1970) and rather higher transport costs from Italy, but it too was compelled to make substantial changes in its structure and performance. In 1966 there were six British producers of conventional domestic refrigerators, producing at volumes of 70,000–100,000 a year, and employing none of the new technologies mentioned above. With the advent of Italian competition, three of these (Hotpoint, English Electric, and GEC) merged to form British Domestic Appliances (BDA), which scooped up the 14 models of the three companies into one plant, with a combined volume of 250,000 a year. Two producers, Hoover and Kelvinator, withdrew from production in the mid-1960s and in 1978 there were just three producers, Thorn, Hotpoint (BDA), and Electrolux. The British industry laboured under two disadvantages, even after these structural changes. Firstly, the volume implications of the new technologies had not been fully taken on board; there was a view in the industry that a volume of 200,000 units a year, which the larger plants in Britain were quite close to in 1967, was in fact the minimum efficient scale.[7] Italian competitors had grasped that it was in fact four times higher. Second, it took some time to achieve economies within the BDA organization. Because the dozen or more models inherited by the BDA from its three constituent parts were of different dimensions it was not possible to install automated, coil-fed, press-lines, or conveyorization until 1969/70. But for the tariff it is doubtful whether as much of the British refrigerator industry would have survived. Just three manufacturers survived, Thorn with around 20 per cent of the British market in 1978, Hotpoint with around 15 per cent, and Electrolux with around 20 per cent, some of which were imported.

The evolution of the Italians' competitive advantage *vis-à-vis* the British industry is illustrated in Figure 6.2 which relates (real terms) wholesale prices to cumulative volumes in each country. In the late-1950s the British industry had a considerable head-start on the Italian industry; in 1957 it had already produced over five million units, whereas the Italians had yet to produce one million. This advantage secured the British producers a modest 10 per cent cost advantage. But the Italians were expanding very rapidly, and from 1958 onwards they reduced wholesale prices, and probably unit costs, in line with cumulative volume all the way down to 1970, at a consistent rate of 13 per cent in real terms per doubling of cumulative volume — a rate which is fairly typical for manufacturing industries. In the late 1950s the British industry was also reducing wholesale prices at a similar rate in relation to cumulative volume but the crucial difference was that the Italian industry's cumulative volume was increasing in relative, and later in absolute, terms at a very much faster rate than that of the British. By 1960, therefore, Italian wholesale prices were 15 per cent lower than those of the British producers. This appeared to energize the latter; the British price structure collapsed, and British producers managed to reduce prices at an exceptionally high rate of 40 per cent with each doubling of cumulative volume from 1960 onwards, in an effort to hold the price differential against the invading Italians. This they succeeded in doing; the differential was 15 per cent in both 1965 and 1970.

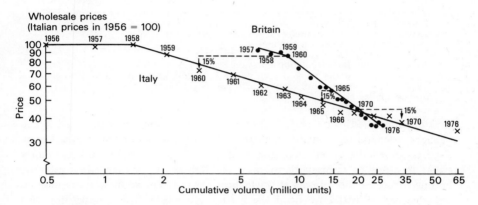

Fig. 6.2. Refrigerators: Italian and British unit wholesale prices in real terms, 1956–1976
(Expressed on a common currency basis, deflated by British GDP deflator)

After 1970, the Italians ran into decreasing returns; they were scarcely able to reduce real wholesale prices much further, whereas the British continued to do so and by 1975 had almost closed the gap. Hotpoint and Thorn considered it worthwhile investing in new refrigerator capacity in the late 1970s. According to one industry spokesman,[8] Thorn, the leading British producer, had secured a cost advantage over the Italians in the late 1970s. These recent developments help to explain why the Italian penetration of the British market was stabilized, at around 20 per cent.

The German refrigerator industry was perhaps better placed to cope with the Italian challenge since it had already structured itself in a way which facilitated economies of scale by 1958, well before the Italians launched their export efforts. Four producers accounted for over 70 per cent of German refrigerator and freezer production in 1958, and this proportion rose to 80 per cent by 1970, mainly as a result of mergers; of the eight largest companies in 1965, five were involved in mergers in the late 1960s. Bosch and Siemens merged their white goods interest, raising Bosch's traditional market leadership to 45 per cent in 1970. Bosch took over the group's production of dishwashers, cookers, and refrigerators, concentrating the production of refrigerators at Gingen.

In summary, the evolution of a Community market in refrigerators was

TABLE 6.5. *Structural Changes in the German Refrigerator Industry*
1958-1970

Company	Production in 1958 (000)	Company	Production in 1970 (000)
Bosch	400	Bosch–Siemens	1000
Bauknecht	240	Bauknecht	350
Linde	200	AEG–Linde–BBC	235
BBC	100	Liebherr	210

Entry: 1958 Liebherr (70,000 units a year)
Exits: 1965 Kupperbusch (15,000 units a year)
        1967 Alaska (60,000 units a year)
        1971 Panzerbode (50,000 units a year)
Mergers: 1967 Bosch (800,000 units) and Siemens (100,000 units). AEG (120,000
         units) merged with Linde (150,000 units) and BBC (100,000
         units), and acquired a 20 per cent share of Zanussi.
Source: Jürgen Müller.

instrumental in bringing about rationalization and economies of scale, which
brought dramatic real reductions in the prices of domestic refrigerators. Italian
exports forced the other three major refrigerator industries in the Community
either to come to terms with the new technologies by merging their interests
in order to secure the volumes at single locations and achieve the scale economies
available, or to withdraw from the market altogether. This competition also
stimulated new channels of distribution which undercut the traditional channels,
with their comfortable margins. The Italian industry itself also underwent
considerable structural changes. Export opportunities allowed the market leaders,
Zanussi and Ignis, to draw ahead of their Italian rivals. This factor, coupled
with the rapid defensive responses of the other Community refrigerator industries,
forced a number of smaller Italian producers out of business in the early 1970s.
These observations provide support for the proposition outlined in Chapter 2,
namely that intra-Community trade stimulates structural change and economies
of scale, both in importing and exporting countries.

WASHING-MACHINES

The integration of the Community's washing-machine sector follows on behind
the refrigerator story and replicates most of its major features. In washing-
machines, as in refrigerators, the Italians led the way with volume production
techniques, achieving cost advantages which were used as a platform from which
to invade neighbouring markets. But the narrative is less straightforward because
competitive modes in the washing-machine sector are conditioned by the product's
relative complexity; the machine is subject to greater demands in use, and requires
more frequent servicing. Brand loyalty and back-up service are therefore more
important, and relative price is less important, than is the case in refrigerators.
    Trade in washing-machines did not really develop until the automatic washing-

machine had become accepted and standardized around its present configuration. The late 1950s still saw housewives manhandling wet clothing out of tub-like machines and drying it with manually-operated wringers attached to the machine. Washing was performed by circulating the water and clothing with rotating discs or impellers, occasionally causing tangling and damage. In British machines a second tub was added for spindrying, which reduced labour but considerably increased the dimensions of the machine. In short, 1950s machines were aids in the traditional 'wash-day'. The automatic machines which followed in the 1960s replaced the wash-day altogether. Automatic machines became possible in Europe through the introduction of the timer from the USA. Washing and drying could be carried out in the one drum; the washing action in the horizontally-mounted drum was achieved through rotation of the drum itself, which increased washing efficiency and reduced damage. Early automatics were accident-prone, occasionally catching fire, flooding, and vibrating badly. They were heavy (100 kg. or more) and expensive. A better machine such as the 1962 Hoover Keymatic, retailed at £120, equivalent to ten weeks' wages of a manual labourer. Many were complicated to use and required the operator to make more decisions than modern machines require, on water levels and temperature, for example. No one country in Europe could be said to have been the technical pioneer at this time; each country produced its own early models which were gradually improved and made cheaper in real terms. By 1965 or thereabouts, a cost-effective design configuration had stabilized sufficiently for international trade on a substantial scale to commence.

TRADE AND STRUCTURAL CHANGE

Intra-Community trade made relatively little impact on the shape of the industry until the mid-1960s. The refrigerator story should have indicated the shape of events in advance, for, just as in refrigerators, there was first a wave of new entrants into the Italian washing-machine sector in the late 1950s, boosting the number of producers from only 5 in 1953 to 50 by 1960 (see Figure 6.3). An intense struggle for survival followed within the Italian market, which rapidly shook out the majority of these producers; by 1964 only 18 survived.[9] The largest producer, Zanussi, by this time accounted for 28 per cent of all the Italian production; the second and third largest producers, Candy and Indesit, for a further 36 per cent. Production leapt and unit costs plunged during these years. Annual volume rose from less than 200,000 in 1960 to 1.5 million in 1965; it actually doubled in each of two successive years, 1962 and 1963. The unit wholesale price of washing-machines halved in real terms in just five years between 1962 and 1967, as Figure 6.4 indicates. Exports played their part in accelerating these developments; as a proportion of total Italian washing-machine output, exports rose from 10 per cent in 1960 to over 50 per cent by 1970.[10] Over this same period the leading producer, Zanussi, increased its share of production from 28 per cent to 40 per cent, and doubled its volume

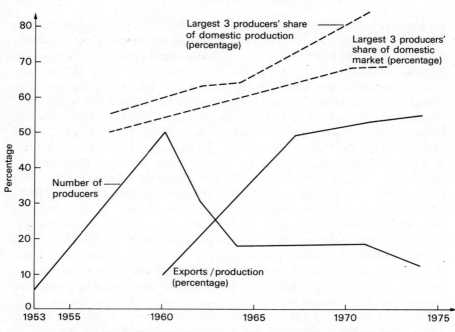

Fig. 6.3. Italian washing-machine industry: trade and structural change

from 500,000 to over 1m. units a year. Predictably, the unit cost reduction, which made possible this expansion into export markets put a number of smaller producers under strain. A crisis in 1968 led to a number of casualties, which were scooped up by Zanussi, with Government encouragement and financial support. These developments provide a vivid illustration of one of the central propositions of this study, that leading exporters achieve greater scale and unit cost reductions both through exporting *and* by displacing less efficient competitors at home.

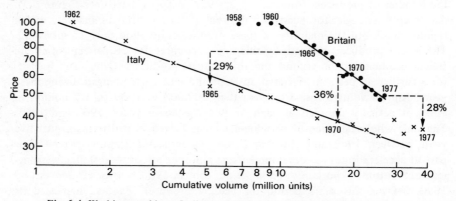

Fig. 6.4. Washing-machines: Italian and British wholesale prices in real terms

The price trends in the major countries help to explain why Italian exports began when they did. In the late 1950s Italian washing-machines cost more (by 10 per cent or so) to make then their British and German equivalents. During the next few years, Italian prices plummeted (see Figure 6.4); by 1963 they had drawn level with British prices; by 1965 the Italians had secured a 29 per cent cost advantage, which they maintained thereafter, explaining why their export effort was launched in 1965 and why Italian exports could be sustained. The Italians' progress in reducing prices in real terms was closely related to their cumulative volume, with prices falling by 15 per cent with each doubling in cumulative volume. Their high costs in the late 1950s were partly the result of low cumulative volume, and the rapid price/cost reductions of the early 1960s appeared to be the result of enormous increases in cumulative volume. Prior to the arrival of the Italians the rate of price reduction in other countries had been relatively sedate. In Britain, for example, washing-machine prices barely fell in real terms, between 1958 and 1961 (see Figure 6.4) but thereafter the British had to reduce prices at the very rapid rate of 40 per cent per doubling of cumulative volume merely to prevent the unfavourable price differential with the Italians from widening still further. In Germany too, it was noticeable that the rate of price reduction quickened after 1965 (see Figure 6.5).[11]

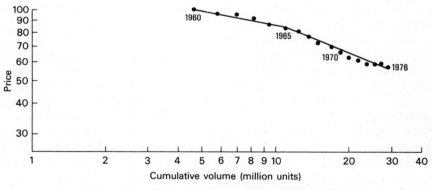

Fig. 6.5. German unit wholesale prices for washing-machines
(Real terms: 1960 = 100)

What impact did the Italians have on neighbouring industries? As in refrigerators, the Italians used 'cover' to gain entry into other washing-machine markets. They lacked marketing expertise and their brands were less acceptable to Germans and British customers than local favourites. Accordingly, they minimized these disadvantages, either by supplying mail order chains (Currys, Comet, and Rumbelows in Britain, Quelle and Neckermann in Germany) with unbranded products, or by permitting their products to sell under the brands of electricity showrooms and local manufacturers where the latter wished to maintain a full product range, even though they could not compete on manufacturing costs at the lower end of the market. Zanussi's products were sold under AEG, Electrolux, and Hotpoint trade marks as well as their own and that of the electricity industry's brand (Electra) in Britain.[12]

France was the nearest and the most vulnerable market. In 1965 its washing-machine sector was as fragmented as Italy's had been five years earlier. There were then 40 producers. Hotchkiss Brandt (150,000 units in 1965) and Amiens (80,000 units) led the field, followed by five others with 50,000 units (Frigidaire, Esswein, Bendix, Arthur Martin, and Hoover), and four others with over 20,000 units (Lincoln, La Laveuse Française, Vendôme, and Flandria). These volumes were insufficient to permit the French sector to achieve the economies of scale available in washing-machine manufacture. For the reasons discussed below, volumes of 300,000 units were necessary in the 1960s to secure these economies; already by 1965 Zanussi (450,000 units) had achieved this volume, Candy and Indesit (each with around 270,000 units) were fast approaching it. According to the cost–volume relationship discussed below, the Italians' scale advantage would have conferred a cost advantage over the French competition of 10–20 per cent. The Italian interest in the French market threatened to cause havoc, and prompted a range of defensive moves, both by the French government and by the industry. The French government devised administrative delays in the form of a Norme Française that laid down safety and performance standards which all appliances offered for sale on the French market had to satisfy before being granted import licences.

The French industry rapidly reorganized itself. In 1966 and 1967 the component supplier, Claret, integrated forwards by acquiring three washing-machine producers, Esswein, La Laveuse Française, and Royal, and was itself acquired later in 1967 by the merged Thomson–Brandt group. Appliance manufacturers outside France, moved in by acquisition; Philips acquired Amiens, the second largest producer, and later acquired Lincoln in 1974; and the Swedish company, Electrolux, acquired Arthur Martin in 1975. Hoover and Flandria eventually withdrew, in 1977. In 1977, five producers (Thomson–Brandt, Philips, Arthur Martin, Lincoln, and Bendix) accounted for nearly 100 per cent of French washing-machine production. Thomson–Brandt increased its volume to nearly 500,000 by 1970, to 750,000 by 1974, and to nearly 1m. in 1977. With the acquisition of Claret's motor and pump facilities it became a fully integrated producer and, in total volume terms at least, had by 1974 achieved the minimum efficient scale relevant to a fully integrated producer. Arthur Martin achieved volumes of 250,000 by 1974 and so too, did the Philips Amiens plant. Thomson–Brandt concentrated the production of six formerly separate producers into just two efficiently sized plants, at Lyon (over 600,000 units a year) and La Roche sur Yon (formerly the Esswein plant, with volumes of 300,000 units a year).[13]

The surprising aspect of this episode is that the Italians failed to gain more than 10 per cent of the French washing-machine market. The speed of the French industry's response was one reason; no doubt the lesson of the refrigerator story was fresh in its mind. The French government played a part. The industry also possessed a national protective advantage in the form of an idiosyncratic French preference for the slim, top-loading machines whereas the rest of Europe opted for front-loading machines. Since the top-loader's construction and methods used in its manufacture are distinct, other countries' scale advantages in front-loaders posed less of a threat to the French industry. Thomson–Brandt actually manufactures top-loaders for importing companies to sell under their own labels — a reverse of the situation in Britain and Germany where local companies market imported machines under their own labels.

In the British market the pioneers were English Electric and Bendix in 1960, followed by Hoover in 1962. By 1964 two Italian machines appeared on the market. They were startlingly cheap, retailing at 20–30 per cent below the British prices but even so, they were not rated as 'value for money' by a consumer magazine.[14] The Italian machine was judged a poor performer; the other (Indesit) was judged electrically unsafe and in danger of debouching hot water should one open the door during the washing cycle. Throughout the 1960s the Italians' rating gradually improved but Hoover's automatic was still judged the 'best buy' in 1970. By 1972, Indesit's model had not improved, to judge from these reports;[15] it spun poorly, its controls were unclear, its electrics were doubtful, and the door could still be opened during its operation, but its price advantage was now over 40 per cent.[16]

By 1970, Italian producers had only secured a 5 per cent market share of the British washing-machine market, but over the period 1970–75 the share of automatics (in which the Italians specialized) doubled from 30 per cent to 60 per cent, helping the Italians to increase their overall market share to 20 per cent. The other factor was that over these years, the Italians offered a price advantage which partially offset the persistent quality disadvantage of their products.

The British washing-machine sector was better structured in the 1960s to face international competition. It was dominated from the beginning by just two producers, Hoover and English Electric (later Hotpoint). In 1966 Hoover produced around 250,000 machines, one-third of British production and close to the minimum efficient scale of 300,000 units. English Electric produced roughly half this volume. By 1971, Hoover's volume reached 400,000 units and remained between 400,000 and 500,000 units during the 1970s — less than half Zanussi's 1.1m. Together, these two British producers accounted for nearly half of the country's output of automatics in 1979. In terms of overall company volumes at least, the bulk of British production was in an efficient configuration. There were two notable casualties, Bendix, one of the pioneers in automatics, and Thorn. It would be too easy to attribute these withdrawals to inadequate scale, since in 1978 three small companies survived, Servis (owned by Wilkins and Mitchell) with around 100,000 units, Philips, and Creda (owned by Tube Investments) with half this volume. There is ample evidence throughout the Community that there is room for the small, high-quality companies.

The German industry also had its traumas. There were 40 washing-machine manufacturers in Germany after the war; in 1978 there were only five:

Bosch–Siemens, AEG, Miele, Blomberg, and Lepper. The first two aim at volume markets and each produce over 500,000 units a year. Miele is the Daimler–Benz of the industry with 400,000 units a year. Blomberg is a versatile specialist, manufacturing 20,000 units a year to specific customer requests, in very small lot sizes. Lepper produces only 50,000 units a year under a special co-operation agreement with the mail order house Quelle. The casualties of the industry – Schauf in 1965, Wamsler and Zimmerman in 1968 – each produced less than 150,000 units a year. A number of producers were acquired by AEG.

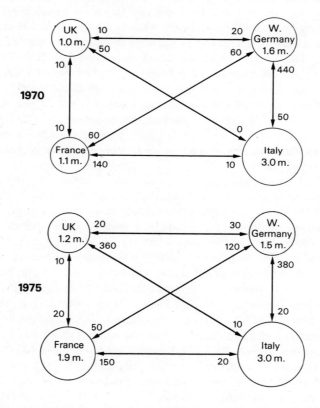

Fig. 6.6. Trade flows in washing-machines between major European producers
(Figures within the circles represent the country's production of washing-machines;
trade flows are in thousands of units)

Two snapshots of the intra-Community trade pattern, shown in Figure 6.6, sum up this discussion. By 1970, the Italians had secured substantial exports to Germany (around 20 per cent of the German market), significant exports to France (10 per cent of the market), but only modest exports to Britain (5 per cent of the market). By 1975, Italy's exports to France and Germany had fallen slightly but its exports to Britain had risen sharply to nearly 25 per cent of the market. Trade between France and Britain, and between Germany and Britain, remained slight, although French exports to Germany had become more significant.

MANUFACTURING TECHNOLOGY, SCALE ECONOMIES, AND COMPETITIVE POSITIONS

The story has so far indicated how intra-Community trade contributed to reshaping the washing-machine sectors of all four countries. It concludes by considering the underlying technology and economics of washing-machine manufacture, and their role in explaining the pattern of trade.

MANUFACTURING TECHNOLOGY AND SCALE ECONOMIES

The washing-machine comprises a pressed steel cabinet which houses a revolving drum (with an inner and outer casing), driven by an electric motor, linked to a water system (pump, valves, and piping) and controlled by a timer which co-ordinates the motor and water system according to pre-selected programmes of washing, rinsing, and spin-drying. The cost structure shown in Table 6.6 indicates that over half the ex-factory cost for the typical manufacturer is accounted for by bought-in items. Direct costs (material content plus direct labour) account for two-thirds of these ex-factory costs; half of these direct costs are accounted for by just four items: cabinet (12–15 per cent), drum (18–21 per cent), motor (11–14 per cent), and timer (7–8 per cent).

TABLE 6.6.   *The Structure of Manufacturing Costs*
(percentage)

Bought-in material and components	53
Direct labour	14
Indirect labour	14
Depreciation	1
Warranty costs	5
Other overheads	13
	100

The product is more complicated than the refrigerator and allows more options to the manufacturer in how he designs and manufactures. There is the option to produce the cabinet using a shell, reinforced with bracing pieces, or using a frame assembly technique. Tubs can either be made from chrome steel, which requires no finish, or from vitreous enamelled steel, which is cheaper but visually less attractive. There are options also in the design of the tub itself: some are manufactured in an oval shape, designed to provide an outlet for the water during the spin cycle; alternatives have complex drainage and/or inter-rupted spin-cycle arrangements to achieve the same effect. One of the basic design problems of the washing-machine is to control vibration during a spin cycle which entails speeds of 500–1100 r.p.m., leading to the well-known propensity of the early washing-machine to 'dance'. One option open to the manufacturer is to increase the weight of the drum with heavy steel back-plates and even lumps of concrete strapped to it, which of course increases the material costs and the energy requirements of the machine. An alternative, more sophisticated, approach, which is cheaper on materials, is to minimize the source of vibration — the uneven distribution of the load — by programming in a pre-spin cycle to distribute the load evenly before the high speed cycle begins. Generally speaking, as well as posing distinct design problems, the speed of the spinning cycle is an important indicator both of the machine's functional performance and quality. Lastly, manufacturers can introduce wider options in respect of the machine's programme, through the introduction of electronics into the timer mechanism.

Since the motor and timer tend to be purchased from specialist component suppliers, along with rubber components for the water system and all extra items, washing-machine manufacture reduces essentially to two operations; metal fabrication (the cabinet shell, drum, and door) and final assembly. In the first operation, flat-rolled sheet steel or coil is fed into press-lines where it is formed and folded into shells and drums, which are completed on welding lines. They then pass into paint-spraying booths and are subsequently stored in overhead assembly conveyors, awaiting to be called off into final assembly. In parallel with these operations, various sub-assemblies will have been completed, such as wiring harnesses, motors, and water systems.

Final assembly lines are much less elaborate than in the car industry; there is a minimum of model-specific tooling surrounding the line and operatives work singly. Testing is integrated into the line (except for thorough off-line testing on a sampling basis). For these reasons it is feasible to vary the model types on the line in a way which is not in car assembly, but there are still economies in restricting the model types on each line. For example top-loaders always have their own line; the simpler and more complex front loaders would each have their own lines.[17]

There is a noticeable distinction between the relatively mechanized, capital-intensive fabrication stage, and the relatively labour-intensive assembly stage. The logic of this is that the two stages are uncoupled, to allow the fullest utilization of the capital-intensive equipment on a two- or three-shift basis, whereas the assembly is carried out on a one- or two-shift basis. A buffer stock capacity is therefore required to cover the period when the fabricating shift is operating while the assembly lines are not. The scale factor bears most strongly on the pressing operations, less strongly on the welding operations on the shell and drum, and fairly insignificantly on the assembly operation. As in refrigerator manufacture, volume allows automated press-lines to be used, which, in one plant visited, permitted the manning levels to be reduced from 28 to 3. Automatic presses and bending lines have a capacity of roughly 400,000 units a year, assuming three-shift operations with 80 per cent utilization. Considerable auto-mation is also possible in the welding operations; at low volumes the formed cabinet and drum pass through a series of manually operated spot-welding machines. With volumes of 200,000 units a year and imaginative design of automatic welding equipment, it is possible to install automated lines and operate them fully. Volume also permits the automation of a whole range of minor fabricating operations such as production of plastic moulding, die-casting the bases of the drums, and machining and winding the armatures on the motor. In assembly, line speeds lie between 50 and 90 an hour which, on a two-shift basis over 220 working days a year, implies an annual volume of at least 180,000 units per model for full line utilization. While Italian producers tend to replicate plants specializing in particular models, British and German producers tend to group several lines under one roof.

These factors suggest that the minimum efficient scale would appear to be at least 400,000 units a year; it would allow full utilization of the press line, two welding lines, and two assembly lines. Much would depend on the model range and the ability of the automated equipment to accommodate different models with rapid change-overs. A manufacturer producing just two main automatic machines might require an annual volume of 800,000 units in order to operate two press lines, four welding lines, and two fast (90 an hour) assembly lines, so as to operate dedicated equipment. A manufacturer with a broader range would suffer some penalty but might argue that rapid change-over could keep this very small. Some manufacturers seemed to think that a volume of 600,000–800,000 exhausted the available economies, but one manufacturer reckoned that for each product type, scale economies continued all the way, at an un-changed rate, from 100,000 units a year up to over 1½m. units a year.

How important are scale economies? Bearing in mind that the washing-machine's production technology is similar but more complex than that of the refrigerator, one would expect to find that scale economies are marginally greater in washing-machines compared to Scherer's calculation for refrigerators (a cost penalty of 6.5 per cent at one-third of the minimum efficient scale). According to one manufacturer, roughly the same relationship applies in washing-machine manufacture (a 10 per cent cost reduction as volume increases from 100,000 to 500,000, implying a cost penalty of 7.5 per cent at one-third of 500,000). But other indications suggest a sharper decline in costs. Pratten sug-gested a cost reduction of 7.5 per cent over the 250,000 to 500,000 range.[18] Balloni's cost–volume relationship for the Italian washing-machine sector over time suggests a 20 per cent cost reduction with each doubling of volume, but this figure also includes other factors (learning, weight reduction over time, technical progress). The most unambiguous and carefully costed statement on the subject received during the enquiry was to the effect that scale economies were specific to model-types and that unit costs declined by 15 per cent with successive doublings in model volume, all the way out to 1½m. units a year.[19]

This then is the range of estimates of scale economies. How did costs relate to scale in practice? The comparative costs of washing-machine manufacture in the four countries in 1978 have been estimated according to methods outlined in Appendix 8 and are shown in Table 6.7. Table 6.7 indicates that Italian unit costs were the lowest in the Community in 1978. An Italian standard machine could be manufactured for less than £80 in 1978; other countries' unit costs exceeded £100. Quality differences probably accounted for some part of these differences. The German unit material costs were considerably higher than elsewhere, but a major reason for the differences in unit cost were differences in unit labour costs for equivalent work content. Italian unit labour costs were only £13; French, British, and German unit labour costs were roughly double this. The Table also compares unit costs using Italian costs as the benchmark. To improve comparability, German unit costs have been treated as if the German bought-in element has been the same as French and British levels (£74 rather than £83); the German machine's higher quality probably accounted for this difference. The Table shows that German, French, and British unit costs of washing-machine manufacture were respectively 20 per cent, 30 per cent, and 40 per cent higher than Italian levels in 1978.

TABLE 6.7.   *Unit Costs of Washing-Machine Manufacture: Four Countries, 1978*[a]

Actual costs: £1978	Italy	Germany	France	Britain
Materials and bought-in items	51	83	58	58
Direct labour	8	17	} 26	15
Indirect labour	5	6		19
Factory overheads	14	15	17[b]	17
Factory price	78	121	101	109
Comparative costs: Italy = 100				
Materials	65	(74)[c]	74	74
Direct labour	10	22	} 33	19
Indirect labour	7	8		24
Factory overheads	18	19	22	22
Factory price[d]	100	120	130	140

[a]   The comparison is made, as far as is possible, on the basis of comparable machines; this is particularly difficult in the case of German machines which are typically of higher quality than the majority in other countries. An adjustment has been attempted, to allow for this in the value-added elements.
[b]   No reliable figure available: assumed equal to British overhead cost.
[c]   German unit materials costs are higher than those in other countries, probably because of higher quality requirements and the complexity of the product. This comparison is made as if German material costs were the same as British and French levels.
[d]   Rounded figures.

For explanations of these differences, one looks primarily to scale factors. Total volume seems not to be the most relevant dimension of scale in this industry.

TABLE 6.8.   *Unit Cost and Scale: Actual and Estimated Positions Compared*

	Italy	Germany	France	Britain
Annual volume per model (000)[a]	250	100	60	100
Expected unit cost on basis of volume per model (Italy = 100)[b]	100	125	140	125
Estimated relative cost	100	120	130	140

[a] Plants in Germany, France, and Italy produced other products in addition to washing-machines (dishwashers in France, tumble-driers in Germany and Britain) usually sharing some of the equipment, e.g. press-lines. For the purposes of the comparison, these items have been included as distinct model types. The French figure of 60,000 may understate the true position, because the company operates two plants, many of whose models will certainly have components in common.
[b] Assuming that unit costs decline by 15 per cent with each doubling of volume per model.

All the manufacturers concerned produced half a million or more units a year; the Italian manufacturer was by no means the largest and, therefore, its cost advantage cannot be explained in terms of overall volume. It was noted above that the clearest statement made on the subject was that scale advantages relate to volume per model and this seemed plausible in view of the advantages in being able to operate press, welding, and assembly lines on a dedicated basis. The ability of this dimension of scale to explain international cost differences is explored in Table 6.8. There were substantial differences in volume per model between the four countries; 250,000 in Italy, 100,000 in Germany and Britain, and 60,000 in France. Reckoning on the basis of the 15 per cent cost reduction with every doubling in volume per model, one would expect German and British unit costs to be 40 per cent above this level. In the German case, there is a reasonable correspondence between the actual and expected cost disadvantage, remembering the uncertainties about the implications of quality differences for both bought-in and factory costs. The French cost disadvantage (30 per cent) is less than the predicted 40 per cent and this may be due to the ability of the French producer to achieve economies in respect of components common to several models. Although its two plants each produced their own model ranges sold under separate marques dating from pre-merger days, they were supplied from a single component plant. British unit costs appeared to be higher than predicted on scale alone, which explains only 60 per cent of the British cost disadvantage. Excessive indirect labour costs seem to have been the main reason for this, arising partly from under-utilization of capacity — itself the consequence of increased Italian penetration of the British market — and partly perhaps from two general difficulties of British manufacturing, namely, the effect of artificial job demarcation in padding out the maintenance functions and the high supervision costs associated with large British plants. Indirect labour costs were 40 per cent less than direct labour costs in the Italian plants and there was a noticeable absence of supervisory staff; the plants appeared almost to run themselves. Had the relationship between indirect and direct labour costs in the British industry been in line with Continental practice (indirect costs equal to 60 per cent of direct costs), British unit costs would in fact have been closely in line with the expected unit costs in Table 6.8, calculated on the basis of volume per model considerations.

To conclude, the manufacturing technology in washing-machine manufacture offers a route to cost reduction via high model volumes. The differing extents to which the four countries have proceeded along this route largely explain their relative costs in 1978, with one variance in the British case which is explicable in terms of a familiar British weakness in the use of indirect labour.

Unit Costs and Competitive Positions

The trade flows in Figure 6.6 now become intelligible, viewed against the cost configurations in Table 6.7, and the positioning of the four national industries in the quality spectrum and in relation to national income levels:

	Unit Cost	Product quality	Income per head
Germany	high	high	high
France	medium–low	medium	high
Britain	medium–high	medium	low
Italy	low	medium	low

Germany is in a class of its own in terms of quality, but the cost penalty that this implies denied Germany any significant exports to the two low income markets, Britain and Italy (only 20,000 units to each in 1975) which could not afford the quality premium. Higher income levels in France may explain the rather higher German exports to the French market (50,000 units). At the lower end of the market, the Italian cost advantage secured substantial exports to Germany (440,000 units); the medium–low costs of the French industry, and its unique top-loading machines, also secured significant exports to Germany (120,000 units). Italy imported hardly any machines at all (50,000 units). German machines were too expensive for its low-income market; French and British producers could not compete on cost and hence price. The Italian cost advantage secured substantial exports (900,000 units to the other three markets), more so in the high-cost German market than in the medium–low cost French market. French medium–low costs provided some opportunities in the German market (120,000). French and British costs and quality were too similar for any worthwhile trade to develop between the two countries. The British consumer was too poor to afford German machines, but was strongly motivated to buy cheap Italian machines. Britian appeared to have little or no export opportunities; it could not compete in Italy on cost, and not having any established quality advantage over the Italians, it was dominated by the latter in both France and Germany.

CONCLUSIONS

The evolution of the European white goods industry vividly illustrates a number of the features of the European economy which were anticipated earlier in Chapter 2. Most striking was the way in which the wider European market offered the larger, low-cost Italian producers opportunities to displace smaller, higher-cost producers in neighbouring markets, and that in both the refrigerator and washing-machine sectors, the aggressive exporters also displaced marginal domestic producers. It was encouraging that defensive moves by beleaguered importers led to restructuring and considerable improvement in performance, which were necessary to match the downward trend in the Italians' prices, if not their levels. These developments all underline the integral links between intra-Community trade, structural change, scale of production, and improved manufacturing performance.

NOTES

1 The Italian industry supplied 80 per cent of the combined imports of Germany, France, and Britain. Germany and Britain exchanged 20,000 units or so; Germany exported 90,000 units to France and a negligible quantity to Italy.
2 Valeriano Balloni, *Origini, Sviluppo e Maturita dell'industria degli Electtrodomestici* (Bologna, 1978), p. 65. These changes are shown in Figure 6.1. The industry's growth in concentration went hand in hand with its increasing orientation towards export markets and was accelerated by it; the leading producers accounted for a larger share of domestic production than their share of the domestic market.
3 I am indebted for this assessment to an unpublished study by J. C. Cousins and P. I. Freeman, 'The UK Domestic Industry', (1966).
4 F. M. Scherer, *Multi-plant Operations*.
5 Most of the casualties in the refrigerator sector were those who failed to achieve volumes in excess of 100,000 units a year; e.g. Arthur Martin, Frigeavia, Whirlpool, and Frigidaire in France; Kupperbusch, Alaska, and Panzerbode in Germany; Hoover and Kelvinator in Britain.
6 The Italian cost advantage was reinforced (probably unnecessarily) by rebates of duties on imported steel, under Italian Law 639, which in practice provided a subsidy related to weight, regardless of steel content and its origin. This practice was contested by France, as being contrary to Article 92(i) of the Treaty of Rome, which rules against state aids which distort competition. France also applied to the Commission for import quotas, which were refused. The case was referred to the European Court of Justice which ruled in December 1965 [Common Market Law reports, 1966, case 45/64] that the Italians were in breach of Article 96, inasmuch as the Italian Government rebated a number of duties (registration tax, stamp duty, mortgage tax) which were imposed on commercial activity generally, not on production as such. Italy reduced its rebates in respect of exports to Community members as a result of this judgement.
7 In fairness to the British management, some had perceived the need to rationalize well before the surge in imports. When Hotpoint was given new management by AEI in 1956 it foresaw that appliance manufacture, like that of motor cars, would eventually be concentrated in the hands of very few specialist firms, and, acting on this belief, proposed to build up a volume through heavy advertising, exporting, and negotiations (largely abortive) to swap production lines with other British manufacturers.
8 George Dorman, quoted in *Electrical Review*, 17–24 Dec. 1977. In July 1975 the cheapest Italian 5-cubic feet refrigerator retailed in Britain (the Indesit 140 LGBT) at £56;

the cheapest British-made competitor was Thorn's Triumph 3515 at £60. By mid-1977, Thorn had matched Indesit's price (£55).

9 Balloni, p. 65.
10 Balloni, p. 228.
11 All prices are deflated by a GDP deflator. The Italian prices are derived from Balloni, p. 104, German prices from the Statistisches Bundesamt, and British prices from trade journals.
12 Discount chains' manner of operation presented the local producers with a dilemma. If they did not react at all, there was the danger that the discount chains would take over the entire lower end of the market, using imported products. If they countered the low-priced imports handled by the wholesale chains by pushing lower-priced models of their own through the same channels, they risked undermining small, high-margin retailers on whom they depended for the bulk of their sales, since it is difficult to convince a well-informed market that the large price difference between cheap models handled by discount chains and expensive models handled by specialist retailers is justified by quality differences. Even if distinct brands are offered to the two distribution channels, consumer magazines are apt to reveal how minimal the quality differences are between the discounted brand and the quality brand intended for independent specialist retailers. This subject is fully discussed by Charles Baden Fuller in 'The Economics of Private Brands, with Special Reference to the Domestic Appliance Industries of the USA and UK', Ph.D. thesis accepted by the University of London, 1980.
13 The company itself reckoned that the minimum efficient volume was 600,000 units, rather lower than Balloni's 750,000 estimate. The Amiens plant was suboptimum in terms of washing-machines alone but effectively achieved efficient volume by using the same presses and painting facilities, and many of the same components in the manufacture of as many dishwashers (300,000 a year).
14 Which?, Nov. 1964.
15 Which?, Jan. 1972.
16 The Indesit Export retailed at £66; Hoover's 3236 at £123 in 1972.
17 In one plant it was pointed out that since the line is 80 metres long, a model change-over would provide no work for operatives towards the end of the line until the early afternoon.
18 C. F. Pratten, Economies of Scale in Manufacturing Industry (Cambridge, 1971), p. 217. It was acknowledged that this estimate was speculative, because no British manufacturer had then produced at the rate of 500,000 units a year.
19 Based on the calculation that costs for the following categories decline with each doubling of volume as follows.

	(per cent)
raw materials	3
components	10
assembly	12–15
parts manufactured in-house	20–25
technical overheads	30–35

CHAPTER 7

THE ECONOMIC BENEFITS OF INTRA-COMMUNITY TRADE

It is a cause for surprise that, although the putative economic benefits of Community membership are fundamental to the Community's existence, and enlargement, so little serious research has been undertaken to establish how significant these benefits might be. References to this subject are vague and tentative. Reviewing developments during the Community's first fifteen years, the European Commission noted the high growth in output per capita in the member countries over this period (5 per cent per annum between 1958 and 1973), and made the diffident observation that: 'It is impossible to give scientific proof that this rapid and sustained growth is due to the formation of the Common Market, or that member countries would not have been able to show an equally rapid expansion if they had taken some other course.'[1] The Report's authors were too modest to claim more than that: 'qualitative indications . . . give the impression that the formation of the Community had been a stimulus to investment and innovation.'

The Commission was no doubt inhibited from advancing bolder claims by the fact that free-trade policies tend to yield less than visible achievements; to use a favourite Commission term, the benefits are not 'transparent'. Their contributions to the enlargement of consumer choice and the more efficient allocation of resources are of such a gradual and diffused nature that they tend either to be taken for granted or disregarded entirely. To the extent that public imagination is seized at all, it is by the incidental hardships in this process, such as the closure of uncompetitive plants in the face of intra-Community competition. Moreover, the spadework necessary to open up this competition, to achieve the adoption of common product definitions and the harmonization of standards, and to document and prosecute commercial practices and government policies which are inimical to cross-frontier trade, is unglamorous, bureaucratic, and open to (occasionally well-deserved) ridicule. The Commission has sometimes appeared to the public to be engaged in unnecessary rituals in pursuit of intangible benefits.

How much worse off would Europeans have been in economic terms if the Community had not existed and if instead, the member countries had merely participated in the GATT? The traditional verdict of economic analysis is: hardly at all. While acknowledging that the Community has stimulated trade, customs union theory attributes very modest benefits to this additional trade. The analysis in Chapter 2 developed the economies of scale approach to trade and arrived at a very different verdict. Trade originates in part from scale-related unit cost differentials, and in turn induces structural changes and efficiency gains in both the exporting and importing countries. A hypothetical illustration, based on the assumption of 10 per cent cost reductions per doubling of volume, suggested that direct benefits from trade could be over half as great as the value of trade itself. This chapter considers the extent to which the case studies support this proposition and estimates the probable magnitude of the aggregate benefits from Community trade. These estimates are unashamedly speculative, and are offered in the belief that it is better to be approximately right about the total dynamics of trade than it is to be precise about static benefits calculated on the assumption, which the foregoing case studies have shown to be highly unrealistic, that economies of scale are fully exploited in the absence of trade.

The quantification of these economic benefits, like most quantification in economics, is complicated by the other, more significant changes which are going on at the same time, most notably, the growth of the industries concerned. The analysis in Chapter 2 abstracted from this by considering a static world in which trade led to resource savings through the reallocation of production within and between countries, in respect to a given quantum of output. What is actually observed is a moving pattern of market growth, enhanced competition, structural change, and real reductions in unit costs, all of which are interrelated. In other words, the static welfare benefits of trade — the subject of the familiar customs union theory — are caught up with the so-called dynamic effects. It is customary when quantifying the benefits of trade to focus on the former, and simply to acknowledge that the dynamic benefits exist, as an unquantifiable bonus. The discussion below attempts to improve on this; it first discusses the nature and magnitude of the static benefits arising in the three industries and then hazards an estimate of some of the dynamic benefits, arising from trade in the white goods industry.

White Goods: Washing-Machines

In 1976, Italy exported 30 per cent of its total washing-machine output (3.4m. units) to three major markets — Britain (430,000 units), Germany (370,000 units), and France (240,000 units), and imported negligible quantities in return. The cost analysis shown in Table 6.7 revealed the following configuration of unit costs:

Italy	Germany	France	Britain
100	120	130	140

These differentials imply that the importers' unit costs were, on a weighted average basis, 31 per cent higher than the Italian levels.

It was also noted that as trade and volume increased, the number of producers in the Italian industry diminished rapidly, from 50 in 1960 to 13 in 1974, and within the largest six producers, which together accounted for 90 per cent of production in 1974, a greater share was progressively assumed by Zanussi (30 per cent of the six producers' output in 1964, 45 per cent in 1974). It is not possible to identify the internal transfers of production which occurred within the Italian industry as a consequence of trade but some idea of their significance can be inferred by considering the industry's learning curve, the relationship between real costs and cumulative volume. Exports to Britain, Germany, and France in 1976 enabled the Italian industry to achieve a volume over 40 per cent higher than it would otherwise have been; and because exports were a fairly steady proportion of production during the industry's growth period (from 1965 onwards), cumulative volume was also increased by a similar amount of this trade. It was estimated on page 129 that the unit costs of the Italian washing-machine industry declined by 15 per cent in real terms with every doubling of cumulative volume. Using this relationship as a basis for calculating the effect of exports on Italian unit costs, it seems plausible to suggest that the industry's combined exports to France, Germany, and Britain, which accounted for 30 per cent of the industry's output, reduced unit costs by 8 per cent.[2]

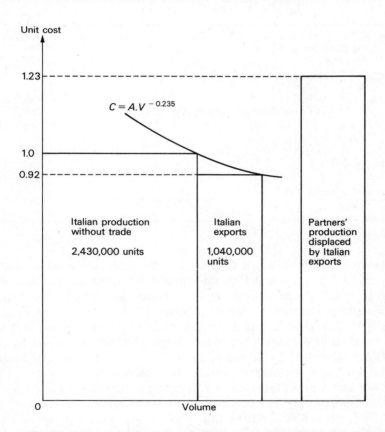

Fig. 7.1. Resource implications of Italian exports of washing-machines

The unit costs of the displaced production in the importing countries can also be inferred. The unit cost differentials between Italy and its partners which are directly observable refer of course to *surviving* capacity in each country. The unit costs of the displaced capacity would, by implication, have been higher than that of the surviving capacity, by perhaps 10 per cent or more. The observed unit cost of the surviving capacity was 31 per cent higher than the Italian unit cost. The unit cost of the displaced capacity would on this basis have probably been at least 34 per cent higher. Setting Italian costs *without* trade as the *numeraire*, observed Italian unit costs were 0.92 (due to the 8 per cent cost reduction achieved by expansion through exporting); the unit costs of displaced capacity in Italy's trading partners were therefore 1.23 (= 0.92 $\times$ 1.34). The resource savings arising from this trade are illustrated in Figure 7.1, and are estimated in Table 7.1 to be equivalent to 54 per cent of the value of the trade itself.

TABLE 7.1   *Trade Benefits: Exports of Italian Washing-Machines, 1976*

Italian production	000 units
Without trade	2430
With trade	3470
Cost of production	
Without trade	
2430 in Italy $\times$ 1.0	2430
1040 in France, Germany, and Britain $\times$ 1.23	1280
	3710
With trade	
3470 in Italy $\times$ 0.92	3190
Resource saving	520

$$\frac{\text{Resource saving}}{\text{Trade}} \quad = \quad \frac{520}{1040 \times 0.92} \quad = \quad 54 \text{ per cent}$$

Cars

In the car industry, it was noticeable that the most substantial increases in structural change experienced by the national car industries tended to occur when an industry was making aggressive moves into neighbouring markets. The increase in German concentration occurred between 1955 and 1970 (see Table 4.4). The three largest companies' share of production increased from 70 per cent to 87 per cent in this period. Borgward withdrew from the industry; DKW, Auto-Union, and NSU ceased to be separate entities and were absorbed by and eventually rationalized within the Volkswagen organization, whose share of German car output increased from 40 per cent in 1955 to 52 per cent in 1970. Concentration also increased in the British car industry between 1965 and 1970, when BMC's relative cost position and export prospects looked favourable. BMC's share of production rose from 37 per cent in 1965 to 48 per cent in 1970. During the 1970s, when both industries moved on to the defensive, (3-firm) concentration in the German industry fell back again (from 87 per cent in 1970 to 81 per cent in 1977); so would have the level of concentration in the

British industry if the government of the day had not intervened with rescues of the largest and third largest companies (British Leyland and Chrysler) in 1975. From 1965 onwards the French car industry improved its export performance. The 3-firm concentration increased from 82 per cent in 1965 to 100 per cent in 1977, with Renault increasing its share of production from 30 per cent in 1955, to 35 per cent in 1965, and to 40 per cent in 1975, at the expense principally of Chrysler whose share of production fell from 27 per cent in 1955 to 15 per cent in 1975.

TABLE 7.2.   *Impact of French Car Exports to Britain on French Producers*

French producers	Exports to Britain (000 units)	French producers' volumes		Percentage increase in volume due to trade
		Without trade (000 units)	With trade (000 units)	
Renault	70	1150	1220	6
Peugeot	25	630	655	4
Citroën	25	590	615	4
Chrysler	10	470	480	2
Total	130	2840	2970	

To convey an idea of the order of the economic benefits directly attributable to trade and these structural changes, an assessment is made of the effects of French exports to Britain in 1976. The French industry exported over 130,000 vehicles to Britain in that year, equivalent to nearly 5 per cent of French production, exploiting a unit cost advantage over British manufacturers of around 15 per cent. The trade had a differential impact on French producers, which is shown in Table 7.2, with Renault gaining most, Chrysler (France) least.

The resource savings are calculated on the following assumptions: that unit costs in the French car industry declined by 20 per cent per doubling in volume (suggested by the Renault equation in Table 4.15); that by virtue of being twice the size of its then domestic rivals, Renault already enjoyed a cost advantage of 10 per cent with an allowance for Renault's wider product range; that the unit cost of displaced British capacity was 10 per cent above that of the surviving capacity, which in turn was 18 per cent higher than the smaller French producers' unit costs. The benefits are shown in Table 7.3. They were equivalent to 53 per cent of French exports to Britain.[3]

Trucks

In the truck industry, Daimler–Benz's penetration of the French market generated benefits of a similar order. French unit costs were 30 per cent higher than those of Daimler–Benz in 1976, largely due to scale differences (130,000 units a year produced at Daimler–Benz, around 20,000 a year at Berliet). This size differential was undoubtedly assisted by Daimler–Benz's simultaneous drive into export

TABLE 7.3.   *Trade Benefits: Exports of French Cars to Britain, 1977*

	Volume (000)	Unit cost	Cost (000 units)
Total costs before trade			
Renault	1,150	0.9	1,035
Others	1,690	1.0	1,690
			2,725
British output displaced by French exports	130	1.30	169
	2,970		2,894
Total costs after trade			
Renault	1,220	0.889[a]	1,085
Others	1,750	0.994[b]	1,740
	2,970		2,825
Resource savings			69
$\dfrac{\text{Resource savings}}{\text{Trade}}$	$=$	$\dfrac{69}{130}$	$=$ 53 per cent

[a] Reduced by 1.2 per cent, due to increase of 0.6 per cent in volume.
[b] Reduced by 0.6 per cent, due to increase of 0.3 per cent in volume.

markets and its rationalization of parts of the German truck industry. Leaving aside those benefits deriving from that rationalization which could be attributed to trade, and the encouragement which the German penetration of the French market gave to rationalization of the French industry (with the merger between Saviem and Berliet), and concentrating on the directly observable effects, one notes that, as in cars, the structure of the German industry adjusted itself slightly in favour of the larger producers as a direct result of exports. Exports to France in 1976 allowed the lowest-cost producer, Daimler–Benz, to increase output by 7.5 per cent, the second largest producer, Magirus–Deutz, by 5 per cent, and M.A.N. by 3 per cent. One could reckon that Daimler–Benz's cost advantage over the other two producers was around 10 per cent,[4] and that the cost disadvantage *vis-à-vis* Daimler–Benz of the displaced French production – the product lines phased out by Saviem and Berliet – would have been even higher than that of the surviving capacity – perhaps as much as 40 per cent. The directly attributable benefits from this trade are set out in Table 7.4 and amount to 48 per cent of the value of the trade itself.

In the three industries, the ratio of benefits-to-trade was 54 per cent in the white goods example, 53 per cent in cars, and 48 per cent in trucks. These ratios cluster very closely around 50 per cent, close to the theoretical estimate offered in Chapter 2. None of these estimates give any credit to trade for any induced efficiency gains among the surviving producers in the importing country. These could be significant; after all, imports from low-cost producers inject formidable doses of competition to which all domestic producers need to respond in order to ensure that they will not be the next to succumb. The French truck industry is a good example. Saviem and Berliet took active steps to rationalize their rambling product ranges in response to imports. In the areas of overlap between the two companies there was scope for cost reductions through scale effects alone, of at least 7 per cent in respect of 40,000 units of production, equivalent to 2,800 units, and probably the same amount again through improved methods. If German imports, which account for 40 per cent of imports, were credited pro rata with inspiring these improvements, the benefit/trade ratio in Table 7.4 would increase from 48 per cent to 67 per cent. These responses are not automatic, however. In the British car industry, government assistance in the 1970s averted the closure of uneconomic capacity (the Chrysler Linwood plant, the Vauxhall Ellesmere Port plant), and probably one or other of British Leyland's major plants (Longbridge or Cowley). In addition, the state's safety net probably delayed the necessary improvements in industrial relations and the reduction in gross overmanning in the assisted companies. Although the indirect benefits of trade are potentially of real significance, they can be blocked by state intervention in the pursuit of job preservation.

TABLE 7.4. *Trade Benefits: Exports of German Trucks to France, 1977*

	Volume	Unit cost	Cost
Total costs before trade			
Daimler–Benz	119,400	0.9	107,460
Magirus and M.A.N.	37,400	1.0	37,400
French output displaced by German exports	12,200	1.26	15,372
			160,232
Total costs after trade			
Daimler–Benz	129,000	0.895[a]	115,455
Magirus and M.A.N.	39,000	0.997[b]	38,891
			154,346
Resource savings			5,886
$\dfrac{\text{Resource savings}}{\text{Trade}} =$	$\dfrac{5,886}{12,200} =$		48 per cent

[a]   Reduced by 0.56 per cent, due to increase in volume of 8 per cent.
[b]   Reduced by 0.28 per cent, due to increase in volume of 4 per cent.

The best opportunity to observe these induced efficiency gains is provided by the response of the British refrigerator industry to Italian competition. In this sector, it has been seen how the leading Italian manufacturers built larger plants and expanded exports, forcing smaller competitors in Italy and in its trading partners either to retire or rationalize their capacity. The difficulty in quantifying these effects resides in identifying the turn of events which would have occurred in the absence of this competition. A device which offers a way of doing this is the 'experience curve' concept. In the course of their evolution most industries achieve continuous real-terms reductions in unit costs through a combination of scaling-up, technological advance, and on-the-job learning. The leading authority on this phenomenon, the Boston Consulting Group, has proposed the general observation that the unit cost of value added characteristically declines by 20–30 per cent with each doubling of cumulative volume. Reckoning that value added typically accounts for 50 per cent of total costs, these figures imply unit costs reductions of 10–15 per cent.[5] The BCG has documented this relationship for a great many industries and termed it the 'experience curve'. These curves, BCG argues, apply consistently across technologies and through time, regardless of cumulative experience.

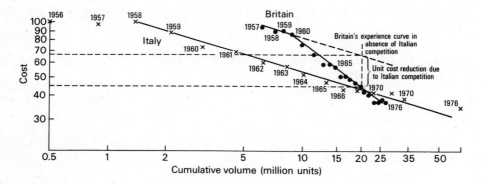

Fig. 7.2. Refrigerators: effect of Italian competition on British unit costs

The significance of this relationship is that it provides a broad guide to what would have probably happened otherwise, against which to assess the actual progress of an industry. Suppose, for example, that in the absence of the pressure of the unusually severe external competition to which it was subjected, the British refrigerator industry would have scaled-up, introduced new manufacturing technology, and learned from experience, at a rate which would have achieved unit cost reductions of 10–15 per cent with each doubling of cumulative volume. But a performance of this order would not have been sufficient to ensure the survival of the British refrigerator industry against the Italian industry, which at any given point in time achieved lower unit costs than the British industry and which moved so rapidly down an experience curve with a slope of 16 per cent, that it would have rapidly widened its unit cost differential with respect to British producers. The latter had no choice but to achieve cost reductions at the same rate over *time* as did the Italians; but because the British were not doubling their cumulative volume as fast as the Italians they had to reduce unit costs with each doubling of cumulative volume that much faster, at 40 per cent. Figure 7.2 illustrates this. Had the British industry followed an experience curve of a typical gradient after 1960 — for example, by reducing unit costs by 16 per cent per doubling of cumulative volume as the Italian industry did — British prices would have fallen to a level of 68 (1956 = 100) in 1970, well above the level of 45 actually achieved. Italian competition, then, can be plausibly credited with prompting a reduction in British unit costs of one-third more than would otherwise have been the case. Since British refrigerator output was 1.1m. units in 1970, this saving was equivalent to 370,000 units (see Table 7.5).[6]

TABLE 7.5.   *Benefits from Trade: Italian Exports of Refrigerators to Britain, 1970*

Source of benefits	Benefits (units)
Displacement of high cost British output by lower cost Italian products (340,000 units × 15 per cent cost differential)	50,000
Induced cost reductions in the Italian industry (5,250,000 units × 0.08 per cent)	40,000
Induced cost reductions in the British industry (1,100,000 units × 34 per cent)[a]	370,000
Total	460,000
$\dfrac{\text{Benefits}}{\text{Trade}} = \dfrac{460{,}000}{340{,}000} =$	135 per cent

[a]   British unit costs were 34 per cent lower than it was estimated that they would have been, on the basis of cumulative volumes.

Italian costs were also lower because of exports to Britain. By 1970, the Italian industry had exported around 1.7m. units to Britain. In the absence of these exports, the Italian industry's cumulative volume in 1970 (34m.) would have been 5 per cent lower. Since Italian unit costs declined by 16 per cent with every doubling of cumulative volume, the effect of exports to the British market could have reduced unit costs for the Italian industry as a whole by 0.8 per cent, equivalent to over 40,000 units.

On this assessment the resource benefits from this particular slice of trade are 135 per cent of the value of trade itself; the indirect benefits (410,000 units) far exceed the effects of displacement of high cost domestic production by lower cost imports. The largest element in the calculation — the incremental reductions in unit costs in the British industry — are also the most hazardous to calculate, since experience curves are only a rough guide to the counterfactual situation. None the less, even discounting for this uncertainty, it appears that trade is capable of exerting considerable leverage on industrial structure and performance.

Would it be valid to generalize the result over all Community trade in manufacturing? It may be argued that the three industries are a small and biased sample, chosen precisely because they exhibit the kind of results which the theory proposed by this study is predicting. Two observations are worth making on this point. First, even if the products studied are, as an aggregate, traded within the Community to a greater degree in proportion to their output than the average, they might not be representative of manufacturing, but they could still be representative of the products *traded* within the Community. It is the latter aggregate which is of interest in what follows, rather than the former. Second, they are in fact reasonably representative of traded products. The white goods industry, it is true, has seen more dramatic trade penetration and restructuring than most industries. Because of the homogeneous nature of its products, and hence the price sensitivity of their demand, low-cost producers have had opportunities to penetrate other markets which are not as easily available to producers of more heterogeneous products. Yet we have seen that in respect to trucks, a product which is both complicated and differentiated, and subject to technical barriers to trade and strong brand loyalties, the pattern of development was much the same as in white goods, yielding resource savings which were pretty much in line with those in white goods. There are, therefore, grounds for supposing that the model of trade proposed in this study is generally applicable across a wide spectrum of industries, and that it provides a basis for proposing an aggregate estimate of the benefits attributable to Community trade.

AGGREGATED BENEFITS OF INTRA-COMMUNITY TRADE

Now is the appropriate point to attempt to assess the economic benefits which the original members of the Community have derived from their membership. To simplify the discussion the effects of the Community's two enlargements will be disregarded. The assessment involves four stages:

(1) drawing on the results of this study to estimate the benefits associated with particular trade flows;

(2) drawing on the extensive literature on trade creation for estimates of the aggregate effect of the Community's existence on intra-Community trade in manufactures;

(3) applying the relationships derived at (1) to the increment of trade identified at (2) to obtain aggregate effects in the manufacturing sectors;

(4) considering wider repercussions in the non-trading sectors.

Two broad types of trade have been distinguished in this study: trade involving exchanges of differentiated products which does not entail any reallocation of resources in the trading partners, and trade which does. This study has been concerned with the latter type of trade and its effects, but it was recognized in Chapter 2 that pure exchange has an important role: the exchange of Citroëns and Volkswagens by the French and Germans, for example, benefits both, but it need not necessarily involve any movement of resources in either country. The formation of the Community may simply have provided the two companies concerned with opportunities to switch some orders from the domestic market to the neighbouring market, to satisfy customers unable to secure their preferred choices of car from the domestic supplier. The discussion of this type of trade in Chapter 2 suggested that if economies of scale operated, at the rate of a 10 per cent decline in unit costs per doubling of volume, exchanges of this kind generated consumer benefits equivalent to something in the region of 20 per cent of the imports involved. It is difficult to judge the proportion of the trade in manufactures which can be characterized in this way. It became clear in the industry studies that some substantial bilateral exchanges took place in the absence of significant cost differences between the two partners, and therefore were presumably driven by consumers' appetite for greater variety: exchanges of washing-machines between France and Germany; of trucks between Germany and Italy. It is suggested that perhaps 25 per cent of intra-Community trade in manufactures originates purely from considerations of wider consumer choice, involving no switching of resources or induced efficiency effects.

The analysis of this study suggests that the bulk of trade — perhaps 75 per cent of it — originates from scale-related cost differences and that these differences generate resource benefits equivalent to 50 per cent of the imports involved, close to the theoretical figure of 60 per cent which emerged from the discussion in Chapter 2. All three industry studies yielded ratios of resource benefits to trade which clustered closely around 50 per cent. There are grounds, then, for having some confidence in this figure. The effects of trade on efficiency — the famous but never quantified dynamic effects, the prospect of which helped to carry Britain into the Community — are far less certain. The one calculation, in the refrigerator sector, which was made in this Chapter of the direct effect of trade on resource saving, combined with its indirect effect on the efficiency of the surviving capacity in the importing country, threw up a resource benefit to trade ratio of 135 per cent. On the basis of only one study it is impossible to generalize, but knowing how a growth in import penetration can cast a long shadow across a threatened importing industry it would not be surprising if the combined direct and indirect effects were equivalent to 100 per cent of the imports involved; in other words, if the induced efficiency effects were as great again as the direct resource saving effects. The judgement, then, is that one-quarter of intra-Community trade in manufactures is of a pure exchange type and generates economic benefits equivalent to 20 per cent of imports; three-quarters of this trade derives from cost differences and generates benefits equivalent to 50–100 per cent of imports.

Turning now to consider the magnitude of the impetus which the Community gave to intra-Community trade, we find a great range of published estimates, employing a variety of techniques. In his review of these studies, Mayes concluded that 'it is clear after such a wealth of research that the bounds of magnitude have been established for the effects of integration on trade (in manufactures) ... the range for 1970 is approximately $8 billion to $15 billion'.[7] This study is concerned with improved use of resources — the substitution of lower cost supplies for higher cost supplies — a process termed 'trade creation'. A component of the additional trade was merely trade diversion — switching from non-Community suppliers to Community suppliers as a result of the preference accorded to the latter. To a large extent this diversion was offset by external trade creation attributable to the fact that the Community's common external tariffs were on the whole lower than members' pre-Community tariffs. But the bulk of the additional trade represented internal trade creation — the substitution of imports from Community partners in place of domestic production. Williamson and Bottrill[8] concluded 'that intra-EEC trade in 1969 was something like 50 per cent greater than it would have been if the EEC had not been created. Most of this rise appears to be attributable to trade creation rather than diversion, while the harm done to other countries' exports by diversion was largely offset by positive external trade creation'. The studies suggest, when taken as a whole, that internal trade creation in 1970 was worth around $10bn. Intra-Community trade in manufactures was worth $33.bn. in 1970. 30 per cent of it was attributable to Community-induced trade creation, which could be said to have raised intra-Community trade by 40–50 per cent. If one allows that the external trade creation roughly offsets the trade diversion effects, in resource allocation terms as well as in terms of the volumes of trade concerned, this uplifting effect of the Community on trade of 40–50 per cent is a good basis for estimating the economic benefits of the Community.

In 1980, trade in manufactures between the Six was worth almost $200bn.,[9] a sixfold increase in money terms over the 1970 level, and a threefold increase in real terms. Whereas intra-Community trade was equivalent to 20 per cent of the Six's manufacturing output in 1970, it was equivalent to 30 per cent in 1980. To what extent was this real increase in trade in the 1970s a reflection of a continuing and growing Community effect, and to what extent was it simply a reflection of general liberalization? The answer to this question has to be a conjectural one because the analytical technique which had served reasonably well in earlier studies of Community effects up to around 1970 became increasingly less appropriate as the Community matured, namely, comparing the trends in imports of the Community from its partners with those from the rest of the world, and attributing the divergence in these trends after the Community's formation to the Community itself. Two important changes took place in the 1970s which made this approach more difficult to pursue.

First, former EFTA countries either joined or concluded free-trading agreements with the Community. Thus the countries which were the most relevant members of the control group of non-members used in earlier studies no longer qualified as such in the 1970s.

Second, there were important supply-side changes in world trade in the 1970s: the increased competitiveness of Japan and of the newly-industrialized countries of South-East Asia in a wider range of industries. This development removed another important group of manufacturing countries from the Rest of the World control group. Japan, for example, increased her exports of manufactures to the Community fifteenfold in the 1970s, from $1.1bn. in 1970 to $17bn. in 1980, and would undoubtedly have made a significant impact whether or not the Community had been formed. The relevant Rest of the World control group narrows to only the USA and Canada, and even their suitability is not at all clear. The year 1971 saw the abandonment of the fixed parity system which had in effect sustained the US dollar well in excess of the parity compatible with the competitiveness of US manufactures. The floating dollar has improved US competitiveness and it must be for consideration how much of increased Community imports from the USA — an increase of nearly five times from $5bn. in 1970 to $38bn. in 1980 — has been attributable to this factor.

These observations illustrate the difficulties in finding suitable controls with which to compare the growth of European integration so long after the formation of the Community. We resort instead to naïve extrapolation, after noting two points. First, integration is a long-term process which in the Community was far from complete in 1970; the level of integration in the Community in 1969 was reckoned to be only one-quarter as complete as that of the USA which had by then already functioned for a century as a customs union. One does not expect the impetus towards European integration to have been exhausted by 1970. Second, the succession of independent estimates of the Community's effects on trade up to 1970 form a progression with a pronounced trend, as Mayes's review records. These two points taken together — the reasoned expectation of a continuing increase in integration towards the American level, and the upward trend in the Community's trade effects recorded in the 1960s — suggest that it would not be implausible to extrapolate from the 1960s experience in respect to the proportion of intra-Community trade attributable to the Community. The search for more complete analytic techniques has its attractions, but however satisfactory they might turn out to be from a technical point of view, they would in the end have to be applied to a historical framework which would involve hazarding guesses about the kind of trading environment which would have evolved if the Community countries had merely participated in successive GATT rounds, which themselves might then have proceeded differently had Community partners participated independently. Would other trading blocs such as EFTA have been formed without the Community? And more generally still, would the OECD countries' commitment to an open trading system have survived as well as it has in the recession since 1973, but for the existence of a European Community for whom such a system is fundamental? The *anti-monde* in 1980 would have been considerably less open without the institutional buttress which the Community has provided for an open trading system.

The consensus of a number of studies attributed to the Community a degree of internal trade creation which raised intra-Community trade in 1970 by close to 40–50 per cent above the level it would have attained in the absence of the Community. If one assumed that the trade-creating effect of the Community on internal trade continued to grow in proportional terms at the same rate in the 1970s as it did in the 1960s, it would have grown from 40–50 per cent in 1970 to 100–125 per cent in 1980, equivalent to $100–125bn. additional trade in manufactures.

By applying the benefit/trade relationships to this $100–125bn. increment of Community-induced trade in manufactures in 1980, we have:

(1) consumer choice-related benefits equivalent to 20 per cent of $25–30bn. of this additional trade, worth $5–6bn.;

(2) resource savings benefits equivalent to 50–100 per cent of $75–90 bn. of the additional trade, worth $37–90bn.

In aggregate, the benefits could range between $40bn. and $96bn., equivalent to between 5–12 per cent of the Six's manufacturing output of nearly $800bn. in 1980.

Indirect Effects on Non-Manufacturing Sectors

In addition to these industrial benefits there were probably substantial indirect effects as well. In market economies, few sectors can wholly insulate themselves from developments in other sectors. The processes described in this chapter have contributed significantly to higher productivity in manufacturing. Since the Six's manufacturing labour force remained constant over the period considered, labour productivity in manufacturing could have risen by nearly 12 per cent, in proportion to the resource benefits in manufacturing, as a result of the Community. The non-manufacturing activities most responsive to these changes are those which compete for the same labour as manufacturing industries — banking, insurance, transport, and professional services. The least affected activities are perhaps public-sector monopolies and public-sector services subject to fairly rigid manpower requirements (staff/pupil ratios in education, staff/patient ratios in health care), but even these are constrained by limitations on expenditure which press eventually in the direction of productivity improvements to offset demands for real increases in wages originating from productivity growth in the manufacturing sector.

Some idea of the importance of these induced effects on productivity outside the manufacturing sector can be inferred from the relative rates at which labour productivity grows in manufacturing and service industries in advanced industrial countries.

Service sector productivity grows more slowly than manufacturing productivity, tending to make services more expensive relative to manufactures. A consideration of a detailed analysis of this phenomenon suggests that the relationship between the two rates of productivity growth is fairly stable; that productivity growth in services follows along at a rate which is between a quarter and a half as great as productivity growth in manufacturing.

This rule of thumb is based on the relative prices of services in the USA and Europe, and the relationship between these relative prices and the differentials in labour productivity which can be presumed to underlie them. According to the calculations of Irving Kravis and his associates,[10] the costs of services in the USA in 1970, relative to the costs of services in Germany, France, and Britain, were respectively 145 per cent, 161 per cent, and 196 per cent. Services (which are defined by Kravis as being wholly provided by labour) cost more in the USA because the American productivity advantage is less in service industries than it is in manufacturing industries, coupled with the fact that American wage levels reflect the American productivity advantage in manufacturing, not in services, because manufacturing products are traded internationally, whereas services, by and large, are not. In other words, American unit labour costs in manufacturing are roughly the same as in Europe, implying wage differentials with respect to Germany, France, and Britain roughly equal to American productivity differentials in manufacturing (138 per cent, 168 per cent, and 194 per cent respectively in 1970). Knowing the relative labour costs in the USA and Europe, the relative costs of services provides the clue to relative productivity in services. For example, American services cost 45 per cent more than German services in 1970, using labour which was paid 138 per cent more than German labour. American productivity in service industries must therefore have been 64 per cent higher than in Germany (238/145-1) to offset the costs of higher wages to the extent that they were. The American productivity advantage in services (64 per cent) was therefore nearly half as great as it was in manufacturing (138 per cent). Similar calculations for France and Britain suggest similar relationships between the two productivity advantages of the USA; 40 per cent in respect to France and 26 per cent in respect to Britain. The range of these calculations suggests that, as manufacturing productivity increases, productivity increased in the non-manufacturing sectors also, but at a slower rate, equal to between one-quarter and one-half the rate of growth in manufacturing productivity. On this basis, the 5-12 per cent increase in manufacturing productivity attributable to the Community would induce a productivity increase of 2-4 per cent in the non-manufacturing sector.[11]

TABLE 7.6.   *Estimated Economic Benefits to the Six Attributable to the Community, 1980*

| | Trade-related resource benefits as a percentage of: | |
	Sector output	Six's GDP[a]
Manufacturing	5–12	1½–3½
Non-manufacturing	2–4	1½–2½
Total		3–6

[a]   Manufacturing accounted for 30 per cent of the Six's GDP in 1980.

Estimates of the aggregated benefits derived from intra-Community trade in manufactures are shown in Table 7.6. They amount to 3–6 per cent of the Six's GDP. This is a substantial achievement by any comparison, particularly compared to the contributions which government policies in the industrial sectors have been able to make, in the positive direction; their contributions in the negative direction can be considerably higher. These benefits from trade will have been reflected in increases in measured GDP which are a good deal higher than 3–6 per cent. National income accounting is perforce obliged to measure many non-market sector outputs (much of the public sector) in terms of their inputs. Thus if real wages in the non-market sector keep pace with those in the market sector, the former is in effect attributed with the productivity growth of the latter, even though, as we have seen above, it is lower. If such conventions were adopted here the benefits from trade might be valued at as much as 10 per cent of GDP. These calculations say nothing about the distribution of the benefits between the member countries. This requires a further study.

Estimates of this order are controversially high. According to the customs union approach to these benefits, the removal of the internal tariffs would stimulate increases in economic welfare which, as a percentage of the trade created, would be *less* than the average pre-Community tariff; of 10 per cent, let us say. If this figure is applied to Community-induced trade ($100–125bn. in 1980), the resource savings turn out to be $10–12bn., equivalent to only $\frac{2}{3}$ per cent of Community GDP. One objection to this approach was developed in Chapter 2; it ignores scale and industrial structure, and the additional inducements which trading opportunities offer to industry leaders to displace high-cost competition. A second objection is that it is not just tariffs which hold back trade, but a whole clutch of factors connected with incompatibility of standards, mistrust of foreign products, inertia, and discriminatory commerical practices, all of which tie domestic customers to domestic producers. These factors can continue to isolate Community markets long after the removal of tariffs; the important implication of this is that the international cost differences which drive the increased intra-Community trade can be considerably greater than pre-Community tariffs. Thus, for example, case studies in the vehicle and domestic electric appliance industries revealed substantial increases in trade, occurring long after the removal of tariffs, associated with international cost differences well above the original tariff levels, i.e. 10–25 per cent.

The estimated benefits could be challenged from a rather different standpoint. They equate resource savings with economic benefits, but resource savings are only valuable to the extent that the resources concerned, principally labour, can be redeployed in ways which are more useful than those from which they were displaced. This basic assumption has been generally self-evident for much of the post-war period, since despite the considerable structural change, and hence temporary unemployment, caused by the upsurge of intra-Community trade, rates of unemployment fell to and remained at very low levels in the Community after 1963 until 1974,[12] while real wages rose rapidly. Large-scale redundancies, it is true, can prove too much for local labour markets to digest in the short term, but studies on re-employment patterns in various industries in several regions of Britain and the USA suggest that even in these cases the majority of the displaced workers are back in work within a year.[13] This surprisingly smooth adjustment process, which contrasts sharply with the impression of ossified employment patterns and predictions of industrial catastrophe whenever this or that industry is threatened by imports, is less surprising when it is viewed against a picture of general mobility of the industrial work-force. In British manufacturing, for example, the numbers of annual job changes is equal to 20 per cent of the total manufacturing work-force. Mobility of this order facilitates the rapid absorption of substantial cohorts of redundant employees, and this even in conditions of recession.

This observation goes some way to meeting the other popular objection to international trade, that a country with, say, three million unemployed 'cannot afford' redundancies occasioned by import competition, and that structural change must be postponed until (1985? 1990?) unemployment is 'back to normal'. The fallacy in this argument is to suppose that unemployment would fall if an economy was locked rigidly in its existing shape by import controls. Levels of unemployment are primarily determined by conditions in the labour markets: by the abilities or otherwise of labour markets and the educational system to match supplies of labour to specific demands at particular locations; by the post-tax incentives to seek work; by wage and locational rigidities; by fiscal inducements to substitute capital for labour; and most importantly, by the ability of unions, with the connivance of managements, to prevent real wages adjusting to market-clearing levels. No amount of tinkering with import controls can raise employment levels, other than temporarily. If introduced multilaterally, import controls are simultaneously self-defeating. But even if they are introduced unilaterally they can only have short-lived effects; a country which blocks imports also promotes its exchange rate (unless it continuously accumulates surpluses and forgoes real consumption), and thereby chokes off exports and jobs commensurate with the blocked imports. The choice, then, between trade and employment, except in the very short term, is an illusion. The real choice is between a higher standard of living with free trade, or a lower standard of living with restricted trade.

Britain's Experience of Community Membership: Beneficial or Not?

Some readers will by now be frustrated by the lack of any reference to Britain's position; to the question whether or not Britain's controversial decisions to join the Community in 1973, and not to leave in 1975, are beginning to pay off in terms of improved productivity. The short answer to this question is: no, but one would not expect favourable results to appear so soon after the removal of tariffs in 1978, still less so, given the structural and institutional rigidities in Britain, the timing of Britain's entry, and the adoption of economic policies in Britain during the years immediately after entry which hindered rather than enhanced market forces.

TABLE 7.7.   *National Income per Head: Purchasing Power Parity Basis*[a]
(USA = 100)

	France	Germany	Italy	Britain
1950	45	36	23	56
1970	74	74	48	62
1973	77	75	60	58
1980	93	88	67	60

[a]   GNP for 1950 and 1970; GDP for 1973 and 1980.
Sources: 1950 and 1970: Irving Kravis, *International Comparisons of Purchasing Power*, p. 11.
1973 and 1980: A. D. Roy, 'Labour Productivity, in 1980: An International Comparison', *National Institute Economic Review*, No. 101, Aug. 1982, Tables 3 and 4.

Britain made hardly any progress towards catching up the USA in the period of its membership. As Table 7.7 shows, Britain's GDP per head, measured in terms of what it could buy, remained at pretty much the same level relative to that of the USA during the 1973-80 period, just as it had during the 1950-70 period before entry. The other Community members continued to close the gap on the USA during the 1970s, and the pattern is very much the same for manufacturing output per head. Britain's manufacturing productivity rose at less than one-half per cent a year between 1973 and 1980. This is not to say that Britain has not obtained any benefits from trade; according to the logic of this study, Britain's miniscule productivity gains would have been even lower, or even negative, without Community membership.

Britain has performed badly since joining but a period so short as seven years is hardly a basis for testing whether or not Community membership stimulates growth. The industry studies suggest that economic integration is a slow process, requiring 15-20 years to show measurable benefits and perhaps 40-50 years for completion, as later discussion makes clear. The foregoing analysis suggests that the Six achieved an increase in GDP of up to 6 per cent through Community membership over a twenty-year period – an increase of less than one-third per cent a year – in circumstances which favoured structural changes necessary to realize these benefits. Even if these circumstances had continued during the period of Britain's membership, Britain would have been hard put to secure this annual rate of differential growth from a standing start, in 1973. To do so, Britain's industrial leaders would have had to have had ready to hand a set of European business strategies of the kind which continental producers had already been evolving for 15 years. The strategies were not conspicuous.

But of course the conditions which favoured growth up to 1973 did not persist. Britain joined at precisely the moment when these were about to deteriorate, following the economic crisis of 1974. By ignoring the Community's formation, by failing to secure membership in 1962, Britain missed the best of the party, and found the best seats taken, so to speak. She paid a high entry fee to join, just as the sun was setting on 15 years of rapid Community growth. In industrial terms, the late arrival was unfortunate because continental producers had already made substantial adjustments to membership, and national champions had had opportunities to emerge in major industries. Predictably, Britain suffered initial shocks on the balance of payments as weak industries such as steel and cars were exposed, and some industries of which great things had been expected, such as trucks, made little headway in European markets. The light which the industry studies shed on this, for what it is worth, is that British managements had not sufficiently grasped the significance of economies of scale nor planned how to achieve them; nor had they fully seized the moral of the truck industry study, that to succeed in Europe it is necessary to have a manufacturing *policy* which simultaneously achieves scale and quick and reliable delivery, and also copes with the diversity of specifications demanded by European markets.

Finally, in the mid-1970s, at precisely the time when the situation demanded confident and aggressive strategies on the part of British managements, they moved on to the defensive in the face of the recession and national policies designed to enhance the bargaining strength, the working conditions, and the job security of the employee, to remove managements' room for initiative with respect to prices, wages, and dividends, and to impose, through policies of industrial support, structural rigidities on an economy which needed above all to adapt its structure to Community membership.

It is perhaps not surprising, in the light of these early difficulties, that Britain's first years of membership have yielded no very visible economic benefits. However, the findings of this study suggest that there is a reasonable expectation that as Britain adjusts to membership, within a framework of economic policies which favour growth and structural changes, Britain will begin to secure visible economic benefits of the same order as those which the original members have obtained from their first 20 years of Community membership.

FUTURE PROSPECTS

Looking still towards the future, how much more can be derived from the Community in economic terms? The bench-mark must be the performance of the USA. Europeans have generally been closing this gap since 1950. Within the Community's lifetime, Germany increased its manufacturing productivity from 36 per cent of American levels in 1960 to 44 per cent in 1978, according to the analysis shown in Table 1.1. This represents an increase, relative to the American level, of 22 per cent. This chapter attributes an increase of 5-12 per cent in manufacturing productivity in the Six to the Community in this period. These magnitudes suggest that, but for the Community, Europeans might have closed the gap on the USA by only half as much as it did.

Is it reasonable, therefore, to look forward to American productivity levels in the advanced Community countries within a generation and levels not too far short of that for Britain and Italy? This prospect looks feasible when it is appreciated, first, that the Community is still, despite its achievements, far less integrated economically than the USA, and second, that the early decades of integration are the most difficult.

A comparison of the degree of integration in the Community and the USA in the late 1960s[14] revealed that after a decade of progress during which internal tariffs had been completely removed, the level of integration in the Community was only one quarter of that in the USA. Even allowing for the progress since this comparison (1967 for the USA, 1969 for Europe), there is still a lot of 'water' in the Community's economies which needs to be squeezed out. The relatively slow progress towards integration is due to several factors; the dead weight of past investment decisions, particularly in heavy industries with durable equipment such as steel; respect for territorial preserves, particularly in industries with traditions of anti-competitive behaviour, reluctant to lock horns across national frontiers; and not least, the ability of threatened industries, such as the car, steel, and shipbuilding industries, to enlist substantial government support in attempts to escape the market's verdict on their lack of competitiveness. Living with market forces and with the structural changes they bring about is a test of nerve for the member governments, but if these hold, or are restored in some cases, there is every reason to expect that market forces will in time generate American levels of preformance, thereby doubling European manufacturing productivity and raising its GDP by one-third.

Whether the Community has the will to complete its integration is a real question. There are those who would argue that the Community has already lost it. An analysis of protectionism in the Community by European Research Associates[15] suggests that after three decades of post-war development towards freer trade, Europe is returning to protectionism as a response to fundamental changes in the world economy which have left the majority of its industries uncompetitive. The authors of this report note the familiar point that newly industrializing countries (NICs) are capable of achieving highly competitive unit costs in a wide range of industrial activities by buying Western capital equipment embodying the latest technology, and operating it on a three-shift basis, using labour paid at one-tenth of European wages, unencumbered with European payroll taxes, restrictions, and rules designed to give the manufacturing workers some of the job security, safety, and comfort enjoyed by public sector employees. The authors then argue that 80 per cent of European industry is vulnerable to this threat; in order words, outside the 20 per cent of manufacturing output which comprises the high technology activities inaccessible to NICs, the latter can knock out any European industry they choose, by 'laser beam' tactics, if permitted market access, in the manner in which the Japanese eliminated the British motorcycle industry. This mode of competition is of a quite different kind to that which has characterized intra-Community trade, which, as this book has illustrated, does not typically eliminate national industries but tends to eliminate the tail of inefficient capacity in most industries, and also encourages those which remain, to adopt specialized positions. Clearly, the internal adjustment problems occasioned by the latter type of competition are far less severe than those occasioned by the fights to the death provoked by NIC competition. In the former, resources are required to shift within industries, and often only within companies; in the latter, resources have to shift from one industry to another, involving a greater degree of retraining and geographical dislocation.

The high growth of the European economy up to 1973 eased the adjustment problem considerably; low growth rates and rising unemployment since that time make adjustment look less attractive politically to European governments today. The question arises then; has the analysis in this book described a golden age of Community trade and economic adjustment? Are the conditions of high growth, low unemployment, and the more accommodating intra-industry modes of competition which have characterized intra-Community trade, essential for its continuation? The authors of 'EEC Protectionism' argue that in their anxiety to protect their industries from NIC competition, Community governments are impeding or even reversing European integration. There are significant failures to agree on harmonization. As was noted in Chapter 4 on the car industry, the adoption of harmonized technical regulations (Whole Vehicle Type Approval) in the Community, has foundered on fears that it would facilitate unrestricted Japanese entry to all Community markets. This is just one element of a substantial programme of thirty Article 100 directives, whose purpose is the harmonization of the regulations under which products can be marketed and retailed, which is blocked in Brussels, awaiting resolution of the Third Country issue. There are also indications of positive steps to impede trade, not so obviously related to the Third Country issue.[16]

TABLE 7.8. *Relative Growth of Trade and Manufacturing Output in the Nine, 1970–1980*

	Manufacturing output[a] (1970 = 100)	Intra-Community trade in manufacturing[b] (1970 = 100)	Differential rate of growth of Intra-Community trade (percentage)
1970	100	100	
1971	111	114	2.7
1972	131	142	5.5
1973	167	195	7.7
1974	185	237	9.7
1975	200	246	−6.8
1976	214	286	11.9
1977	243	328	1.0
1978	304	404	−1.5
1979	358	518	8.9
1980	393	581	2.2

Source: [a] National Accounts, OECD.
        [b] Eurostat Monthly External Trade Bulletin.

This dire picture painted by Hager and his associates of a Community driven
remorsely on to the retreat from its *raison d'être* by NIC competition overlooks
the most ancient but ignored truth about trade, that no country can specialize
in everything. In recognizing that NICs could be competitive almost wherever
they choose, the authors overlook the fact that in choosing a few industries in
which to specialize the NICs must as a matter of logic reject the majority;
there is a confusion between 'any' and 'all'. While it is uncomfortable to major
sections of European industry to know that they are vulnerable to NIC competition, they should also reflect that NICs can only attack effectively on a
limited number of points and in earning foreign exchange from these invasions,
they offer new markets for European industry. However, they are right to point
out that creeping protectionism is undermining the Community's purpose
and in the 1970s has retarded the growth of trade in the Community, relative
to the growth in manufacturing output.[17] Table 7.8 shows that the differential
rate of growth in intra-Community trade in manufacture declined in successive
business cycles: over the 1970–4 cycle, intra-Community trade grew by 28 per cent
relative to manufacturing output; in the 1974–9 cycle, it grew by only 13 per cent.

This study has indicated the scale of the economic benefits which are at risk
as a result of the Community's loss of momentum and argues for a return by
the Commission and Member States to a relentless attack on distortions to the
Community markets, due to the erection of non-tariff barriers, nationalistic
public purchasing, and capital subsidies. The Community's priority must be
the completion of the market, because, as this study has demonstrated, this
opens the way to increases in the Community's real incomes, without adding to
unemployment.

NOTES

1 Commission of the European Communities, *Fifteen Years of Community Policy*
  (Brussels, 1973), p. 9.
2 A 15 per cent unit cost reduction per doubling of volume, implies the following cost–
  volume relationship, where C is unit cost, V is volume, and A is a constant:

  $$C = A \cdot V^{-0.235}.$$

  The 30 per cent of production implies a 43 per cent volume increase and an 8 per cent
  unit cost reduction.
3 This assumes that capacity is displaced, rather than merely used at lower utilization.
  In the short run, imports will tend to reduce capacity utilization and increase unit costs,
  but this will in turn force domestic producers to retire marginal capacity.
4 Although the cost–volume relationship in Table 5.9 (which implies a 7 per cent decline
  per doubling of volume) suggests a higher differential (20 per cent or so), the volume
  differences exaggerate the like-with-like comparison; Daimler–Benz's product range
  spans a wider spectrum of vehicle weights than those of the heavy truck specialists,
  Magirus and M.A.N.
5 Boston Consulting Group, *Perspectives on Experience* (Boston, 1970). Learning or
  experience curves have been documented since 1936, when they were first studied in
  the US aerospace industry; T. P. Wright, 'Factors Affecting the Cost of Airplanes',

Journal of Aeronautical Sciences, vol. 3, 1936. For an assessment of their significance, see Annex C, *Review of the Monopolies and Mergers Policy*, Cmnd. 7198, HMSO (London, 1978).

6 Of course it could be argued that in the absence of Italian imports the British industry would have enjoyed a higher domestic market share and therefore have achieved a higher cumulative volume by 1970, and hence lower unit costs than is assumed in this calculation. But this overlooks the fact that because of the price reduction induced by the Italian competition, British domestic demand was higher than it would otherwise have been, by perhaps two-thirds, assuming a price elasticity of demand of −2. Moreover, with higher unit costs the British industry might have exported fewer units than they did (300,000). On balance, the assumption that the British industry's cumulative volume was as high with Italian competition as without, seems reasonable.

7 David G. Mayes, 'The Effects of Economic Integration on Trade', *Journal of Common Market Studies*, Sept. 1978, p. 20.

8 John Williamson and Anthony Bottrill, 'The Impact of Customs Unions on Trade in Manufactures', *Oxford Economic Papers*, Nov. 1971, pp. 323–51. This estimate is comparatively cautious. Whereas Williamson and Bottrill estimate an EC uplift of $9.6bn. in 1969, the estimates reviewed by Mayes range between $7.2bn. to $20.8bn.

9 This calculation refers to trade in manufactures classified in SITC categories 5–8, which do not include trade in fuels, food or food manufactures, and raw materials. Source: Eurostat Monthly External Trade Bulletin, 1980.

10 Irving Kravis and Associates, *A System of International Comparisons of Gross Product and Purchasing Power*, International Bank for Reconstruction and Development (Washington DC, 1975), p. 192.

11 These estimates do not take account of any benefits which may derive from any Community-induced trades in non-manufacturing tradables. On the other hand, they do not take into account either the resource misallocations associated with the Community Agricultural Policy (CAP). Since CAP expenditure is devoted to encouraging the Community's farmers to produce increments of food which Europeans do not want (at the artificially high price levels contrived by the CAP), which have no conceivable strategic significance and which have to be dumped on the world market, Europeans are worse off by roughly the amount of the expenditure on the CAP, equivalent to one-half per cent of Community GDP in 1980. Whether or not this waste of resources can be laid at the door of the Community is a debatable point. It may simply have replaced part of the expenditure of member states, who in 1980 spent over twice as much as the CAP on support for agriculture for 'social' and 'structural' reasons. Agricultural support was not a Community innovation; it reflected pre-Community practices. These national policies, and the dogged support for CAP, reflect muddled ideas about self-sufficiency, and sentimental attitudes which the predominantly industrialized Europeans exhibit towards the rural way of life, or perhaps a wish on the part of urban populations to maintain marginal farms as gardeners of the landscape, on aesthetic grounds. Whatever the motive, it seems likely that in the absence of a Community agricultural policy, European governments would probably have pursued national policies of agricultural support of equivalent cost to the CAP.

12 From just below 4 per cent in 1958 to below 2 per cent between 1963 and 1974.

13 For example, a study of the Firestone Company's major closure (1,300 redundancies) at Brentford, by the Manpower Services Commission ('*Redundancy, Re-employment and the Tyre Industry*', Manpower Services Commission, Apr. 1981) showed that 76 per cent of those surveyed had worked since the closure seven months before; 73 per cent were still in work at the time of the survey. Of those who had held single jobs since the closure (58 per cent of respondents), half had found work within two weeks, three-quarters within six weeks. The local unemployment rate was 4.1 per cent, 60 per cent of the national average. Other redundancy studies, conducted in the 1976–80 period, showed comparable figures for the percentage of workers who had worked since the redundancy; 78 per cent after 11–12 months at Fife, 66 per cent at Maidstone after 4–10 months, 70 per cent at Linwood after 10–13 months. A lower figure was recorded at Tyneside (22 per cent after 11–13 months) but this concerned an elderly group of workers volunteering for redundancy (Tyre study, p. 6.5).

14 G. C. Hufbauer and J. G. Chilas, 'Specialisation by Industrial Countries: Extent and Consequences', Conference on Problems of International Division of Labour, Institut für Weltwirtschaft an der Universität Kiel, July 12–15, 1973. For purposes of the analysis, the USA was divided into four regions, each of the same size as the four major European economies. The degree of inter-regional specialization within the USA was then compared with that between the latter and was found to be four times higher.
15 *'EEC Protectionism: Present Practice and Future Trends'*, vol. I, Michael Noelke and Robert Taylor, vol. II, Wolfgang Hager and Robert Taylor (Brussels, 1981).
16 European Research Associates claim that: 'there are now more than 400 cases of suspect or downright illegal barriers to trade among member states under investigation by the Commission at any one time. The rate has risen fourfold in the past six years. *EEC Protectionism*, vol. II, p. 297.
17 This point does not undermine the argument developed earlier, that the uplift in intra-Community trade attributable to the Community has continued to increase in the 1970s as a proportion of trade. On the contrary, it strengthens it: but for the Community the restraints on trade would have been very much greater.

CHAPTER 8

CONCLUSIONS

This final chapter draws together the threads of this study and highlights their major implications. The study addressed itself to two aspects of the Community's economics which require explanation. The first concerned the pattern of trade within the Community. In a Community of member states which are similarly endowed with factors of production, is the pattern of intra-Community trade explicable in economic terms or not? Is it more predictable, for example, than the results of an athletics contest? Just as the results of the various athletic events depend largely on whether particular successful personalities emerge in one country rather than another, is the pattern of intra-Community trade just a reflection of particular companies' performance, or are there features of the Community's economies or of the structures of individual industries which predispose particular companies to do well?

The second aspect has to do with the *raison d'être* of the Community itself. What is the explanation for the fact that, on the one hand, policy makers and the European public at large regard the economic benefits of Community as worth working and making certain political sacrifices for, while on the other hand, the verdict of economic analysis is that these economic benefits are derisory? Has the public been deluded, or have economists been missing something important?

Chapter 2 proposed economies of scale as the key to both these aspects. It offered a theory of trade which assumed away differences of factor endowments altogether, and focused on scale-related unit cost differentials within industries and the incentives for low-cost producers to displace higher-cost producers. This introduced industrial structure and provided a very simple way of integrating an account of international trade with that of industrial structure. Industries which were quickest to achieve economies of scale would tend to dominate their neighbours in intra-Community trade; and this trade would induce structural changes which could generate economic benefits of a vastly greater magnitude than those predicted by conventional customs union theory.

In the empirical Chapters (3–6), the scale factor fully lived up to the role which Chapter 2 cast for it. The 1964 bilateral trade patterns within the original Community were explicable in terms of relative plant size. In all the three industry studies, the link was established between trading performance within the four major Community markets and scale of production. In each industry, lowest-cost producers were the most successful; Renault in cars, Daimler–Benz in trucks, and the Italian producers in white goods. And these cost positions depended in large part on superior scale. In general the study discovered that the relative cost positions achieved in practice conformed fairly closely to the theoretical positions calculated on the basis of engineering estimates of scale economies.

The study tried to probe the origins of these economies, where possible, by considering, for example the operational features of a car body press shop, a machining shop in the truck industry, and of assembly lines in general, and also attempted to build up estimates for total unit cost from the individual elements of cost. The links between scale, manufacturing philosophy, production control, and delivery performance in the truck industry were important from a competitive point of view; they were in some respects counter-intuitive, and provided, in the context of a study of this kind, a novel analytical dimension.

What was the study's overall verdict on the functioning of the Community market? The North Americans who wrote the Scherer study, accustomed to the open prairies of American competition, were disappointed by the fact that intra-Community trade was inhibited by artificial restraints imposed by governments or by spheres of influence understandings among potentially competing national industry groups. Achieving integration is undoubtedly uphill work. Non-tariff barriers were in evidence in all three industry studies, and they undoubtedly had a bearing on the widespread divergences between prices and costs that weakened links between relative plant size and trade performance in the formative stages of the Community, and which were explored in Chapter 3. None the less, despite the persistenceof non-tariff barriers, the growth in intra-Community trade has been sustained, and in each of the industries studied the European market could be said to function reasonably effectively in the sense that the linkages between relative costs could be traced in the trade patterns. The spheres of influence mentality undoubtedly prevailed in the Community's early years but in so far as it was to be found in oligopolistic industries, inhibiting effects on cross-frontier trade were more than offset by another, structure-related phenomenon which emerged from the discussion in Chapter 2. It seems that unit cost differences within industries, which would tend to be greater in concentrated industries with their relatively high company size dispersions, provide an incentive to trade. In general, and noting the exceptional (and explicable) behaviour of car prices in Britain after 1978, there were strong indications that the degree of integration within the Community increased as the Community matured.

In their fledgeling states, Community markets tolerated very substantial international differentials in prices. These differentials narrowed sharply as the Community market developed, probably because intra-Community trade became progressively more responsive to these international differentials. All three industry studies revealed that, by the late 1970s, a close relationship existed between relative costs and trade performance. These findings add up to an encouraging verdict on the Community's progress towards integration in those sectors outside the influence of public sector purchasing or regulation.

The study offers some speculative and therefore controversial estimates of the economic benefits from intra-Community trade—between 3 per cent and

6 per cent of the GDP of the original Six. They suggest that the Community's economic performance is of an order which begins to justify the efforts and political sacrifices involved in its formation. It is interesting to consider, if this analysis is even broadly correct, the question: how was it that so many economists, some of whom were among the justly celebrated of the academic profession, pronounced otherwise? What critical factor did they leave out? International trade theory, on which they based their analyses, disregards industrial structure. It assumes that all producers in an industry operate at the minimum efficient scale, at the 'production frontier'. Yet those who study individual industries recognize that business life is quite otherwise, and, indeed, that production at the minimum efficient scale is atypical. Industries achieve internal equilibria in which the efficient producers find it just not worth while to incur the short-term losses necessary to displace their high-cost competitors. Even competitive conditions tolerate wide dispersions in unit costs, much of which are scale-related. It is a short step to recognize that trade offers favourable opportunities for the low-cost producers to disturb these equilibria, and to provoke structural changes whose economic benefits are substantial, of the same order as the increment in trade which provoked them.

Some useful lessons for business strategists emerged from the study. First, the achievement of competitive cost positions through scale is critical. The study illustrated how essential it is in investment planning to understand the economies of scale which the latest technology makes available. All three industry studies showed how changes in technology and production management had raised the minimum efficient scale, from 1m. to 2m. units in cars, from 200,000 to 800,000 units in white goods, and from 15,000 to 100,000 in trucks. In all three industries there appeared to be competitors which were slow to appreciate these changes and grasp their competitive implications, with dire consequences. There was an understandable tendency among companies operating below the minimum efficient scale to look to other advantages, such as the unique features of their product, to pull them through, overlooking the fact that their competitors with scale advantages could not only offer attractive product features, but by virtue of their underlying cost advantage could also afford to compete more effectively on product features.

Second, it is important to identify which dimension of scale is important; in cars it appeared to be the company, in white goods the product line. The trade analysis in Chapter 3 indicated that, in general, relative plant size was more important than relative firm size; that economies of scale resided in manufacturing rather than in the overhead functions performed by the company. A number of acquisitions have been made in the mistaken belief that company size is important in itself; but this study suggests that company size is important mainly in so far as it enables managements to rationalize manufacturing operations to achieve commonality of specifications and plant specialization. Third, the study underlines a lesson which successful European managements have learned over the last twenty years; that exporting is necessary to survive in their home market. There was a time when managements regarded their domestic sales as their basic business and exports as a bonus which would be secured if resources permitted. This erroneous view still informs the protectionist patter of some industrial interests and siege economy protagonists. The theoretical discussion in Chapter 2 demonstrates that leading companies can achieve greater profitability by securing lower unit costs through expansion at the expense of marginal producers in both the export and the domestic market. The case studies suggest that this perception informs the actions of successful competitors. In such a world it becomes necessary for all competitors to compete in export markets in order to achieve the scale and unit cost position from which to defend their domestic positions.

Finally, what is the broader political significance of these conclusions? The Community's prime function is to create the opportunity for Europeans to make themselves materially better off through trade. There are many who, understandably, regard this as an insufficiently uplifting aspiration and would like to see the Community evolving politically to a position in which Europeans could develop, through the institutions of the Community, a capacity to influence events which is consistent with their collective economic strength. But the majority of Europeans, one would judge, look to the Community primarily for tangible economic benefits. Yet these benefits are not visible. Neither the Commission nor member governments make any claim in respect to them, so that although Europeans are aware that they have become considerably better off over the last twenty years they are not able to associate any substantial part of these improvements directly with Community membership. This book has described some of the competitive processes released by the Community and has attached numbers to the benefits which they might imply. If these competitive processes, and the benefits associated with them, were better understood, it is possible that Europeans would have a better relationship with the Community and be more disposed to see its institutions develop. They would see connections between the efficient functioning of European markets, the achievement of greater prosperity, and the provision of greater levels of security than are enjoyed today. They would for these reasons be more strongly disposed to see the Community complete the important task of integrating Community markets.

PROFIT-MAXIMIZING RESPONSES TO CHANGES IN COSTS

This note sets out in formal terms the link between unit cost changes and producers' competitive responses.

Suppose that a producer is confronted with market opportunities represented by a demand function:

$$x = k M^\alpha p^\beta \tag{1}$$

where x represents unit sales, M expenditure on marketing, p the price level, k is a constant; α and β are parameters: $0 < \alpha < 1$; $\beta < 0$. If the producer's unit cost is c, its profit, π, is:

$$\pi = px - cx - M \tag{2}$$
$$= kM^\alpha p^{\beta+1} - ckM^\alpha p^\beta - M$$

The first-order conditions for profit-maximization are:

$$\frac{\partial \pi}{\partial p} = (\beta + 1)kM^\alpha p^\beta - \beta\, ckM^\alpha p^{\beta-1} = 0 \tag{3}$$

$$\frac{\partial \pi}{\partial M} = \alpha M^{\alpha-1} (kp^{\beta+1} - ckp^\beta) - 1 = 0 \tag{4}$$

From (3) $p = \dfrac{\beta}{1 + \beta}\, c$ $\tag{5}$

From (4) $M = [\alpha kp^\beta(p - c)]^{-1/(\alpha-1)}$ $\tag{6}$

Substituting for p in (6):

$$M = \left[-\alpha k c^{1+\beta} \cdot \frac{\beta^\beta}{(1 + \beta)^{1+\beta}} \right]^{-1/(\alpha-1)}. \tag{7}$$

The question of interest is how the producer will vary price and marketing expenditure in response to changes unit cost. From (5) it is clear that provided demand is price-elastic ($\beta < -1$), the lower is unit cost, the lower is price and the greater is x. The marketing response can be deduced from (7):

$$\frac{\partial M}{\partial c} = \frac{\alpha k}{\alpha - 1} \left[-\frac{\alpha k \beta^\beta}{(1 + \beta)^{(1+\beta)}} \cdot c^{1+\beta} \right]^{-\alpha/(\alpha-1)} \left(\frac{\beta}{1 + \beta} \right)^\beta c^\beta. \tag{8}$$

The expression $\alpha k/(\alpha - 1)$ is negative, since $0 < \alpha < 1$. So too is $\beta^\beta/(1 + \beta)^{1+\beta}$, if $\beta < -1$. Thus the expression in square brackets is positive. The expression $(\beta/1 + \beta)^\beta$ is also positive. Combining these signs, (8) itself is negative; the lower are unit costs, the higher is marketing expenditure. This makes intuitive sense; if the producer is initially in equilibrium, and unit cost is reduced by some means, the producer's profit margin will increase initially by the same amount. The marginal profitability of marketing expenditure will increase, prompting the producer to spend more.

Marketing responses to unit cost changes reinforce the effects of price responses to these unit cost changes. If other factors remain equal, a reduction in an industry's unit cost is predicted to induce the industry to take steps to increase its market share in both its domestic and export markets, turning the balance of trade in the positive direction.

APPENDIX 2

BENEFITS OF GREATER CONSUMER CHOICE OFFERED BY TRADE WHEN ECONOMIES OF SCALE APPLY

Let the volumes in which the firm produces Models I and II be represented by Y and X. The unit manufacturing costs of Models I and II are respectively AY^α and AX^α, where α is negative, reflecting economies of scale. The transformation curve Y_1AX_1 in Figure 2.1 describes the combinations of Y and X which can be produced within a given total cost, C, such that:

$$C = AY^{1+\alpha} + AX^{1+\alpha}.$$

If unit costs decline by 10 per cent with each doubling of volume:

$$A(2Y)^\alpha = 0.9\,AY^\alpha$$

$$2^\alpha = 0.9$$

$$\alpha \log 2 = \log 0.9$$

$$\alpha = -0.1521.$$

Y_1AX_1 intersects the axes when Y and X and $(C/A)^{1/(1+\alpha)}$. At A, $Y = X = (C/2A)^{1/(1+\alpha)}$. $OB = 2(C/2A)^{1/(1+\alpha)}$. The gain in real income at T compared to A, measured at post-trade prices, is:

$$BY_1 = (C/A)^{1/(1+\alpha)} - 2(C/2A)^{1/(1+\alpha)}.$$

Imports are equal to $ST = \frac{1}{2}(C/A)^{1/(1+\alpha)}$

$$\frac{\text{Welfare Gain}}{\text{Imports}} = \frac{(C/A)^{1/(1+\alpha)} - 2(C/2A)^{1/(1+\alpha)}}{\frac{1}{2}(C/A)^{1/(1+\alpha)}}$$

$$= 2(1 - 2(\tfrac{1}{2})^{1/(1+\alpha)})$$

$$= 23 \text{ per cent.}$$

DATA ON BILATERAL TRADE AND CONCENTRATION

France–Germany

Industry N.I.C.E. classification	Bilateral trade (US $000)	Combined industry output (US $000)	Average 8-firm concentration (× 1000)
235	4,240	346,997	475
236	985	275,560	490
237	38,329	1,526,596	130
239	52,239	1,086,426	120
243	30,362	3,691,282	55
245	4,865	131,830	135
251	18,658	678,178	65
253	3,168	715,233	25
255	1,587	206,266	125
259	1,802	220,070	125
272	21,392	1,665,766	120
280	7,275	3,062,420	85
291	24,142	571,531	365
292	1,756	465,649	95
301	41,913	2,015,039	525
302	9,703	1,192,058	130
303	40,329	846,891	975
304	3,235	186,414	870
311	170,999	6,860,645	510
312	63,718	1,463,894	225
313	31,592	2,936,437	165
320	61,435	5,890,819	845
331	27,211	463,339	140
332	20,600	1,100,596	390
334	5,492	895,942	490
335	4,648	1,149,843	185
345	24,701	2,110,449	270
353	14,133	1,970,182	205
354	10,090	1,280,745	295
362	59,501	818,741	795
364	40,747	616,853	375
365	16,251	1,107,835	220
368	41,097	700,632	370
371/373	65,262	4,988,412	460
374/375	65,020	3,635,079	495
376/377	30,141	1,361,391	385
378	2,564	200,036	875
381	7,093	1,134,507	540
382	1,854	391,120	690
383	254,398	9,091,272	585
385	3,011	432,073	455
386	18,272	1,209,762	755

Industry N.I.C.E. classification	Bilateral trade (US $000)	Combined industry output (US $000)	Average 8-firm concentration (× 1000)
391	7,984	803,813	305
392	3,811	180,379	185
395	4,085	290,551	150
397	8,349	332,610	220

France–Italy

Industry N.I.C.E. classification	Bilateral trade (US $000)	Combined industry output (US $000)	Average 8-firm concentration (× 1000)
232	31,974	1,942,771	210
233	2,938	1,884,645	235
235	7,508	305,412	485
236	54	205,857	550
237	35,846	1,016,383	95
243	17,870	1,877,750	35
244	996	102,837	295
245	2,477	59,041	180
251	10,355	303,557	50
253	320	459,030	20
255	1,156	57,511	150
259	1,000	147,704	225
271	6,223	1,249,227	350
272	6,724	997,107	95
280	21,995	2,253,288	115
291	8,527	393,347	225
292	737	253,302	195
301	21,266	1,479,208	580
302	4,829	687,521	110
303	26,447	942,920	970
304	3,832	93,085	955
311	76,584	3,276,125	455
312	29,401	1,590,686	455
313	14,035	2,691,769	230
320	32,266	3,124,443	740
331	6,685	444,680	130
332	14,164	881,056	330
333	2,578	449,603	295
334	1,491	640,641	465
335	3,311	506,150	225
339	7,370	258,428	115
341	80,491	4,322,119	650
342	3,097	636,101	735
344	6,121	1,040,770	535
345	9,509	1,208,591	175
352	2,184	1,000,657	65
353	3,074	735,506	185
354	797	722,025	360

France–Italy (*cont.*):

Industry N.I.C.E. classification	Bilateral trade (US $000)	Combined industry output (US $000)	Average 8-firm concentration (× 1000)
355	17,002	1,973,866	90
361	23,307	653,683	315
362	27,402	655,281	890
363	18,017	983,025	165
364	11,744	458,032	395
365	3,865	427,688	195
366	13,137	1,049,725	255
367	8,244	180,840	775
368	14,029	206,762	395
369	41,455	2,091,795	275
371	2,695	308,896	600
372	17,023	1,494,075	375
373	6,125	717,799	615
374	13,115	400,300	525
375	4,578	1,369,875	490
376	19,841	565,170	470
377	4,883	223,034	770
378	678	113,014	840
381	5,504	918,330	610
382	1,164	310,514	620
383	99,789	6,210,019	690
385	2,244	531,070	585
386	14,793	1,021,789	810
389	174	49,824	105
391	2,211	556,379	370
392	965	64,928	205
393	4,508	148,731	405
394	2,381	178,184	375
395	3,704	219,121	120
396	908	33,845	375
397	6,765	196,028	240
399	1,841	137,231	210

Germany–Italy

Industry N.I.C.E. classification	Bilateral trade (US $000)	Combined industry output (US $000)	Average 8-firm concentration (× 1000)
235	1,173	264,257	580
236	59	133,181	390
237	58,401	1,348,487	105
239	15,208	944,224	130
243	46,513	3,003,134	50
245	3,932	116,919	165
251	5,559	566,415	75
253	237	540,513	25

Industry N.I.C.E. classification	Bilateral trade (US $000)	Combined industry output (US $000)	Average 8-firm concentration (× 1000)
254	128	118,890	110
255	1,764	248,267	125
259	2,379	152,310	100
272	10,786	1,229,711	135
280	5,928	2,279,576	100
291	12,341	455,232	340
292	2,429	377,857	95
301	43,546	1,694,221	535
302	12,232	1,030,367	140
303	37,765	719,019	995
304	2,739	119,911	915
311	125,768	5,694,872	495
312	45,966	1,844,728	410
313	22,637	2,282,526	175
331	9,009	619,003	100
332	15,622	993,712	445
335	2,971	1,061,775	120
343	31,365	805,670	340
345	12,691	2,110,449	195
353	6,088	1,249,472	140
355	5,271	616,288	455
361	18,405	1,101,215	310
362	26,156	719,152	845
364	35,784	767,461	420
365	12,494	1,038,127	225
368	34,098	751,840	305
378	1,012	137,856	815
381	3,645	1,063,213	650
382	2,549	279,390	680
383	173,622	7,690,333	655
385	3,910	502,051	520
386	53,816	316,981	865
391	17,663	277,100	315
392	2,447	180,379	270
395	25,746	256,930	140
397	9,332	194,174	280

APPENDIX 4

RECONCILIATION OF TRADE AND CENSUS CLASSIFICATIONS

The basis on which N.I.C.E. industry definitions used to compile the census of production (Résultats définitifs de l'enquête Industrielle de 1963 EES 69/2 Statistical Office of the EEC) were reconciled to the S.I.T.C. product classifications is indicated below. In some cases 4 or 5 digit S.I.T.C. categories have been allocated to 2, 3 or 4 N.I.C.E. categories.

N.I.C.E.	S.I.T.C.
232	262.20, 262.60, 262.70, 262.30, 262.90, 651.2, 653.2, 656.61.
233	263.1 (x.50), 263.2, 263.3, 263.4, 651.3, 652.1.
235	265.1 (x.66), 265.2 (x.75), 265.3 (x.75), 651.5, 653.3.
236	264.0 (x.75), 265.4 (x.75), 265.5 (x.75), 265.8 (x.75), 651.92, 651.93, 653.4.
237	841.4, 653.7.
239	654.0, 655.5, 655.1, 655.4, 655.8, 655.9, 656.1, 656.2, 657.4, 657.5, 657.6.
243	655.7, 841.1, 841.2, 841.3 (x.33), 841.5, 399.4.
244	821.03, 656.91 (x.50).
245	842.0, 613.0.
251	243.1, 243.2, 242.2, 242.3, 242.4, 243.3, 242.9, 631.8.
252/4	631.1, 631.2, 631.4, 632.1, 632.2.
253	632.4.
255	632.7, 632.8.
259	633.0, 899.22, 899.23, 899.24.
271	251.2, 251.5, 251.6, 251.7, 251.8, 251.9, 641.3, 641.5, 641.6, 641.7.
272	641.2, 641.4, 642, 641.9.
280	892.1, 892.2, 892.3, 892.4, 892.91, 892.94, 892.93.
291	611.2, 611.3, 611.4, 611.9.
292	612.1, 612.2, 612.9, 612.3 (x.50), 841.3 (x.66).
301	231.3, 621.0, 629.1, 629.3, 629.4, 629.9, 841.6, 663.8, 851.02 (x.50), 894.23 (x.50), 894.22 (x.50), 894.24 (x.25), 894.42 (x.50).
302	893.0.
303	266, 651.6, 651.7.
304	599.5.
311	231.2, 512, 513, 514, 521, 561, 431.1, 431.2, 431.4, 581.
312	431.3, 532, 571.1, 571.2, 571.3, 531, 551, 599.6, 899.32, 241.2, 599.2, 599.7, 599.9, 271.1.
313	541, 553, 554, 862.3, 641.95 (x.25), 895.23, 895.91.
320	331.0, 332.1, 332.2, 332.3, 332.4, 332.5, 332.6.
331	662.
332	664, 665.
333	663.9, 663.7, 666, 812.2 (x.50).
334	661.2, 661.1, 273.2 (x.50).
335	661.83, 663.61, 663.62.
339	661.3, 663.1, 663.2, 663.5.
341	671, 672, 674, 673.4, 679.

N.I.C.E.	S.I.T.C.
342	723.23, 678.2, 678.3, 678.4, 678.5.
343	673.1, 673.2, 673.5, 693.1, 693.2, 693.31, 693.41, 675.
344	681, 682.1, 682.21, 683.1, 683.21, 684.1, 684.21, 681.1, 685.21, 686.21, 686.1, 686.21, 687.1, 687.21, 689.
345	682.22–26, 683.22–24, 684.22–26, 686.22–23, 687.22–24, 678.1, 698.82, 697.11 (x.50).
352	694, 698.3, 698.6, 698.81.
353	676, 691, 719.66, 731.7 (x.25).
354	692.1, 692.3, 711.1, 711.2.
355	692.2, 695.1, 695.21–23, 698, 697.11 (x.50), 697.12, 698.1, 698.2, 698.5, 698.83, 698.85, 698.9, 812.3, 812.42, 894.3, 951.04, 951.05, 697.2, 697.9.
361	712.
362	714.
363	715, 695.24–26, 719.99.
364	717.1 (excluding 717.15), 717.3.
365	718.3, 719.62.
366	718.4, 719.3.
367	719.7, 719.93.
368	717.15, 717.2, 718.1, 718.2.
369	711.3, 711.5 (x.75), 711.3, 719.1, 719.2, 719.63, 719.65, 719.92, 951.01, 951.02, 951.06.
371–3	723.1, 723.21, 723.22, 722, 729.1, 729.41, 729.6, 729.92, 729.95, 729.96.
381	735.
382	731.1–6, 731.7 (x.25).
383	711.5 (x.25), 732.1–8.
385	732.9, 733.1.
386	711.4, 734.
389	733.3 (x.33), 894.1.
391	861.8, 861.91 (x.50), 861.92, 861.93 (x.50), 861.95 (x.50), 861.96, 861.97 (x.50), 861.98 (x.50).
392	861.7, 821.02 (x.33), 899.62 (x.33).
393	861.1–6, 861.91 (x.50), 861.93 (x.50), 861.95 (x.50), 861.97–98 (x.50).
394	864.
395	897, 961.0.
396	891.4, 891.8, 891.9.
397	894.2, 894.4.

CALCULATION OF PLANT AND FIRM SIZES

Estimates of the average size by employment of the largest twenty plants and firms in France and Italy were obtained from Phlips (1971, appendix, tables A5 and A6). Germany presented problems because in the 1963 EEC industrial census the employment in the largest size class in many German industries is suppressed for disclosure reasons, as well as the employment in at least one other size class, to prevent accurate calculations of the employment of the largest firms by subtraction from the total industry employment. In many cases, however, employment in the smaller suppressed class(es) can be approximated using an assumed class mean size: if the employment in the largest size class appears to be large in relation to that in the smaller suppressed class(es), errors in the assumed mean(s) have relatively small effects on the estimate of the employment in the largest size class. In most industries this was adjudged to be the case, enabling the calculation of the employment in the largest twenty firms and plants using tables F of the Enquête Industrielle 1963[1] (*Données sur les Entreprises, Ventilées par Classes d'Effectifs*) and tables G (*Données sur les Unites Locales, Ventilées par Classes d'Effectifs*) which give both the number of firms (plants) and total employment in each size class. In several industries, the employment of the largest few firms is more effectively concealed by the merger of the largest class with the second or even third largest classes, preventing credible estimates of top-20 firm and plant sizes. More problematic is the known concealment of joint ownership in reporting firm size. However, what tends to be understated is common ownership, rather than operational control. It is the presumed scale economies in the latter which is of primary interest in this study. The calculations of the size of the largest twenty firms or plants typically involved the addition to the employment in the largest size class the employment of those largest firms in the immediately lower size classes required to make up the chosen number of firms. The interpolation required by this procedure can be done in various ways, depending on what use is made of the only information available about the class within which the interpolation is done, the number of firms it contains, and their mean size. Phlips favours Bain's (1966) method of averaging maximum and minimum estimates of the employment of the largest firms to be selected to make up the desired number (8 or 20). The method works like this: the maximum possible size of the selected firms is estimated on the assumption that all other firms in the class are of the minimum size of the class. The minimum possible size of the selected firms is the mean size of the class in question. These extreme estimates are then averaged. This method is open to the criticisms that it yields the average of two highly improbable extremes and that it fails to make the fullest use of the limited information available. Moreover, changes in the number of the largest firms to be selected from a size class need not, according to this method, imply a change in their mean size, which is highly improbable. In this study, a different method has been used for the calculation of the mean sizes of the twenty largest firms and plants for Germany. According to this method the mean of the largest n firms, $\bar{x}_n$, of a size class of N firms of mean size $\bar{x}_N$ and with an upper size limit, x_u, is given by

$$\bar{x}_n = x_u - (x_u - \bar{x}_N)n/N.$$

An example illustrates this and Bain's method. Suppose that a 200–500 employees size class contains 20 firms of mean size 300, and the mean size of the four largest firms is required. According to the Bain method the maximum estimate of this mean is $[6000 - (16 \times 200)]/4 = 700$. Since this exceeds the upper class limit, the latter is chosen as the maximum estimate. The estimated mean size of the four largest firms is therefore the average of this maximum estimate and the minimum (300), i.e., 400. According to the method employed in this study the mean size of the largest four firms is

$$\bar{x}_4 = 500 - (500 - 300) \times 4/20 = 460.$$

In this fairly representative example the Bain method yields the same estimate of the mean size of the largest firms (400) regardless of whether the largest 1, 2, 3, 4, 5, or 6 firms are selected. The interpolation formula obtained above was developed for calculating the top-60 per cent plants and firms. The problem here involved determining the number of the largest firms in a size-class, n, which accounted for a certain number of workers, L, needed to top up the number of workers in larger size-classes to 60 per cent of the industry total. The total employment in these largest n firms is:

$$n\bar{x}_n = nx_u - (x_u - \bar{x})n^2/N = L.$$

The required n is then solved from this quadratic equation. When interpolation was required within the largest open-ended size class, a variation on the formula was used, based on the lower size-class limit.

NOTE

1 *Résultats Définits de l'Enquête Industrielle de 1963*, Etudes et Enquêtes Statistiques, Brussels, Statistical Office the EEC, 1969.

DATA ON TRADE PERFORMANCE AND INDUSTRIAL STRUCTURE

TABLE 1.   *Trade Performance*

	Industry N.I.C.E. classification[a]	Trade peformance[b]		
		TP_{fg}	TP_{fi}	TP_{gi}
1	232	0.52	0.15	−0.45
2	233	0.26	0.59	−0.37
3	235	0.56	0.86	−0.73
4	236	0.94	0.07	−1.00
5	237	0.49	−0.82	−0.50
6	239	0.42	−0.26	0.39
7	243	0.24	−0.66	−0.80
8	244	0.17	0.18	0.43
9	245	0.78	−0.44	−0.23
10	251	0.71	0.98	0.87
11	252/4	0.58	−0.49	−0.49
12	253	−0.19	−0.16	−0.56
13	255	−0.30	−0.74	−0.40
14	259	−0.09	−0.76	−0.45
15	271	0.20	0.52	0.13
16	272	−0.15	0.42	0.50
17	280	−0.40	−0.68	0.30
18	291	0.71	0.71	−0.34
19	292	−0.19	−0.55	−0.57
20	301	0.28	−0.35	−0.57
21	302	−0.29	−0.33	−0.43
22	303	0.06	−0.69	−0.15
23	304	0.56	0.38	0.81
24	311	−0.28	0.06	0.28
25	312	−0.24	0.20	0.69
26	313	0.00	0.29	0.78
27	320	0.91	−0.84	−0.59
28	331	−0.63	−0.45	0.00
29	332	0.33	0.30	−0.48
30	333	−0.88	−0.20	0.72
31	334	0.88	0.90	−0.06
32	335	0.23	−0.92	0.86
33	341	0.07	0.70	0.60
34	342	−0.78	0.33	0.24
35	343	−0.30	0.83	0.09
36	344	0.19	0.12	0.00
37	345	−0.40	0.19	0.34
38	352	−0.78	−0.13	0.67
39	353	−0.45	0.52	0.65
40	354	−0.61	0.10	0.73
41	355	−0.54	−0.58	0.47
42	361	−0.59	−0.18	0.73
43	362	0.13	−0.34	0.11

	Industry N.I.C.E. classification[a]	Trade performance[b]		
		TP_{fg}	TP_{fi}	TP_{gi}
44	363	0.67	0.68	−0.24
45	364	−0.69	−0.23	0.56
46	365	−0.74	−0.49	0.63
47	366	−0.24	0.00	0.63
48	367	−0.28	0.44	0.28
49	368	−0.87	−0.63	0.70
50	369	−0.60	−0.38	0.45
51	371/2/3	−0.28	0.29	0.67
52	378	0.08	0.93	0.87
53	381	−0.59	−0.29	−0.59
54	382	−0.52	−0.41	0.76
55	383	−0.30	−0.23	0.07
56	385	0.25	−0.31	−0.86
57	386	0.75	0.13	−0.75
58	389	−0.40	−0.30	−0.37
59	391	−0.68	0.33	0.28
60	392	−0.58	−0.62	0.90
61	393	−0.62	−0.05	0.45
62	394	−0.38	0.57	0.53
63	395	−0.32	−0.74	−0.86
64	396	−0.84	−0.81	0.28
65	397	−0.44	−0.40	−0.20

[a] Nomenclature des Industries Etablies dans les Communautés Européennes, Brussels, Statistical Office of the EEC, June 1963.
[b] *Foreign Trade: Analytical Tables for 1964*, Brussels, Statistical Office of the EEC.

TABLE 2.   *Size of Largest Plants and Firms*

	Mean size of 20 largest plants in industry			Mean size of 20 largest firms in industry		
	France	Germany	Italy	France	Germany	Italy
1	1,530	1,361	1,717	1,869	−	2,416
2	924	2,227	1,561	2,267	−	3,029
3	479	625	413	655	764	557
4	517	425	325	773	445	259
5	786	992	619	1,074	1,658	735
6	457	859	678	490	879	597
7	750	1,114	927	1,014	1,929	757
8	174	241	107	216	291	123
9	92	142	118	103	144	116
10	142	300	106	163	390	129
11	535	708	283	801	744	305
12	216	301	276	216	325	276
13	61	400	197	58	473	226
14	190	218	128	240	229.	138
15	905	1,274	761	1,503	2,230	1,140
16	441	926	337	528	1,344	372
17	1,232	1,784	827	1,621	1,825	1,013

TABLE 2. (*cont.*):

	Mean size of 20 largest plants in industry			Mean size of 20 largest firms in industry		
	France	Germany	Italy	France	Germany	Italy
18	364	850	329	418	998	326
19	277	421	204	309	499	234
20	2,496	3,246	1,516	3,066	3,622	2,017
21	440	1,124	398	437	1,267	461
22	1,339	2,303	1,554	1,696	3,510	2,540
23	167	289	29	192	288	138
24	1,833	9,039	1,924	3,692	11,858	2,474
25	617	912	976	924	958	2,829
26	988	1,798	991	1,738	2,178	1,391
27	1,140	1,305	487	1,521	1,905	569
28	235	356	318	386	504	590
29	1,187	1,904	605	1,928	2,050	697
30	674	1,204	573	959	2,772	910
31	332	788	389	655	1,266	802
32	467	652	372	637	650	596
33	5,901	9,310	2,950	10,638	18,722	4,381
34	925	2,326	1,412	660	1,188	1,124
35	763	1,316	248	980	1,303	228
36	1,021	2,191	865	2,184	3,167	1,071
37	1,260	2,401	831	1,861	3,271	519
38	461	1,351	294	492	1,504	313
39	569	1,451	470	689	1,411	598
40	800	1,720	156	1,187	1,898	132
41	970	1,999	630	1,399	–	679
42	897	2,202	384	985	2,486	338
43	1,078	2,400	975	1,436	2,785	1,562
44	681	1,673	619	967	1,722	530
45	432	1,878	782	480	2,086	1,111
46	315	1,388	355	383	1,923	379
47	685	3,212	496	943	3,318	702
48	148	2,678	842	162	–	907
49	213	1,415	302	232	1,614	348
50	2,305	4,087	1,108	3,338	7,205	887
51	2,584	4,978	1,052	4,138	14,122	2,221
52	515	544	120	524	600	142
53	3,278	3,195	1,847	2,145	3,293	2,368
54	1,395	1,034	945	1,016	1,028	652
55	9,112	13,553	4,405	12,438	15,403	6,904
56	625	688	981	661	779	1,154
57	2,646	1,228	590	3,897	1,353	349
58	31	168	94	31	184	94
59	1,273	870	74	1,608	950	81
60	123	480	127	145	524	117
61	157	1,938	360	172	2,054	394
62	411	864	224	455	973	250
63	219	351	240	244	402	253
64	85	287	159	101	328	165
65	346	465	164	387	541	175

TABLE 3. *Net Output per Employee and Relative Industry Size*

	Net output per employee[a]			Relative industry size[b]		
	France	Germany	Italy	France Germany	France Italy	Germany Italy
1	3,161	3,522	2,701	1.45	1.38	0.95
2	2,784	3,337	2,309	0.82	1.29	1.57
3	2,927	3,188	2,944	1.27	1.74	1.37
4	3,485	3,890	1,896	1.72	5.49	3.20
5	2,772	3,331	1,984	0.64	1.42	2.22
6	3,264	4,173	2,553	0.45	1.73	3.86
7	2,591	2,894	2,085	0.53	2.16	4.05
8	3,221	4,052	2,989	0.51	3.04	6.02
9	3,282	4,293	3,003	0.39	1.68	4.30
10	3,435	3,876	2,281	0.44	2.16	4.91
11	3,567	3,792	2,005	1.42	2.80	2.80
12	3,092	3,930	2,146	0.80	2.80	2.23
13	2,662	3,427	2,038	0.04	0.16	3.99
14	3,191	3,221	2,073	0.96	2.69	2.81
15	5,823	5,719	4,538	0.77	1.64	2.14
16	4,118	4,111	2,984	0.76	2.55	3.38
17	4,551	4,151	4,493	0.98	2.06	2.10
18	4,091	3,477	2,729	0.80	1.84	2.29
19	3,234	3,305	1,919	0.58	2.06	3.57
20	4,350	4,753	4,761	0.81	1.55	1.92
21	4,081	4,342	2,901	0.55	1.61	2.92
22	7,530	6,449	5,602	1.72	1.31	0.76
23	7,402	9,152	5,309	0.75	6.00	8.02
24	6,834	7,646	5,372	0.48	2.10	4.40
25	5,653	6,734	5,390	0.70	0.61	0.87
26	5,999	6,536	7,072	1.32	1.64	1.24
27	35,159	31,864	23,283	0.76	4.43	5.81
28	3,561	4,610	2,515	0.45	0.48	1.06
29	4,285	4,368	3,412	0.81	1.28	1.57
30	3,389	3,700	3,313	0.30	0.72	2.42
31	8,378	8,677	5,687	0.53	0.93	1.77
32	4,567	5,985	2,274	0.35	1.42	4.08
33	5,435	5,401	5,063	0.59	2.21	3.74
34	6,277	5,242	4,445	0.77	0.63	0.82
35	4,114	4,812	3,341	0.50	4.73	9.46
36	5,819	4,685	3,949	1.07	2.88	2.70
37	4,202	4,074	3,393	0.67	2.38	3.52
38	4,316	4,306	2,049	o.74	5.05	6.86
39	3,374	4,096	3,481	0.37	0.67	1.83
40	4,053	4,409	3,577	1.18	23.85	20.19
41	3,671	4,186	3,102	0.46	2.00	4.39
42	4,143	4,613	3,678	0.50	2.28	4.52
43	5,801	4,972	5,518	0.85	1.36	1.59
44	5,098	4,429	3,995	0.55	2.01	3.66
45	4,167	3,933	4,198	0.33	0.51	1.52
46	4,715	4,634	3,932	0.29	1.39	4.80
47	4,190	4,406	4,359	0.43	2.27	5.27
48	3,646	4,671	4,357	0.04	0.14	3.84
49	5,440	4,637	4,094	0.13	0.60	4.83
50	4,547	4,315	4,134	0.58	2.84	4.89
51	4,539	3,979	3,982	0.46	1.66	3.60

TABLE 3. (*cont.*):

	Net outper per employee[a]			Relative industry size[b]		
				France	France	Germany
	France	Germany	Italy	Germany	Italy	Italy
52	3,882	4,528	3,704	0.78	3.45	4.42
53	3,726	3,132	3,149	0.77	1.17	1.51
54	3,771	3,534	3,518	1.17	2.12	1.81
55	4,560	5,610	5,705	0.72	1.58	2.20
56	3,954	3,508	3,837	1.14	0.77	0.67
57	5,127	4,449	4,643	3.79	14.84	3.91
58	3,472	4,004	2,039	0.75	3.90	5.18
59	4,450	3,808	3,053	2.06	36.51	17.68
60	3,313	3,592	2,648	0.37	3.03	8.16
61	3,826	3,245	3,632	0.12	0.37	3.10
62	3,505	3,152	3,518	0.80	4.18	5.23
63	4,306	3,887	1,936	0.77	1.36	1.77
64	2,883	3,293	1,642	0.23	0.59	2.54
65	3,095	3,444	1,983	1.01	5.81	5.74

[a] Net output per employee refers to value added, in plants employing ten or more employees, table B44, *L'Enquête Industrielle de 1963.*
[b] Relative industry size relates to gross output, in plants with ten or more employees, table 37, *L'Enquête Industrielle de 1963.*

TABLE 4. *Representative Plant and Firm Sizes*

Industry N.I.C.E. classification[a]	Industry description	Mean size of largest plants accounting for 60 per cent of industry employment			Mean size of largest firms accounting for 60 per cent of industry employment		
		France	Germany	Italy	France	Germany	Italy
232	Wool	583	–	477	883	–	652
233	Cotton	390	–	712	1,063	–	1,699
235	linen and hemp	376	750	398	660	1,286	1,176
236	Other textiles fibres	506	541	384	1,820	1,180	322
237	Hosiery	257	257	71	368	433	80
239	Other textiles	104	266	62	122	290	97
243	Garments	86	147	20	96	218	20
244	Mattresses and beds	101	149	27	138	179	32
245	Fur goods	16	28	33	17	28	28
251	Saw mills	20	45	19	20	48	22
253	Frames and floors	13	14	11	19	14	11
255	Other wood products	17	102	45	17	116	52
259	Cork products	32	86	25	40	88	24
271	Pulp, paper, and board	630	801	479	996	1,897	905
272	Paper products	173	313	100	218	413	114
280	Printing and publishing	167	236	87	233	256	108
291	Tanning	189	725	108	237	1,060	109
292	Leather products	42	98	34	44	116	36
301	Synthetic rubber	1,016	2,610	1,347	5,503	5,535	4,404
302	Plastic materials	149	323	94	150	352	103
303	Synthetic fibres	2,165	5,915	2,832	10,713	9,740	12,399
304	Starch, glue, and gelatine	590	714	11	1,350	1,163	814
311	Basic chemicals	840	12,049	1,260	3,595	18,527	3,022
312	Industrial and agricultural chemicals	188	324	338	476	344	12,607
313	Chemicals for domestic consumption	297	903	363	615	1,077	591
320	Petroleum	1,311	1,865	611	5,707	5,139	1,030
331	Baked clay products	104	96	101	167	124	150
332	Glass	894	1,034	195	2,270	1,216	228

TABLE 4. (cont.):

Industry N.I.C.E. classification[a]	Industry description	Mean size of largest plants accounting for 60 per cent of industry employment			Mean size of largest firms accounting for 60 per cent of industry employment		
		France	Germany	Italy	France	Germany	Italy
333	Pottery	427	861	239	797	1,857	350
334	Cement	249	475	199	958	1,461	556
335	Concrete products	95	116	63	141	131	83
339	Stone and non-metallic mineral products	24	–	29	29	–	36
341	Steel mills	6,027	5,111	2,661	20,092	14,127	13,340
342	Steel tubes	2,198	2,763	2,079	4,548	4,979	3,635
343	Wire-drawing	656	787	239	1,311	859	243
344	Primary non-ferrous metals	762	371	543	3,957	388	826
345	Foundries	526	1,169	226	782	1,843	161
352	Second transformation of metals	79	371	40	75	388	42
353	Metallic construction	333	441	100	413	420	118
354	Boiler-works	204	1,107	241	278	1,308	195
355	Metal tools	155	–	121	179	–	131
361	Farm equipment	492	1,812	180	655	2,413	170
362	Office machines	1,852	4,451	3,685	7,334	7,722	20,410
363	Machine tools	276	798	207	372	842	185
364	Textile machinery	305	1,428	718	361	1,913	1,193
365	Food products machinery	134	649	240	164	833	230
366	Mining and construction machinery	324	1,576	256	483	1,624	420
367	Transmission equipment	386	3,902	1,759	898	6,459	5,680
368	Other specific machinery	213	769	147	291	652	192
369	Other machinery	1,018	2,303	306	2,292	4,387	274
381	Shipbuilding	3,689	4,358	2,656	3,126	4,591	9,967
382	Railway vehicles	895	1,353	1,524	1,760	1,959	1,078
383	Motor vehicles	10,137	13,458	7,532	28,115	22,689	37,003
385	Motorcycles	560	588	1,891	839	728	3,078
386	Aircraft	2,594	1,485	1,664	11,623	4,308	1,620
389	Other transport equipment	8	19	15	8	19	15

391	Measuring equipment	521	409	69	952	456	80
392	Medical equipment	20	67	46	22	73	43
393	Opthalmic and photographic equipment	165	1,446	218	210	2,028	282
394	Watches and clocks	250	538	32	310	719	39
395	Jewellery	49	84	35	59	89	38
396	Musical instruments	72	170	103	108	207	109
397	Games, toys, and sports equipment	122	227	119	155	264	132

a Nomenclature des Industries Etablies dans les Communautés Européennes, Brussels, Statistical Office of the EEC, June 1963.

Source: Résultats Définitifs de l'Enquête Industrielle de 1963. Etudes et Enquêtes Statistiques, Brussels, Statistical Office the EEC, 1969, tables F and G.

DATA ON FRANCO–GERMAN CAR TRADE
(relating to Table 4.11)

Year	TP_{fg}	RC_{fg}	MI_{fg}	$RC_{fg} \cdot MI_{fg}$
1955	0.876	100.00	1.038	103.80
1956	1.194	96.22	1.143	109.98
1957	1.354	90.95	1.138	103.50
1958	1.548	81.42	1.459	118.79
1959	1.591	88.56	2.676	236.99
1960	1.635	76.64	3.869	296.52
1961	0.597	71.93	4.668	335.77
1962	1.133	74.36	6.159	457.98
1963	0.782	68.78	7.040	484.21
1964	0.536	69.00	7.338	506.32
1965	0.794	62.71	6.579	412.57
1966	0.849	62.29	6.505	405.20
1967	1.583	57.45	6.388	366.99
1968	1.517	56.09	7.555	423.76
1969	1.171	52.76	7.279	383.04
1970	1.659	45.92	8.727	400.74
1971	1.877	42.68	9.806	418.52
1972	1.777	42.28	9.455	399.76
1973	1.504	40.34	10.546	425.43
1974	1.753	35.09	8.969	314.72
1975	1.554	45.64	8.568	391.04
1976	1.070	44.83	9.181	411.58

COMPARING COSTS OF WASHING-MACHINE MANUFACTURE

The comparison of manufacturing costs was built up from engineering analyses of the materials content of different countries' machines, and from assessments of the costs of the value added element based on the inputs used in different manufacturing locations. In so far as the latter involved comparable products the comparison was reasonably straightforward since Italian plants in particular tend to be specialized by product type; allowance has been made for differences in work content (e.g. motors were assembled in one assembly plant, not in another), reckoning that the value added components of the items in question were proportional to the latter's material costs derived from the engineering estimates. Where the product mix was broader and different between countries (e.g. comparing costs in a German plant, which produced top-loading as well as front loading models of an up-market type, with those in an Italian plant) the comparative cost of a German unit of production was calculated in the following way:

(i) the German product was identified as broadly equivalent to a reference Italian machine in terms of specifications (e.g. a low-priced front-loading automatic with a spin speed of 350 r.p.m., compared to a 400 r.p.m. Italian machine);

(ii) the product-mix in the German plant was converted into an equivalent volume of the reference machines, on the basis of estimates of the budgeted direct man-hours per unit for the final assembly of each product type; the latter figures were derived from a production programme specifying the manning requirements and expected daily throughputs of each assembly line. This calculation translated the German plant's annual volume of various machines into an equivalent volume of reference machines;

(iii) the four major elements of manufacturing cost were identified (materials and overheads by management; direct and indirect labour costs from head counts, estimated wage levels, and employers' contributions) and divided by the reference volume figure.

AUTHOR INDEX

SUBJECT INDEX